Officially Noted

2/00 AL

Working Women for the 21st Century

50 Women Reveal Their Pathways to Career Success

Nelda LaTeef

Williamson Publishing • Charlotte, Vermont

Copyright © 1992 by Nelda LaTeef

**Library of Congress
Cataloging-in-Publication Data**

LaTeef, Nelda, 1958-
Working Women for the 21st Century: 50 Women Reveal Their Pathways
to Career Success/Nelda LaTeef.
    p.   cm.
   Includes index.
   ISBN 0-913589-64-4 (cloth) – ISBN 0-913589-66-7 (paper)
    1. Women in the professions – United States – Case studies.
   2. Success in business – United States – Case studies. I. Title.
   HD6054.2.U6L38 1992
   331.4 – dc20   91-46230
                                              CIP

Cover design: Trezzo-Braren Studio
Typesetting: Superior Type
Printing: Banta Company

Williamson Publishing Co.
Box 185
Charlotte, Vermont 05445
(800) 234-8791

Manufactured in the United States of America
10 9 8 7 6 5 4 3 2 1

Notice: The information contained in this book is true, complete and accurate to the
best of our knowledge. All recommendations and suggestions are made without any
guarantees on the part of the author or Williamson Publishing. The author and publisher disclaim all liability incurred in connection with the use of this information.

To my parents,
who taught me, in the words of
William Blake, "No bird soars too high,
if she soars with her own wings."

Contents

Acknowledgments

I would like to acknowledge at the outset the participation and cooperation of the fifty women who animate this book. I see these women as emblematic of a first generation of women to face an unlimited and unprecedented array of career opportunities. These women have launched successful careers in such diverse fields as the law, the military, the arts, and public affairs. These women speak to us all, but, in particular, they speak to those individuals confronting career choices – whether starting out or looking for change. I am grateful to these fifty women for the refreshing candor with which they discussed the hurdles and rewards of the career paths they chose.

As a senior at Harvard, their views would have made a world of difference to me as I took long walks along the Charles River pondering career choices. Several years ago, listening to my younger siblings express similar concerns, it occurred to me how helpful it would be to have the experience and advice of outstanding role models representing a range of professions. To capture a watershed in gender relations, I decided to focus on women and, specifically, American women.

To begin, I wrote letters outlining my idea to Sandra Day O'Connor, Ellen Goodman, and Geraldine Ferraro. I received almost immediate responses. Ellen Goodman wrote to tell me the idea was a "terrific" one; Geraldine Ferraro's assistant called to arrange an interview for me; and Sandra Day O'Connor wished me luck and agreed to respond to my questions.

From that point onward the project became a passionate commitment. I perused references, publications, and biographies in search of role models. I called upon professional associations for possible leads and suggestions, and sought their opinions about candidates.

More about the selection process. In addition to demonstrated excellence in one's field, I looked for a generosity of spirit. Also, I was searching for individuals who took their responsibility as role models seriously and who were willing to give of their time to encourage others. Not one of the women, when asked to participate, inquired, "Why me?" In fact, all fifty women felt that this book would be a valuable resource in helping others explore career options.

Unfortunately, the strictures of space necessarily precluded the inclusion of many exemplary women – trailblazers as well as unsung heroes. My toughest predicament was narrowing the selection in a given field of endeavor to a single individual. Also, bearing in mind that successful people by definition tend to be busy people, a very pragmatic consideration was accessibility. However, despite such obstacles, these women made time and permitted me to get through to them. I hope the reader will understand my predicament and not become sidetracked over alternative choices.

Delving into the lives of these fifty women has been personally broadening. Their willingness to share their professional and life experiences made getting up in the morning a joyous adventure. Kahlil Gibran's observation, "We live only to discover beauty" is applicable to the active lives these women lead. They have a wonder and zest for life that is truly contagious.

My family was indispensable in this endeavor, too. They kept my spirits high with their nurturing encouragement. I always looked forward with great anticipation to my father's comments after he would read an interview, and my mother's amused reminder to him, "But you said the last one was the very best!" To Noel, who makes everything seem possible with his sage counsel, no words of thanks are adequate. To Nora, a heartfelt hug for always pitching in when I needed assistance, no matter what the hour. To Ned, a special word of thanks for assisting in transcribing interviews when my deadline loomed. And, last but not least, a note of acknowledgement to our cat, Ninja, who never failed to remind me that there are three meals in the day.

I owe a deep measure of gratitude to my publisher, Jack Williamson, for his enthusiastic support. Finally, let me express my thanks to my editor, Susan Williamson, for her many valuable contributions.

Introduction

Thornton Wilder observed in 1951 that "Americans are still engaged in inventing what it is to be an American...at once an exhilarating and a painful occupation." On the cusp of the twenty-first century what do women bring to this occupation?

Few people will dispute that women today have made great strides in every walk of life. The question, therefore, may be whether any individual, man or woman, can make a difference in this time of uncertainty, confusion about values, and apparent lack of direction, as unprecedented change looms on the horizon. I believe that the fifty women interviewed for this book demonstrate that this question can be answered with a resounding "Yes!" What is more, I believe that these women, representing diverse professions, are a source of instruction and inspiration on how to make a difference. They are role models for us all.

Their proficiency speaks for itself. But more important, these women share a sense of responsibility for moral and social education that heightens public sensibilities. The individual and collective abilities of these women to shape our values extends to all levels of human interaction, from the family to society at large.

Many of these women will have a profound impact in redefining what it means to be successful in our society. Cathy Black, former publisher of *USA Today,* is a case in point. She says, "A CEO running a Fortune 500 company by and large puts that job first and foremost in his or her life. As women get into that ring, we may be able to humanize things more." Telling, too, is the maxim cited by attorney Alice Young: "No one on their deathbed has ever said I wish I had spent more time at the office." These women share a contextual view of life and an idealism that stands out at a time when a disturbing indifference exacerbates urban violence, poverty, homelessness, and hunger.

As a society, these women's values are imparted to us in many ways—not the least of which is by osmosis. When asked about the driving force in her life today, professor Mary Catherine Bateson cited her growing involvement with social issues, "particularly the need to give people a better understanding of the importance of cultural diversity, partly because I see some kinds of prejudice coming back—things that we thought we had made a lot of progress on." Bateson further observed, "I don't think that we can count on that progress holding. I'm very concerned that the position of women should continue to improve and not deteriorate, that racism should not have a resurgence in this country, and that a value for human differences should become more and more deeply embedded in the educational system."

These women are helping to shape a new reality. Psychiatrist and attorney Judianne Densen-Gerber, who calls herself "a reluctant dragon," has combined training in law and medicine to pioneer in drug rehabilitation and to draft legislation against child abuse and child pornography. Attorney Alice Young is an active member of the Aspen Institute, a corporate think tank committed to teaching values to leaders of corporate America and to tackling difficult issues of the day. Elizabeth Dole stepped down from her cabinet post to head the American Red Cross. In assuming her new position, she decided to forgo a $200,000 salary. When asked why, she said simply, "The best way I can let volunteers know of their importance is to be one of them." By her example, Dole is helping to transcend the greed and selfishness of the eighties and is setting in motion a new ethic of community spirit.

Many of these fifty women embarked on careers mindful of how such careers would affect society. When asked what drew her to law, Justice Sandra Day O'Connor said, "I took a class as an undergraduate at Stanford from an inspiring professor. He was a lawyer, and he showed how the law could serve society in beneficial ways." O'Connor attributes the progress women have achieved to "strong advocacy and government and private action to raise the public consciousness." These role models, by virtue of their obvious accomplishments, are ensuring that this progress will be sustained. Yet these strides cannot be taken for granted, and the shaping of public consciousness relies heavily on the capacity of women such as these to share their values with us all. As La Rochefoucauld said, "Nothing is so contagious as an example. We never do great good or great evil without bringing about more of the same on the part of others."

The shaping and sharing of values is a highly complex process, but these women provide insights into that process and the sacrifices it entails. While there has been public discussion of the "supermom" syndrome with the toll it takes on women's health, it is all the more remarkable that these women are willing to take on, in anthropologist Laura Nader's words, "a triple shift," by contributing to the great public debates that affect this nation.

This sense of responsibility for, and willingness to engage in, the shaping and sharing of values may be traced to the noteworthy fact that twenty-one of the women have been teachers at some point in their careers. Currently, twelve are teaching, and three are contemplating going into teaching.

More statistics about these women. Their median age is forty-seven. The youngest, born in 1961, is musician Nadja Salerno-Sonnenberg, and the oldest, born in 1924, is theater producer/director Zelda Fichandler.

The women represent a wide range of educational backgrounds and academic degrees: seven women hold Ph.D.'s, four hold M.D.'s, seven hold J.D.'s, seven hold graduate school degrees, fifteen hold B.A.'s, four hold B.S.'s, five did not complete college, and two ended their formal education at the high school level.

Forty of the women are currently married, and thirty-four have children. Two of the women stated that they deliberately chose not to have children because they wanted to devote themselves full-time to their careers. Seven of the women had children only after they had established themselves in their careers.

In the interviews, I made it a point to ask a core set of questions that would provide readers with information regarding many different career paths. The differences, as well as the similarities, in responses are illuminating, particularly with regard to gender discrimination.

When asked if they had experienced gender discrimination in their work, thirty-one of the women said yes (eight said they continue to experience discrimination on an ongoing basis), twenty-one said no, and one said probably. Senator Nancy Kassebaum noted, "There still are times I experience discrimination! But I never felt that you should dwell on it because that takes up a lot of energy in a destructive sort of way." Geraldine Ferraro said, "There was discrimination even when I ran for national office. I mean, you tell me why people said genetically I wasn't able to understand throw weights. Evidently, they thought genetically I wouldn't be able to be the commander in chief if I were called upon to do so."

Architect Joan Goody responded, "There still are a fair number of people who are reluctant to give responsibility to a woman because they are prejudiced or they have limited experience or just don't think that a woman can handle it. . . . So I think as a woman, one has to be all the more thoughtful, strong, and careful and to project that image. That is just one additional burden in a profession that has many." Professor of electrical engineering Irene Peden said, "The older I get, the more I would say there is discrimination." Judianne Densen-Gerber said, "There is no way of overestimating the amount of discrimination that one experiences professionally because one is a woman. . . . There is definitely a glass ceiling." Laura Nader noted, "You have to be naive not to see discrimination." She then added, "I was treated the same in some ways: I didn't have maternity leave, but neither did the guys. I was treated differently in terms of promotion and pay. I never dwelt on it, though, until it became obscene."

Literary agent Jean Naggar and editor Paige Rense spoke of a different kind of discrimination. Naggar explained, "It isn't overt discrimination. It's much more subtle. It's a tendency to see me as – I hate to say this – 'that nice woman' rather than as 'that tough literary agent.' " Rense reported, "I do notice a tendency in some men to regard women as not their intellectual equals. And yet I notice a tendency in other men to absolutely delight when a woman says something wonderful. They are both forms of discrimination."

Professor Mary Catherine Bateson spoke about the lack of mentoring: "Women often don't get mentoring; they don't get guidance – the same kind of guidance from senior people in their field that young men get. They sometimes get caught believing the official myths about how things work. In every system, there is an official way that things work and then there is a good deal of informal negotiating going on: people doing favors for each other, old-boy-network things that are *sous-entendu* in the way people support each other. I think women have to watch for that."

Pediatrician Marianne Neifert voiced similar concerns about the ten years she spent in an academic track: "There were clear differences in my mind between what happened to junior female faculty and what happened to junior male faculty. I had a definite lack of mentorship. I feel I was pigeonholed in low-level positions. I was naive and blinded to the fact that many men were on track with proper mentorship to take their careers somewhere. I was viewed more as a drone. . . . What I lacked were mentors who invested in me."

It is interesting to note that, almost across the board, women in their thirties and forties, as opposed to those in their fifties and sixties, viewed instances of discrimination with a carefree, almost feisty attitude. In the former category, Anna Perez, the first lady's press secretary, noted, "I just do whatever I'm doing, and if people have a problem with that, I figure it's their problem, not mine." Terrie Williams, head of her own public relations firm, said, "That only gives me inspiration and the fuel to say, 'Well, I'll show you!' " Chef and restaurateur Elizabeth Terry explained, "If someone says, 'You can't do that because you are a woman,' I think you should do it and show them 'Ha! I can do it better!' There is great fun in that." Entrepreneur Debbi Fields said, "I never felt discrimination because I wouldn't let people make me feel that way."

Some of the women view discrimination as a given and believe that the way to combat it is to work twice as hard. The mayor of the District of Columbia, Sharon Pratt Kelly, said, "It's hard being a woman in any profession because often you have to work twice as hard to prove your worth." Gail Wilensky, administrator of the Health Care Financing Administration, recounted, "When I was finishing graduate school and starting to look in the job market, one of the older professors took me aside and said, 'You need to understand that if you ever are in direct, head-on competition with a man and you are equally qualified, you are going to lose every time. But if you are noticeably better, you'll have a fighting chance.' " She continued, "I was pretty angry at this fellow for having said that. It never occurred to me, up until then, that might be an issue. But after I calmed down, I decided I could live with those rules. My personal experiences have been that if you can demonstrate that you really are clearly better than other choices, you've got a fair shot."

Alternatively, some said that being a woman helped their careers. Susan Heilbron, general counsel and vice president of Maxwell Macmillan Group, noted, "One of the reasons I've been successful is because I am a woman. Unfortunately, society expects that successful men have to be unusually tough, unusually aggressive, to be respected. I think that often gets in the way of getting things done. People don't have such silly expectations of women." Financial planner Laura Waller shares this view: "In some ways, being a woman has been an asset. Many people choose a woman because, right or wrong, they perceive us as being more honest and fair. I've also found that my high-pressured male clients feel more comfortable talking to me about areas of finance that they don't know much about than they might if I were a man."

When asked to identify their role models, the women said that they had different role models at different stages in their lives. Three of the women said that they never had role models because they were breaking new ground. In fact, many trailblazers chose as role models their parents, teachers, siblings, husbands, coworkers, and bosses, as well as historical figures such as Eleanor Roosevelt (mentioned by two of the women), Thomas Jefferson, Abigail Adams, and General George C. Marshall. One woman cited as role models Hollywood actresses Ginger Rogers and Rosalind Russell, who played the parts of "career women."

It is interesting to note that while these women's mothers were rarely in a position to act as mentors in a business or professional setting, they inspired their daughters to fulfill their highest aspirations. One can only speculate how the growing number of professional women now in a position to mentor their daughters, as well as their sons, will change advancement opportunities.

Striking a creative balance between their careers and interpersonal relationships is one of the overarching challenges of these women's lives. Accountant Barbara Pope said, "I waited to have a child until I was a partner in the firm. At that point, I had a bit more control over my schedule, but it's still difficult. . . . It would be one of life's great pleasures to pick my seven-year-old daughter up from school at 2:30 in the afternoon." Prize-winning chemist, Jacqueline Barton, who had her first child at age thirty-eight said, "I can't imagine having a child at a younger age when you are coming up in the ranks. It's a constant struggle."

Striking this balance is difficult on many levels, but one of the most difficult aspects is dealing with feelings of guilt for not always being there for their children, even if they can afford nannies and housekeepers. Chriss Winston, former director of speech writing at the White House said, "It isn't easy at all. You do feel guilty. It wasn't hard when it was just my husband and me . . . but once a baby enters the picture, that really changes your life. That's been the hardest part, because I'd like to spend a lot more time with my little boy than I do. I try to do that on the weekends, and, he stays up so I can see him at night. But it isn't easy." Newspaper publisher Cathleen Black, often described as "the most powerful woman in publishing," admitted, "Some days are better than others. . . . There are some days when I feel conflicted, but I have not yet had to miss anything important in my son's life."

Shortly after I interviewed Winston and Black, they resigned from their positions. One of Winston's colleagues said, "She really had to wrestle with the decision. She loved her job and loved to travel with the president, but she also knew she was missing really precious time with her son, Ian, and he was growing up and she wasn't seeing him. I don't know if I would have been willing to give up such a position for my child." And thus, we see, the intense struggle played out in the lives of these achieving women.

Advertising executive Agi Clark and literary agent Jean Naggar, who both had to work out of necessity when their children were young, expressed regrets about not being home with them. Clark said, "There are very few things in my life that I would do differently, which I guess is a nice thing, but I do think I would do this differently. If I could have, I would have liked to stay home with my son, at least for his first three or four years." Naggar said, "I tried not to shortchange anyone at any point and did what I felt was best for everybody, but I look back now and regret a lot of the time I wish I could have spent with my children when they were younger. . . . There was no other choice for me, but looking back, now that the children are all grown and have left home, I regret that I didn't have more time."

Attorney Alice Young sees the balancing of one's professional and personal lives as maintaining a sense of priorities: " . . . when you have a sick child and a meeting to attend, you go to the sick child. It's not so difficult to figure out what makes sense."

An emerging trend expressed by these women was a desire to create a linkage between their professional and personal lives rather than perceiving them as two separate worlds. Young noted, "Coping with my children, I think, has forced me to be more mature than I otherwise would have been and has been invaluable in my learning to cope with my practice. So I don't view any of it as having to choose one or the other. It's always been trying to put everything in balance."

Almost without exception, the women who are married cited their husbands' support as essential to pulling off the balancing act. Such support takes many forms including, in the case of veterinarian Peregrine Wolff, having her husband, an ornithologist, put his career on hold to move with her to her new position as director of animal health at the Minnesota Zoological Garden. Others credited the assistance of siblings and parents as well. Six women cited the means to hire outside help as enabling them to maintain the balance.

All the women share a passion for what they do, as well as enormous self-discipline. Justice O'Connor's brother said of his sister, "All her life, whatever she did, she would just do it to perfection, whether it was important or unimportant, semi-important or very important, she would just do it to perfection. . . . If you said, 'The job is to wash dishes well,' she would do it better than anyone else."

When asked what she thinks accounts for her success, Jacqueline Barton responded, "The pursuit of excellence and doing it right are important to me." Cartoonist Cathy Guisewite said, "I'm really competitive with myself. I'm never satisfied with what I've done. I'm always trying to be better than I was the day before." Agi Clark noted, "Whatever I do, I throw myself 100 percent into it, and I do it with all my concentration, all my attention and caring. Also, I think I'm pretty damn talented!" *Voilà!*

Arts

Catherine Murphy

Profession: Artist

Currently: Free-lance Artist; Art Teacher, Yale University

Date of birth: January 22, 1946

Education: B.F.A., Pratt Institute, 1963-1967
Skowhegan School of Painting and Sculpture, 1966

$\mathcal{H}$ilton Kramer, art critic for the *New York Times,* heralded Catherine Murphy as "one of the most accomplished realist painters of our generation" and described her paintings as "at once familiar and mysterious – a dream made up of entirely wide-awake observations."

The composition of Murphy's work is noted for its distinct American aura. Her subjects are commonplace, but as art historian Susan Willard observed, her paintings "transcend the commonplace and arrive at an enigmatic almost mysterious reality . . . intimate in scale and yet distant and aloof."

Murphy produces only a few canvases a year. Working from nature, her technique is painstaking as she strokes detail upon detail onto the canvas. She begins with a broadly brushed, expressive underpainting, which becomes progressively more precise as she works over the canvas with finer and finer brushes, producing a vibrant "felt" surface.

Recognized as a master of realism by the age of thirty, Murphy was "discovered" in 1971 when the prominent art critic John Canaday came across her work at an exhibition on Long Island. He reviewed a portrait of her mother for the *New York Times,* describing it as "going far beyond mere likeness . . . beyond the suggestion of character to fuse both within an evocation of mood and place."

Murphy has been a recipient of grants from the National Endowment for the Arts and the Guggenheim Foundation. She has held numerous individual exhibitions and has participated in selected group exhibitions. Her paintings have been collected by museums and corporations, including the Whitney Museum, Phillips Collection, Hirshhorn Museum, Chase Manhattan Bank, and Exxon Corporation.

Murphy was born in Lexington, Massachusetts, the daughter of a musician who supported his family by working for the U.S. Post Office. She is married to Harry Roseman, a realist sculptor. They live in Poughkeepsie, New York. Once a week, she commutes to New Haven to teach art at Yale University.

What drew you to a career in art?

The word *career* is misleading. Art picks you. You don't pick it. You don't do art unless you have to. It is very difficult to do – to continue doing. When you are a child, you have a little bit of talent and your teachers tell you that you are very good and then you like doing it. But most people who go to art school, most people who study art in college, even graduate school, don't continue being artists once they are out of school, because if you have a choice and you don't *need* to be an artist emotionally, then generally you don't continue being an artist. So *career* is a strange word because I never thought I would make a career in art. I just was an artist, but luckily, since *career* implies making a living at it, I have a career in art.

Did you always know you were going to be an artist?

Yes, I knew I was going to be an artist. I'll tell you a story about my confirmation at around the age of twelve. I was brought up Catholic. My parish was outside Boston in Lexington, Massachusetts, and Cardinal Cushing confirmed us. He was a very impressive man, and he had a very strange Grrr . . . Grrr voice. After he confirmed us, he had an informal chat with the kids, and he asked, "Do any of you have the vocation?" Nobody raised their hand. So I raised my hand – I was always an outgoing child – and I said, "Yes! I am going to be an artist!" My friend Terry Reardon raised his hand and said, "I'm going to be an airplane pilot!" That started a domino effect. Finally, Cardinal Cushing said, "No! Stop! That's not what I meant! What I meant by vocation was if any of you were going to be a priest or a nun." (Laughter) So in answer to your question, yes, it seems like I always knew I was going to be an artist, but I also dabbled in other things in the arts, like music and theater.

What aspect of your work do you find most challenging?

Continuing . . . always to be brave . . . never to get comfortable. You can never be comfortable. You can never think you know something, because the minute you think you know something all is lost. That is, as far as my work is concerned. Where my career is concerned, it's just the fact that it is so unstable.

Where do you get your inspiration?

From everywhere, everything. It's a very complicated question. Mostly from aspects of my own life. Much of the work is based on formal ideas that are part of my own life.

Are you influenced by other artists?

Sure, I think everyone is. Probably less than I was when I was a student, but I often go to shows, and ideas occur to me in those shows. So, of course, I am.

Which artists have influenced you most?

So many. Off the top of my head, I have to say Cezanne, Giovanni Bellini – there are just too many to mention.

Could you describe a typical workday?

I start work around 8:30 in the morning. Because I work from life, my work is very dependent on the kind of light that is available. If it is a sunny day, I work from 8:30 to 12:00. I take a break for lunch. Then I work on a different painting from 1:00 to about 5:30. If it's a cloudy day, I work on the same painting all day. I make dinner, do a few chores, and then, intermittently, work after dinner for another couple of hours.

How do you deal with pressure?

I scream. I cry. I talk. I work.

If you unexpectedly had a month off, how would you spend it?

That would be difficult. I have never taken a month off except to travel. Since graduating from college, I've only taken, probably, a week off.

Is it because you never felt the need to take time off?

Well, I can't. I am not happy unless I am working. So I work all the time. If I took a month off, I would probably spend it reading – lying on a beach somewhere just relaxing. If I had a month to travel, I would go to Italy.

Do you consider painting to be your hobby as well as your work?

No, my work is my work. I garden, and I do other things. It is quite easy to separate the two.

Has it been difficult juggling a career and a family?

I don't have children. I have a husband, and he is an artist, too. I didn't have children on purpose so that I could concentrate on my work. I think it is extremely difficult to do both, especially when you work at home. Many of my friends who are artists and have children have had a great deal of difficulty finding time to work because the children are home and you are home, too. It is very hard to do both, so I didn't.

As a woman, have you experienced discrimination in your profession?

Probably, but not to my face. I think at the beginning of my career, it was very helpful for me to be a woman. People helped me because I was a woman. On the other hand, I probably have been turned down for things I don't even know about. But nobody ever stopped me from being a painter. Nobody ever said to me, "You can't do that because you are a woman."

Who was your role model?

When I was growing up, it was definitely my father. He was a musician. Unfortunately, he had a family to support. I think that is another reason I didn't have children. I saw how hard it was for him. He was a musician who had to take up another job to support us.

What advice could you give someone interested in pursuing a career in art?

Well, if they were going to pursue it as a career, I would tell them not to do it. But if they were going to pursue it because they had to, I would say you have to. I know many, many more poor artists than rich artists. I teach one day a week at Yale, and I tell my students, "Nobody really wants you to be an artist, especially people who love you." It's very difficult.

What do you think accounts for your success?

Well, if it is success in my work, I don't know – I have no idea because it is just so ephemeral. Sometimes I have success; sometimes I have failure in my work. (Laughter) But in my career, I was in the right place at the right time. Certain events happened, and I am amazed by my luck.

Cathy Guisewite

Profession: Cartoonist

Currently: Creator of the comic strip "Cathy"

Date of birth: September 5, 1950

Education: B.A., University of Michigan, 1972 (English)

Cathy Guisewite is described by a former colleague as "an incredibly nice person and immensely talented . . . someone who could sit down and turn out ten scripts in a day, and they would all be good." Guisewite is the creator of the popular comic strip "Cathy," which humorously and realistically depicts the trials of surviving as a young, single, working woman. The strip is syndicated in more than one thousand newspapers.

Her career as a cartoonist began accidentally. At her mother's insistence, Guisewite sent Universal Press Syndicate eighteen tongue-in-cheek drawings she had sent her parents illustrating everyday events in her life. Almost immediately upon receiving the material, the syndicate's executives unanimously agreed to offer her a contract. Lee Salem, the managing editor of Universal Press Syndicate, is quoted as saying, "We felt that Cathy the character was real . . . we were struck by the honesty of her sentiments." Indeed, what is particularly appealing about "Cathy" is her balancing act as she fretfully straddles the line between ardent feminism and die-hard traditionalism.

The first "Cathy" strip appeared on November 22, 1976, in sixty newspapers, but it was not until nine months later that Guisewite steeled herself to leave the security of her advertising job at W. B. Doner & Company to become a cartoonist full-time. Having no formal art training, she trained herself to draw cartoons by following instruction books and studying the strips of cartoonists she admired.

Today "Cathy" is so popular that the strips are gathered annually and published as a collection. Published editions of selected strips include *Sorry I'm Late, My Hair Won't Start; The Salesclerk Made Me Buy It; Stressed for Success; My Cologne Backfired;* and *It's More Than a Pregnancy, It's a Religion.* Guisewite also has done several television specials, one of which won an Emmy Award for best prime-time animated program. In a *World Almanac and Book of Facts* poll of newspaper editors across the United States, Guisewite was selected in 1984 and 1986 as one of "America's Twenty-five Most Influential Women."

In 1980, Guisewite left her hometown of Detroit to settle in the tranquil town of Santa Barbara, California. Three years later, feeling she needed anxiety to keep producing her strip, Guisewite moved to Los Angeles where, she insists, "even a trip to the drugstore produces anxiety."

When not working on her comic strip, Guisewite designs and writes copy for a number of "Cathy" novelty products. During her time off, she enjoys tennis, skiing, and watching old movies. Guisewite lives in a spacious, home/studio in the Hollywood Hills with her dog, Trolley.

How did you become a cartoonist?

When I was young, my mother always told me to write about my problems instead of talking to people about them. She used to say, "Don't go blabbing to your friends. Write about it!" So starting at age ten, I got used to writing out my feelings. After college, I was working in the advertising business. My career was going well, but my love life was miserable, so it was only natural for me to write about the confusion, the conflicts, and whatever depressions and frustrations I was feeling.

One night, instead of just writing about it, I drew a picture of what I looked like sitting there writing these depressing things and eating everything in the kitchen. I was really overweight at that time. Just to let my mother know that I was coping with life without talking to anybody, like she always taught me to do, I sent the drawing home with a letter. I began sorting the day's events using little drawings I would send home to my mother. She insisted the things I was writing and drawing were universal and I should send them in and try to sell them. I was humiliated by that concept. It was very personal stuff and me at my worst.

My mother finally went to the library, looked up comic strip syndicates, and wrote me out a list of whom she thought I should send my work to. So I sent some drawings to the name on the top of her list, just to get her off my back. That was Universal Press Syndicate.

In spite of the fact I really didn't know how to draw at the time and my work was not even in comic strip form, they signed me up. The syndicate had been looking for a comic strip that dealt with the changing world for women in a realistic way. They felt that my drawings were honest and captured that experience. Cartoonists generally work for years developing strips. Mine was a very bizarre and lucky situation.

What made you decide to name the main character and comic strip after yourself?

When they said they wanted to make it into a comic strip, the syndicate based their decision on drawings I had done when I was literally illustrating my own life. I fought very hard to name the main character something else. I thought it would be embarrassing to name her Cathy. So I bought a book of baby names and I sent in strips using different names. But the syndicate really liked the idea that the main character would be named Cathy.

When a comic strip comes out, do you get inquiries regarding what is going on in your life, or have you distanced yourself sufficiently from Cathy at this point?

There really is a part of me in all the characters. I think the people who know me know which parts of me are like Cathy, Irving, and Mr. Pinkley. The characters of Mom and Dad in the comic strip are the only ones that I don't even try to disguise. They are pretty much direct quotes from my own conversations with my parents. I think my friends see little pieces of themselves show up now and then, but there isn't any one character who represents any one person in my life, except for the parents.

What is your primary job as a cartoonist?

I think my job is to offer a couple of minutes of relief during the day. Different comic strips have different functions. Mine is – especially for women – to let them feel they are not alone. A woman can read my strip and say, "I'm not the only woman who balances my check book by switching banks and starting all over. I'm not the only woman who buys fifty dollars of fresh fruit and vegetables at the grocery store and then stops at McDonald's for a Big Mac on the way home." We need to laugh about the little things that bog us down. That's what makes it possible to go on and keep trying!

What do you find most challenging about your work?

Writing the strip is the hardest thing. It is such a small space, and it is such a public display of work. I always feel so honored to have that chunk of space in the newspaper every day, and that feeling only increases with time. So it becomes this horrible, hideous pressure to not just write some little joke for the day, but it becomes "Oh, my God, what could I possibly think of writing that is worthy of having this space in the paper?" I make myself fairly nuts about the writing. I spend a long time on the writing. I throw out a lot, and I rework it a lot. I like to take the drawing home to do and watch old movies on TV while I draw. My comic strip is different that way. It is a lot more word-oriented than art-oriented.

On average, how much time do you spend on a strip?

There is no way to say on the writing. Sometimes it takes a few minutes; other times I will work on an idea for most of the day. On the drawing, it usually takes about an hour and a half to draw a daily strip and maybe four and a half hours to draw a Sunday strip. But that's after I have the words figured out, exactly how they will go.

Cathy's problems always seem to be on the cutting edge. Where do you get your ideas?

I'm lucky because I do a strip that is so close to daily life. I don't have to think of miscellaneous, obscure jokes. I can pretty much look around my office to see what I should write next. If I can't get started on a theme for the week, sometimes I'll buy women's magazines and flip through them to see what people are talking about, or thinking about. A trip to the mall is always good for inspiration. And if I'm really desperate, I'll call my mother!

When you finish a strip and it's a real winner, who is the first person you want to share it with?

I never like anybody to see anything. The only person in the world I would ever try an idea out on is my younger sister, who works as an advertising copywriter in Detroit. If I'm having a problem with the strip, for instance, I'll write one with three different endings. I'll call my sister and ask her which one she thinks really works. Or I'll call her up to ask if she thinks other women do this or that, or if it is just some neurotic thing only women in our family do that we don't necessarily want revealed in the paper. (Laughter) She is usually very blunt and usually very right!

But other than my sister, I can only write the strip if I am pretending nobody else is going to read it. That's not to say I don't every now and then do a strip I think is brilliant and I'm excited to open the paper knowing other people are seeing it, too. I almost never feel that way at the time they are coming out. I always think, "Oh, gee, that could be better. It could've been done this way." But then I feel that ability to torture myself is one of the qualities that makes it possible for me to write this strip. (Laughter) It's what people identify with. It's part of the package!

What is the most frequent problem you encounter in your work?

Not being able to think of anything to draw! But you get used to that. It's sort of a low-level panic that is always with me, but that's okay. I can cope.

How do you deal with the pressure?

I used to eat! (Laughter) Fortunately, I quit doing that. To write this strip, I need to feel that I'm going to be totally by myself for a while with no interruptions. So that means either I have to be home alone in the evening or I need to close the doors in my office. I play depressing music and just sort of relax into it and pretend there isn't total chaos going on around me. It's really like going into a trance because I usually play the same tape over and over. I've been playing the same tape now for maybe a year.

What tape is that?

It's a tape called *Famous Blue Raincoat* by Jennifer Warren. Somebody gave it to me, and it had the right sound. There are a couple of depressing songs on it that are real killers. (Laughter) They get me in the exact right mood to be humorous.

What qualities are you often called upon to use as a cartoonist?

Insecurity. (Laughter) A star quality. I think it takes a real blend of insecurity and total confidence to be able to write a strip like mine or like "Peanuts," or some of the other really personal strips. I think you really have to feel the stuff you are writing, but you also have to be confident enough to feel it's good enough to be printed or that somebody else could learn from it or might be amused by it. It's that combination. Also, I have great stamina. I really like to work! If I have a free evening, I always spend it trying to write strips. I'm always trying to get ahead. I never do! I'm always totally optimistic; I'm right at the brink of getting three months ahead. In fact, I've been doing the job for fourteen years, and I'm still hanging on to my deadlines with my fingernails.

What do you think accounts for your success?

I'm really competitive with myself. I'm never satisfied with what I've done. I'm always trying to be better than I was the day before, always trying to make the strip better.

If you had a month off, how would you spend it?

(Laughter) Getting ahead! That's funny because I fantasized about that. I thought, "If I could only take a month's vacation, what would I do?" And I know what I would do: I'd rent a hotel room somewhere and try to get ahead on my comic strip.

Do you think it would be difficult juggling a career and a family?

Being single has allowed me to live a very self-indulgent life, as far as my work goes. I can work on it at night, on the weekends, whenever. Except for my dog, I basically don't have any other real responsibilities. I am not looking to live the rest of my life this way! When you hit forty, the alarm clock starts sounding. I definitely want to have a family, and I know that I have to have it like tomorrow. Almost all the cartoonists I know are married and have children. For example, Lynn Johnston spends a huge amount of time with her family and still manages to have a very successful strip "For Better or For Worse." I think it is certainly doable.

Who were your role models?

Charles Schulz always was and still is a role model for me. I feel that "Peanuts" really paved the way on the comic pages for a strip like mine. It was the first strip that dealt with real human feelings, real insecurities, and frustrations in the comic pages. I still really admire Charles Schulz. He still writes and draws every single strip himself. He is still just as excited to go to work in the morning. He's just as pleased with himself when he writes a good one, just as depressed when he can't think of anything to write. I think he has a lot of integrity.

What advice would you give someone interested in pursuing a career as a cartoonist?

I would say, "Call my mother!" (Laughter) Short of that, the most important thing is to go with your instincts. My editor at the syndicate gets a lot of submissions from people trying to copy other people, either in art style, writing, or speech. What the syndicates are always looking for is a totally new point of view, a strip that is unique. So I would say that is probably the most important thing. It's a hard business. It's very competitive, and it seems to be getting worse. A lot of towns used to have two or three newspapers with different comics; now most towns have only one paper. When a newspaper adds a comic strip, they have to drop an old one because they never allow more space for the comics. I certainly am proof that it is possible! I would encourage anybody to try it. It makes for a wonderful career, and it's a wonderful way of expressing yourself. It's fun, you get wonderful feedback from people, and it's all about keeping a sense of humor about life.

Judith Jamison

Profession: Choreographer/Dancer

Currently: Artistic Director, Alvin Ailey American Dance Theater and Alvin Ailey American Dance Center

Date of birth: May 10, 1943

Education: Judimar School of Dance, 1950- 1961
Fisk University, 1961- 1962 (Psychology)
Philadelphia Dance Academy, 1962- 1964

"$\mathcal{J}$n motion, she blazes with a fearful intensity hurtling through the air," wrote Hubert Saal in *Newsweek,* "like a spear plunged into the heart of space." When Judith Jamison appears onstage, her proud, commanding presence elicits an instant ovation. Jamison emerged in the 1970s as the first black superstar of American dance. Her five feet ten inches stature, her elegant, imperial manner, and her impeccable technique incorporating classical ballet, modern dance, tap, acrobatics, jazz, and primitive dance, produced a strikingly unique style.

In 1964, Agnes de Mille discovered Jamison during a master dance class at the Philadelphia Dance Academy and invited her to make her New York debut in de Mille's ballet *The Four Marys.* After an audition, which Alvin Ailey happened to observe, she was invited to become a member of the Alvin Ailey Dance Theater. From 1965 to 1980, she toured the United States, Europe, Asia, South America, and Africa. Deborah Jowitt, writing in the *Village Voice,* described her as "extravagantly tall with a purring kind of strength and a leap that looks as if she had been poured upward." Recognizing Jamison's extraordinary talent and captivating stage presence, Ailey choreographed some of his most enduring works for her, most notably the tour de force *Cry,* a solo depicting the nobility and suffering of black women in which Jamison played both a slave and a queen.

In 1984, Jamison choreographed her first work, *Divining,* for the Alvin Ailey American Dance Theater. She went on to create new works for many other companies. In 1989, she choreographed her first opera, Boito's *Mefistofele,* for the Opera Company of Philadelphia. Her PBS special, "The Dance Maker," aired nationally during the spring of the same year.

Jamison is also a lecturer and master teacher, a past presidential appointee to the National Endowment for the Arts (NEA), and a recipient of honorary doctorate degrees from numerous universities. In 1988, she debuted her own company, The Jamison Project, and embarked on a critically acclaimed U.S. tour one year later. Shortly after the death of Alvin Ailey in 1989, she was appointed artistic director of the Alvin Ailey American Dance Theater and Alvin Ailey American Dance Center, the official school of the Ailey company. According to *Dance Magazine,* "Under her leadership the company has entered a new and exciting period of creativity and growth."

Judith Jamison is the subject of the book *Aspects of a Dancer.* She has said, "Dancing is like the aura I feel in church. I walk into a church and there is a warmth, a safeness, a haven. The stage is like that for me, a vacuum where I can express myself."

What drew you into the field of dance?

Well, I was put into dance when I was six years old – "put in" meaning that I had parents who had the wherewithal to understand that they had a daughter with so much energy that they had to point her in some direction. That's what did it!

What aspect of your work do you find most demanding?

Doing interviews! (Laughter) They take me out of a rehearsal that I need to be in or from a lecture demonstration or master class. Words take me out of where I want to be at the moment. My basic form of communication is through movement. I'm very spiritual in what I do. It has nothing to do with verbiage.

Are you eager to get up and go to work in the morning?

Yes, because I don't consider it getting up and going to work. I have a very blessed life. This is what I want to do. There are not very many people who can say that. This isn't work. This is pleasure!

What do you find challenging about your work?

Working with dancers; working with different choreographers; holding a company together; being a psychiatrist, a policewoman, a bottle washer, a mentor, a choreographer, a dancer – being myself.

What are you most proud of having accomplished?

Living! Living for forty-nine years and enjoying it and keeping my sense of humor! Loving what I am doing and being committed to it for lo these many years and wanting to share that kind of commitment with young people.

Is it necessary for a choreographer to also be a dancer?

No, not these days. Apparently, there are a lot of people who understand shape and know the vocabulary. I think it's ideal if you dance, so you know what it feels like. But a lot of choreographers have not danced professionally in front of an audience. It's an enhancement to be a performer before you choreograph, but that does not necessarily turn you into a wonderful choreographer in and of itself. You never know where the talent is going to come from.

Where do you get your ideas and inspiration?

Life! Anything from life, any experience that you've had. That's the whole idea about dance. You bring what you've experienced onto the stage with you. Otherwise, you have someone up there just doing steps.

How do you deal with pressure?

I don't have time to have it! (Laughter) Pressure to me means negative. So you don't let things build up. By the time I get home, I'm too tired. What did I just read about George Abbott, a Broadway choreographer? He is 103 years old and he says, "I leave it. I don't worry about anything." You know, that's it. I leave it! If you are carrying something around with you that you don't need, you've got to get rid of it, or you can't work.

When you've choreographed a piece and you are watching it performed from the back of the house, what do you look for? What thoughts are running through your mind?

Everything from "Did I take the garbage out this morning?" to "Oh, did they do that step right?" It's just a lot of things. It cannot be pinpointed. I mean, your life goes on right before your eyes because you are entrusting other human beings to translate what is in your innermost self. So that's everything. You can stay glued to the back wall and be nervous, or you can realize that the curtain goes up and there is nothing you can do about it because you already had enough rehearsal. The dancers know what they are doing, and you have to trust them. You are thinking a million things.

What do you think accounts for your success?

Family. A very strong upbringing. I have very strong parents and grandparents. I have a lot of people around me going in the same direction – ever upward; people who care about their lives and realize that they have great gifts and it is a privilege for them to be here on this earth and to share whatever they have.

Who was your role model?

Every woman who has ever achieved something in her life. Not just women – everyone who has achieved something in their life and cut their own niche. I don't have any names to drop on you. It would take too long!

What advice would you give someone interested in following in your footsteps?

I'd suggest number one that they don't follow in my footsteps; that they have their own shoes to wear and they should wear them and they are sufficient. To have deep faith and trust in your commitment, your dedication, and your love of what you are doing – no matter what you are doing – just as long as it is positive. Be generous and keep a sense of humor!

Kay Unger

Profession: Fashion Designer

Currently: Partner and Designer, Gillian

Date of birth: May 22, 1945

Education: Washington University, 1965 (Art)
              B.S., Parsons School of Design, 1968 (Fashion Design)

"*I* understand my customer because I have been dressing her for nineteen years," Kay Unger says. "We have grown together." Unger insists that her customer is a lot like herself: active, self-confident, assertive, and feminine. As a fashion designer, she has garnered a reputation for designing clothes that work for today's woman, taking her from office to dinner, conference to cocktail, and day to night. This design philosophy has made her company, Gillian, one of the most successful dress companies in the marketplace, with annual sales of more than $100 million.

Unger's trademark as a designer has always been innovation and originality of color combinations. She developed a keen eye for color and design during early training as a painter in her native Chicago. Unger studied fashion at Washington University and at New York's Parsons School of Design. After assisting designers Jo Copeland, Gayle Kirkpatrick, and Geoffrey Beene, she went on to design boutique and sports collections for Teal Traina.

In 1972, she launched Gillian with her partner Jon Levy. Today she presides over a multimillion-dollar business with eight divisions. While each division has its own focus, the Gillian lines work together to meet all the fashion needs of the executive woman.

Unger is active in the business community as a founding member of the Committee of 200, a leading group of American women entrepreneurs, and as a member of the executive board of the Fashion Group. She is also very much involved in her community and maintains a rigorous schedule of charity commitments. Unger serves on the board of trustees of the Boys Clubs of America and founded an organization called Children Taking Action Against AIDS. She also directs the Epstein Fine Arts Fund, founded by her father in 1954, which assists deserving students in the arts.

When not running her business and keeping up with professional and volunteer associations, she spends time with her husband Gerald, a plastic surgeon, and their two sons.

What drew you to a career in fashion design?

Designing was always in my soul. When I was seven, I wrote a letter saying that I wanted to be a professional skater so I could wear gorgeous costumes. But if I couldn't be a skater, I would be a designer and make the gorgeous costumes. I've always loved clothing. My mother was very involved in fashion, so I was exposed to very fine clothes as I grew up. As a kid, I taught myself how to sew. Then I went to college to be a painter and discovered that I was an okay painter but that I didn't think that I could make a living at it. The school I was attending, Washington University in St. Louis, had a really nice design department, and I decided to try it.

How did you first get started in the fashion business?

While attending Washington University, I heard that the finest design school was the Parsons School of Design, so I went there. At Parsons, I set goals. I decided if I did well, I would go the next step and apply to work for a designer. I did do well and I started working for some people who are no longer in the business. Then I spent a year working for Geoffrey Beene, where I gained very good experience. I was able to work with very fine clothing, and I learned a lot about how to merchandize. Then I went to work for Teal Traina and designed my first collection.

After a year and a half, I tried somewhere else. Within six months, I ventured out on my own. I bought fabric and negotiated a very good deal where I didn't have to pay for the fabric until after I had shipped the garments. I just dove in and started making clothing, not knowing anything about business. Eventually that was my biggest problem. I didn't know how to cost the garments, and I didn't know anything about production. To be free to design, I needed help in other areas, so I took in two partners and started Gillian.

What aspect of your work do you find most challenging?

I think growth is what I find most challenging – going from being a designer who did everything herself to having a rather large staff, inspiring people, and knowing how to tell them you are disappointed when things aren't going well. It's really easy to pat your staff on the back when things are good. It's difficult to tell them when things aren't good. I really think growing into being a boss has been my most challenging job.

What do you enjoy most about your work?

The fact that fashion is forever changing is the part I hate about it and love about it. I swore I would never be in the business for more than ten years. Now it's about twenty-five years that I've been doing it! The customer is constantly changing, and consequently her needs change, too. It is challenging to fill fashion gaps, pursue opportunities, and grow into new products. It's very exciting. Sometimes I hate it, but most of the time I love it.

How do you select your fabric?

I search the markets. I just came back from two weeks in Korea, where 90 percent of the time I was searching for fabric. First you look at what is already out there, what material people are responding to. There were years when they didn't want silk. They only wanted washables. There were years when polyester was considered wonderful, and then it was awful. Sometimes surface texture is important. You have to keep in touch with the customer. I look for fabrics that take color well and are interesting, fabrics that have an expensive look. I look at fabrics from Europe, America, and Asia, and I also develop my own fabrics. We don't make terribly expensive clothing, but I'll look at the most expensive fabrics, try to get inspired by them, and try to inspire my suppliers to make something similar.

As a fashion designer, what special pressures do you experience?

I would say always trying to stay ahead and know what the next trend is; determining how far you can push your customer; keeping in contact with them, which I'm really good at; and trying never to underestimate them. My customer has changed so much from the time I started designing. She really is my age, although there is a span of at least ten years either way. It used to be that she never understood half of what I made because I was farther along than she was. I was more advanced, more adventurous. This woman was still at home, not working. Now this customer is pushing me to do the most that I can do for her.

Is the hem length a major source of concern for you each season?

It really is. We notice that the short dresses often sell faster because they look newer, younger, and wonderful on a hanger. Yet stores really don't want them. In the spring, they sell very quickly, but if you carry them through to the fall, they don't. In winter, women want to cover their legs. Then with the career clothes you have to remember that a lot of these women work in banks, law firms, etc., and they need the length, whether they are young or old. So we sell some dresses in two lengths. That doesn't show indecision; it shows that there are two sets of customers.

How do you relax?

Easily! I love movies – old films, new films, whatever. I stay up late and watch movies on television, and that helps me relax. If I can get out once a week to a movie, I'm just in heaven! I like to listen to music. I like rock music. If I just go out to dinner or to my country house for one day on a weekend, I'll relax. I can turn off my work pretty easily.

Could you describe a typical workday?

Typically, I'd say it starts between 8:00 and 8:30. I usually come to the office and pass out lists of everything everybody needs to do that day or at least that week. I have several divisions, so usually by 9:30 I have a meeting with one of the divisions for about two hours, and then I meet with a couple of people to get them started on whatever they have to do. I usually do fittings for one or two hours in the middle of the day. After that, I have another design meeting or I sit with the designers – one each day – and discuss some ideas that they should be working on.

The rest of the day is a little less scheduled. I may meet with the print designer, have a budget meeting with my partner, go to the showroom and meet with buyers, look at fabrics, or meet with people who have special projects they need to discuss with me. There is always some urgent problem that has to be squeezed into my schedule. I try to get out once in a while, though I don't get out much. On Mondays, I work sometimes until 10:00 at night. Some of the people stay late with me, and we go over all the presentation boards for whatever season they are working on. I do charity work, so some nights I make a list of what needs to be done or who needs to be called, and I have my secretary make the phone calls to check where we are on certain projects.

When you design, where do you get your ideas?

From magazines – European magazines, menswear magazines, home furnishing magazines, lots of magazines. I look through stores to see what people are doing at more expensive levels. I just keep my eyes open. Ideas could come from museums, Broadway shows, movies, books – anything. They could come from going to the Empire State Building and seeing the art deco doors.

Is your wardrobe made up of your own designs?

Mine and others. I don't just wear my own designs. I find it interesting to try other designers who may use more expensive fabric than I can afford. We have to limit ourselves to a certain price level, so it's nice once in a while to be able to wear more expensive fabric and get inspiration from something that's far more expensive than what we would normally make. I feel it, wear it, and get ideas from it. It's fun.

What do you think accounts for your success?

Hard work. At Parsons, they taught us that it's 97 percent hard work and 3 percent talent. In my case, I can't give you a percentage of my talent, but certainly hard work, drive, perseverance, and caring count for a lot of my success.

What are you most proud of having achieved?

I think I'm most proud of still being in business after nineteen years, having watched people more famous and much bigger than we are come and go. We're not the largest, but we are the longest in the business, just about. I'm really proud of that.

As a fashion designer, do you enjoy getting dressed up?

It's a constant pain! I'm definitely the happiest in tights and a sweatshirt. If I have to go out for a black-tie occasion, I hate it. Basically, I like to dress for comfort and for getting a lot of work done. Because I work with bolts of fabric and my office happens to be in a loft-type building, I'm more comfortable being casual. But I love trying new things. I'm pretty slim, so I can try all kinds of shapes and wear pretty much anything. It just depends on my mood. I certainly like to change. I just don't like to have to get dressed up every day.

I save everything. I have clothes that I've saved for years. I don't wear 90 percent of them, but every once in a while, I'll dig something up that's really old and pull it together with a new look. I like to play with that and color combinations. It's a lot of fun!

Has it been difficult juggling a career and a family?

It's very difficult. I know everybody does it, but it still pulls at me. My kids still call me the minute they get home from school to ask, "When are you coming home?" I came home after two weeks of traveling in Korea because they kept calling to say, "Please come home; we miss you."

It's nice to walk the kids to school in the morning and do all kinds of things with them. It's hard getting enough time to plan special things, buy gifts, and not have my secretary do everything.

As a woman, have you experienced discrimination in your profession?

Yes, certainly, with banks. Earlier in my career when I went to a bank to obtain a loan to buy an apartment, they wouldn't loan me the funds, but they would loan money to my male partner, even though we both drew the same salary.

Who were your role models?

Liz Claiborne and Anne Klein.

What advice would you give someone interested in pursuing a career in fashion design?

If you are a designer, the advice would be to learn as much as you can about the making of the garments. The more you know, the less you have to depend on others. If you know how to make the pattern yourself, how to drape the garment, and how to sew it, you will certainly feel more secure. Learn whatever you can about the business side: costing of garments, how to do a business plan, how to borrow money, how to read a spread sheet.

How does one break into the fashion field?

Go to the stores, look at the clothes, and identify the designers you respect. Then, if you are just coming out of school, go and beg that person for a job, even if you have to work for free to learn. You pretty much have to go on your own from there. The days of finding an investor to back you are practically gone. The only way to do it is to work your way up from within a company and to become noticed that way.

Susan Seidelman

Profession: Filmmaker

Date of birth: December 11, 1952

Education: B.A., Drexel University, 1973 (Film)
M.F.A., Graduate School of Film and Television, New York
University, 1977

Susan Seidelman has been described as "one of the most successful filmmakers to have emerged in the United States in the 1980s." Her films are most noted for "the beautiful fluidity of her storytelling and the offbeat authenticity of her character development." A member of the Directors Guild of America, Seidelman has amassed such film credits as *Smithereens* (1982), *Desperately Seeking Susan* (1985), *Making Mr. Right* (1987), *Cookie* (1989), and *She-Devil* (1989).

Seidelman, the eldest of three children, was born and raised in Pennsylvania. She freely admits that she does not look like your typical movie director: "I'm slightly under five feet, so the first day on the set, guys in the crew think I'm there to bring them coffee." When she begins to direct, however, that misconception is quickly laid to rest. Often described as a "serious perfectionist" and a "human dynamo," she features in her films ebullient, high-energy women not unlike herself.

Three years after earning her M.F.A. [Master of Fine Arts], Seidelman independently produced her first feature-length film, *Smithereens.* The film was a hit at the 1982 Cannes Film Festival, launching Seidelman's career.

Her next film, *Desperately Seeking Susan,* was funded by Orion and starred Rosanna Arquette and a little-known rock singer named Madonna. During the filming, Madonna achieved stardom. Taking advantage of Madonna's breakthrough, Seidelman completed the postproduction work in only four months, so impressing Orion executives that she was offered a three-picture contract. *Desperately Seeking Susan* grossed $30 million at the box office — six times its cost.

Seidelman lives in Manhattan in an airy, sparsely furnished apartment at the edge of Soho with Jonathan Brett, an independent film producer, and their infant son, Oscar. Seidelman acknowledges that although Los Angeles is the center of the film industry, she prefers the bounce of New York City.

How did you get started in filmmaking?

Actually, I wasn't really interested in movies as a kid. My interest developed when I was in college. I went to school originally to be a fashion designer, but I got disillusioned with the course. I took a film course because I thought it would be fun to watch movies. I had no deep interest in filmmaking, but I had this wonderful teacher, and he made me think about movies in a new way. I took Film Appreciation I, II, III, IV, and V. I kept taking his course over and over again, and by the time I got out of college, I knew that I loved watching movies. But I never really thought I would have the opportunity to make them.

On a whim, I applied to NYU's graduate film school, not thinking I would get in. I was shocked when I got accepted! This was in 1974, and it was a three-year master's program. At NYU you got hands-on experience. You actually went out with a camera, shot short films, and edited them. From the moment I started filming, I knew it was something I loved.

What aspect of your work do you find most demanding?

Filmmaking is physically exhausting because you are working sometimes sixteen hours a day. When you are actually in production, you are getting up at 6:00 in the morning and going to bed at 12:00 or 1:00 at night. After the first few weeks, you get really tired. Just to have the stamina to continue getting up in the morning when you are drained is demanding. I also think there is a certain amount of pressure, especially if you are making films that cost millions of dollars. The average film costs $17 million. You feel a responsibility to the studio, and the bigger the budget, the more people are looking over your shoulder. So there's a lot of business and politics involved. That can be emotionally demanding.

How do you deal with pressure?

I try to put on blinders. I think that's the only way! Sometimes you can get overloaded, especially on a movie set, where you are working with about eighty people daily. There are a lot of demands on the director, and it can get overwhelming if you don't try to stay focused and deal with one problem at a time.

Could you describe a typical workday when you are in production?

You start rehearsing with the actors by 7:00 A.M. That might take an hour or two. After you've blocked out the scene, the actors go off to their trailer for hair and makeup. Then you work with the director of photography [DP] setting up the shot. The actors come back out to the set around 10:00, and you shoot until 1:00, then break for lunch. It's a half-hour lunch, and at 1:30 you start again.

Usually, if it's an afternoon scene, you shoot until you lose the light – that might be until 6:00 or 7:00. Then you drive back to the city and go to dailies. [Dailies are when you go to the lab and watch what you've filmed the day before to make sure it turned out okay.] That may take another hour or so. After that you might meet with the DP to discuss what you need to do the following day and make sure you have all the equipment you'll need.

I usually get home around 11:00, grab a bite to eat, and fall asleep around midnight. After a while, your body gets physically drained. On Saturdays, you are usually meeting with the DP and the storyboard artist to block out the scenes for the following week. I try to take Sundays off so I can catch up on sleep and just vegetate.

What do you look for in a script?

The characters. That's the thing that appeals to me the most. A strong female protagonist will just grab me. I'm not an action or technical director.

All that kind of stuff doesn't really appeal to me. But often there's something about the characters or the theme of a script that I can relate to and hope other people will be able to relate to also.

What are you most proud of having accomplished?

I think the thing that is most satisfying to me is when I meet people who say, "I saw that film, and it really had a big impact on me" or "It really moved me." For example, I've met people who have said that after seeing *Desperately Seeking Susan,* they decided to move to New York. Cinema can be very persuasive. Sometimes I'm unaware of how powerful it is in spreading ideas and getting people to think about things.

What do you think accounts for your success?

Staying focused and tenacity—not taking no for an answer. I think that you have to believe in yourself because no one else is going to believe in you if you don't. When you stop believing in yourself, other people begin to lose confidence in you, too. This is especially important for women involved in filmmaking because, let's face it, there haven't been a lot of female role models in the movie industry. Filmmaking, particularly directing, has been very much a male-dominated profession. Therefore, women have to pave their own way, and part of that is figuring out what we as women want to say and not taking no for an answer. If Hollywood is not going to give you the opportunity, you have to make the opportunity for yourself. That's why a lot of female directors come out of the independent film world, as opposed to going through the studio system. I started out in New York making a very low-budget, independent film because I knew I wasn't going to get a break in Hollywood and I didn't want to waste my time knocking on closed doors.

If you unexpectedly had a month off, how would you spend it?

Well, I do have months off. The thing about filmmaking is that, unlike a lot of other jobs where you work nine to five, Monday through Friday, with filmmaking you may have one year on, then one year off. It's a different kind of rhythm because essentially it's a free-lance job. There might be a full year where you are not working on a particular movie, where you are just trying to develop various scripts or fill your head with new ideas.

What advice would you give someone interested in pursuing a career in filmmaking?

Well, two things. One of the best ways to learn to be a filmmaker is to make films. I think it's like being a painter. You can't be a painter without picking up a paintbrush and applying paint to canvas. It's fine to read film books and watch movies, but the best thing is to get your hands on some equipment and actually make a film, whether it's Super-8, 16mm, or video. The second thing is not to sit around and wait for opportunities to come to you. Try to create your own. You don't have to live in Hollywood or have a relative in the film business to do that.

Has it been difficult juggling a career and a family?

I'll see! I don't really know yet because I just had a baby about seven months ago. That's one of the reasons I've taken the last couple of months off. I really want to be around my son and watch him grow. But I am planning to go back to work this coming year. I would imagine it's going to be difficult but not impossible, I hope. Certainly children, especially young children, are incredibly demanding, and so is being a director. Unfortunately, directing isn't the kind of job where you can go home and turn it off easily. I know it's possible to do both things, but I think I'm going to have to figure it out as I go along.

As a woman, have you experienced discrimination in your profession?

There is a lot of discrimination in my profession, especially when you look at the statistics. Look at the number of women who are directing movies compared to the number of men. It's pretty horrendous. I can think of maybe ten women who are directing feature films. When I started eight years ago, I could think of three. So I guess its gotten a little better over the past few years, but it's still pretty slim.

Did you have any role models?

It's weird, because before I started film school, which was in 1974, I didn't know of any female directors. I had heard about Ida Lupino, but I had never seen any of her movies. While I was in school, there was one Italian female director, Lina Wertmuller, who I thought was wonderful. She made several films in the mid-seventies that were inspirational for me: *The Seduction of Mimi, Love and Anarchy,* and her most popular movie, *Seven Beauties.* I just thought she was brilliant. What I thought was great about her films was that they had real guts; they weren't timid. She wasn't afraid to make strong statements, and for me that was inspirational.

Nadja Salerno-Sonnenberg

Profession: Musician

Currently: Concert Violinist

Date of birth: June 10, 1961

Education: Curtis Institute of Music (Philadelphia), 1969- 1975
Juilliard School, 1975- 1981

$\mathcal{V}$ iolinist Nadja Salerno-Sonnenberg's rousing performances have earned her great respect and acclaim in the world of music. Her talent has been called "so intense and original, it is positively frightening." Audiences and critics alike have been captivated by the mixture of passion and eloquence in her performances.

At the age of twenty, in 1981, Salerno-Sonnenberg was the youngest performer ever to win the Walter W. Naumburg International Violin Competition, widely recognized as the most prestigious annual musical competition in the United States. The following year, when she made her major New York debut with the American Symphony Orchestra at Carnegie Hall, she was praised by a critic for her "ability to make her instrument speak in very personal ways." She has since appeared with the world's most renowned symphonies and has made numerous festival guest appearances.

Salerno-Sonnenberg was born in Rome and moved with her family to the United States at the age of eight to study the violin at the Curtis Institute of Music. She was the youngest student ever admitted into its precollege division. She later studied with Dorothy DeLay at Juilliard, where she was presented with a $15,000 violin paid for by an anonymous donor. She has done numerous recordings for Angel Records and has written a book, *Nadja: On My Way,* published in 1989. Her passions outside of music include baseball, auto racing, and old movies. She resides in a spacious apartment overlooking New York's Central Park.

What made you decide to become a professional musician?

The decision was made when I was about nineteen years old. Like most teenagers, I had to think about my future. I was coming out of a confusing time. I had been playing the violin since I was five and never really thought about what it would be like to do this for the rest of my life. At that point, I didn't play the fiddle for about seven or eight months. I realized that it would be a shame not to pursue the violin, a shame to throw away all that work and talent. I realized I loved making music so much that I was ready to make it my life's work.

What aspect of your work do you find most demanding?

It's a combination of things. What's very demanding is the lifestyle. It's not so much playing the concert but getting to the town and the planes and the hotels and the rehearsals and the waiting and everything that goes wrong in between. It makes getting onto the stage difficult.

As far as actually playing the instrument is concerned, it's demanding because you never get to a point where you can say, "Okay, now I have mastered it! I can't get any better!" It never happens in the performing arts. Always there are things to improve. You get to one level of playing, and you realize there is yet another level and another level. It's like climbing a mountain. You think you can see the top of the mountain when you are at the bottom, but when you get to a certain point, you see there is more. That is demanding, and sometimes it is frustrating, but most times it is rewarding because it never becomes boring or tiresome.

Are you eager to get up and practice in the morning?

No. Maybe I shouldn't say that! For instance, if I have a concert coming up and I have to play a Tchaikovsky concerto or something that I already know, then it's a matter of getting that piece back into shape. Within a couple of days, it's ready to be performed, but it's not in great shape if I haven't played it for a year. So that kind of practice is necessary. It's tedious, but it's necessary. If I'm learning a new piece, especially a piece that I adore, that is exciting, that is something I look forward to getting up and doing.

How do you deal with pressure?

I'm not sure I have a definite answer for that. I deal with pressure in many different ways. There are times when I just sit down and do a crossword puzzle and try not to think about it. Or I'll just stay and work in my house. There are things that I do that take my mind away from the career. Mostly, it's fixing, building, and making things better in the house or seeing my friends. Living with pressure every single day, you get used to it, but it's hard. Some concerts are very important in the season, and the pressure mounts the closer you get to that concert. It takes its toll.

What do you think accounts for your success?

My approach to playing. In other words, I look at the violin as my tool: that's the instrument I know; that's the instrument I've been working on since I was a kid. My goal is to make music. It is not necessarily to play the violin better than anyone else. I've never considered myself to be a violinist but, rather, a musician. There are many different approaches to a particular instrument. I have never approached the violin as an instrument to master. My goal has always been to play a piece of music in a certain way. I am very committed. I think musically that is why I am where I am. As far as the media, there is something about my personality that people love or hate. I have become very popular in that way. I think the combo is why I am here professionally.

What qualities are necessary to succeed as a professional musician?

That's a loaded question! You must have some innate musical talent. That is extremely important. Some incredibly successful professionals – lawyers and doctors – love music and would do anything to be successful with an instrument but cannot. So you have to be born with some sort of natural talent: an ear, a rhythm, an intonation. Of course, all those things are developed through your training. You require different things at different stages. I required a certain something when I was in school. Now that I am a concert artist and this is what I do with my life, I require other things. Also, if you are dedicated and take pride in your work, if your goal is not just to get by but to be proud of what you have done – no matter what it is – that is a formula for success.

Who were your role models?

Musicians. Mostly opera singers whom I adored musically and theatrically as I was growing up. There was my teacher, who taught me so much about how to deal with the business – not just playing the violin but how to deal with the business. She prepared me so well for that! Many people I have met along the way have helped me. Conductors have helped me so much musically and otherwise. My mom and grandmother have been a constant inspiration as far as character is concerned.

If you unexpectedly had a month off, how would you spend it?

A million different ways! I would love a month off! I have a lot of varied interests. I think that is also partially why I play the way I play and I am the way I am. My life hasn't been just violin or just music. Music is what keeps me going, but I have interests in so many things: writing, inventing . . . gosh, just name it, and I would be interested in it. I love sports! If I had more time, I would be more athletic. I love building things in my apartment. I am very good at building and fixing things: shelves and floors and things like that. I'm like the perfect wife and the perfect husband! I love working out a mystery. I like to write. I like politics. I like so many things that if I had a month off, I wouldn't know where to begin. Believe me, I wouldn't be bored!

Is there any other profession you would rather be pursuing?

I am a very organized person, and I can be very convincing. I think, because of that combo, I would probably make a very good lawyer.

As a woman, have you experienced discrimination in your profession?

Never! Not at all.

Wendy Wasserstein

Profession: Playwright .

Date of birth: October 18, 1950

Education: B.A., Mount Holyoke College, 1971 (History)
M.A., City College of New York, 1973 (Fine Arts)
M.F.A., Yale School of Drama, 1976

"*J* want to entertain, but I also want to use the theater to shake things up a little bit," Wendy Wasserstein says. "I want to make people think." Wasserstein has been described by the *New York Post* as "a popular and highly regarded playwright, who has earned a reputation as a wry social commentator, chronicling the evolution of women over the past two decades."

Her Broadway hit, *The Heidi Chronicles,* spanning the 1960s to the 1980s, was described by one critic as "a memorable elegy for her own lost generation." The play celebrates one woman's wish to stand by her beliefs while coping with a changing world. In 1989, in addition to winning a Tony Award and the Pulitzer Prize for drama, the play won virtually every major New York theater award, including the Susan Smith Blackburn Prize, given annu-ally to the best play written by a woman, and the Hull-Warriner Award, presented by the Dramatists Guild to the author of the best play dealing with controversial subjects involving politics, religion, or social mores.

Wasserstein's other well-known plays include *Uncommon Women and Others* and *Isn't It Romantic,* both of which had respectable off-Broadway runs. In 1983, with the aid of an $18,000 Guggenheim Fellowship, Wasserstein collaborated with Jack Feldman and Bruce Sussman on the musical *Miami,* which was commissioned by Playwrights Horizons, a nonprofit theater with a reputation for nurturing promising young writers. *Miami* was presented to the theater's subscribers as a "musical-in-progress" in January 1986.

While a student at Mount Holyoke College, Wasserstein attended a drama class given at Smith College and was encouraged by her instructor to consider Yale Drama School. Upon graduating from college, unsure whether to follow her instructor's advice or attend Columbia Business School, she returned home to New York and studied to be a playwright with Israel Horovitz and Joseph Heller. Two years later, she received simultaneous acceptances from both Columbia Business School and Yale Drama School. After some deliberation, she decided to go to Yale. Much to her delight, the dean of Columbia Business School sent her a note years later with the message "You made the right choice!"

Wasserstein has written for publications ranging from the *New York Times* to *Interview* and is the author of *Bachelor Girl,* a book of essays. She has participated in numerous workshop productions of plays, and has taught at Columbia and New York University.

Wasserstein grew up in Manhattan, the youngest of four children. She describes herself as "a perpetual graduate student who just gets older and older." Wasserstein resides in a sunny Greenwich Village co-op with her cat, Ginger. She says with an infectious ripple of giggles, "Can you think of any other job where you can work all day in a flannel nightshirt and slippers?"

Why did you become a playwright?

I've always loved the theater, and I still love the theater. Even when I am agitated and full of anxiety, if I can get myself inside of a theater and around theater people, I really feel better. I get a sense of belonging from it. Also, at the end of writing a play, you literally get to play with theater people like Dan Sullivan, Swoosie Kurtz, and Thomas Lynch. We all get together and do something – it's communal. When my book *Bachelor Girl* was published, I felt after it was done there was just me and the editor. You couldn't go visit it like you can a play.

How would you describe your plays?

They are about people. They are serious plays that are funny, have real characters, and raise real issues that hopefully will strike a chord in some people who see them.

What is it like seeing your play performed onstage in front of a receptive audience that laughs and cries in all the right places?

I can't think of anyplace I would rather be than in a theater and, when we're cooking, it is beyond great.

What do you find most exciting about your work?

When I am in the middle of writing something and it is actually going well, it is exciting because the piece exists. Also, the rehearsal process and actors coming in are exciting, but it can also be terrifying. The possibility of creating something new and hopefully an authentic piece of some value is exciting – especially something that you can grow and see, because you don't really know how you've grown or changed until you see what you've done.

What qualities do you think are important to be a playwright?

Stamina more than anything else; being able to see yourself through good times and through bad times. In a sense, the ability to have vision and remain perceptive also are important, as is a generosity of spirit.

Where do your ideas come from?

Most of my ideas come from observations of the lives of people around me. I am more of a watcher and listener than I am a reader or researcher.

Do you view the world as a stage?

Most often the world does not reach the comic or tragic potential of the stage, and when it does, the overwhelming random despair is almost unstageable.

When you attend a play, what do you look for?

I want the play to be good because I want it to excite me about being in the theater. I want it to make me want to write plays. I recently resaw my friend

John Guare's play *Six Degrees of Separation,* and it made me very happy because it was good and it made me want to work.

What do you think accounts for your success?

I take my work very seriously. I think all writers do. Writing is extremely hard. I think that maybe I came of age at a time when, in terms of writing about or writing for women, there wasn't that much around. In some cases, I created characters who hadn't been put on the stage, whose voices hadn't been heard. It always seemed so obvious to me that their stories should be told. They are such great people.

Have you ever feared success?

Yes, sure. All the time. Success is a twofold thing, because sometimes if you become successful, there are other ranks of success, like so-and-so is making more money, and so-and-so is this, and so-and-so is that. Then there is also this thing about "Can I do it again?" I think you have to separate that stuff out. It's just so hard to write a play, and that is the most important thing. Success is isolating because you don't have that many people who have had the same exact experience and you aren't used to competitiveness, jealousies, and insecurities about whether you can do it again. It comes with its own imbroglio.

Do you consider your profession stressful?

Yes, I think it is very stressful because you have external stresses and internal stresses. I can't think of a profession that isn't stressful. I know some friends who say, "Oh, I'll just be a florist or work in a bookstore." But that's stressful, too. I have a friend who always says, "I'll work in a shoe store." And I think, "Yes, but if you were a shoe salesman, it would be so hard!" Imagine bringing out ten different pairs of size eight shoes. I'd rather write a play! (Laughter) Plays are stressful because you're on the line. It's your baby. You can't hide. That's really hard.

Who is your best critic?

I think you have to listen to the audience. I listen to my close friends. I've worked with the same producer, Andre Bishop, for a long time now, and I think he is a very good critic. I also listen to a friend who is a literary manager and to the neighbor, who I think is very good. But basically, you have to listen to an audience.

What don't you like about being a playwright?

So many things. The guilt that you are not working all the time. You sort of want to be with people, but you don't want to be with people because if you are with them, you are not working. You are always insecure. I am a very insecure person. You never know if what you are doing is good or not. That is scary. You don't know whether people will like it or not. You don't really know how you are going to keep making a living. All of those things.

Have you ever felt discriminated against in your profession because you are a woman?

I am always asked if I am a feminist writer. I wish more men were asked about their attitudes toward women.

What have you learned that, had you known earlier, would have made your life easier?

Things take time. There are ups and downs, both of which one will survive. I wish I had been much more disciplined when I was younger and realized that discipline has a lot to do with talent. I wish I was more secure. In some ways, I almost work too hard. If I could just put out what comes off the top of my head, sometimes it's not that bad. But I work things a little bit too much.

What else? I think one has to have a balanced life. I think you have to almost give everything over to the work, which I still sort of believe (laughter) but wish I didn't.

What person or persons have made the greatest difference in your life?

I've been most influenced by my colleagues in the theater, like Christopher Durang. I am amazed by their gifts and their integrity. They, in many ways, are my moral and artistic center.

Who were your role models?

Betty Comden, Lillian Hellman, Carolyn Leigh, and Gwen Verdon.

Do you think it's a man's world?

That is a complicated question. Yes and no. In the arts, especially, there is an effort not to make it a man's world. There is an effort towards more plays by women and minorities. There are more women running theaters now, for instance, although that makes me think, "Is it because, in the larger picture, people think theater is nurturing and therefore not lucrative?" I don't know. I think men still have the power in this world. In many ways, women are reacting to that.

Annalisa Kraft

Zelda Fichandler

Profession: Theater Producer/Director

Currently: Founding Director, Arena Stage Theater; Artistic Director, The
 Acting Company (New York City)

Date of birth: September 18, 1924

Education: B.A., Cornell University, 1945 (Russian Language and
 Literature)
 M.A., George Washington University, 1950 (Theater Arts)

$\mathcal{T}$he late director Alan Schneider once said, "To my mind, there are three seminal figures in the greater American theater. First, Margo Jones, who created a theater in an Esso tank somewhere in Texas. Then Tyrone Guthrie, who brought artistry and grandeur to the provinces. But he was an exotic transplant. He imported the castle fully built and dumped it down in Minneapolis. And finally, Zelda, who built the castle from the ground up, brick by brick, and made it truly American in a sociological sense."

Zelda Fichandler's personal style, eloquence, and total commitment to the world of theater have made her a leading national figure in the performing arts. Her Arena Stage, in Washington, D.C., is a model for theaters around the country. Since its inception in 1950, Fichandler has been the guiding spirit and artistic force behind Arena.

Fichandler's leadership style is intimate and infectious. She has been described by JoAnn Overholt, Arena's administrative director, as "a great leader because, although it's her vision, she has made us feel that it is ours." Under Fichandler, Arena Stage has grown into a three-stage institution with a budget of $9.5 million. The success of the facility can be measured in consistently strong audiences, continuous critical acclaim, and the presence of a strong resident acting ensemble.

In all, she has produced more than four hundred shows at Arena and garnered an impressive string of firsts. Arena Stage was the first theater company outside of New York to win a Tony Award, the first regional theater to stage a Pulitzer Prize-winning play and the first American theater company to be selected by the U.S. State Department to perform in the Soviet Union.

Fichandler assumed the artistic leadership of The Acting Company in New York City in July 1991, and continues to direct one play a year at Arena. She also serves as artistic director of the Graduate Acting Program at New York University's Tisch School of the Arts.

Fichandler's marriage to Thomas Fichandler, ended in 1975, but the two remain close friends. Thomas Fichandler worked as executive director at Arena Stage until his retirement in 1986. He has said of his wife: "She may be a tiny person, but, like Napoleon, she's tiny. Look what Napoleon did. He turned over a world. That's what she did in the theater in this country." The Fichandlers have two sons.

What drew you to the theater?

I guess I always loved the theater. I earned my first dollar when I was about ten for writing an essay for the *Washington Star* saying why I wanted to be an actress when I grew up. Then my interest shifted to other things – political things. I was also a premed student. I've always been interested in human behavior. I thought I would be a psychiatrist. Then I switched into the theater. My interest is a combination of the social, emotional, psychological, and visual, and it seems that the theater combines all of my attractions in the world. I think I found the right profession, because the theater requires that you have an interest and skills in a wide variety of fields, the center of which is an interest in human behavior – why people do what they do.

What aspect of your work do you find most demanding?

I guess the hardest part of my profession is to reconcile the economic survival of an institution that exists only to cradle the art, and producing art in such a way that it doesn't compromise itself, but fulfills the demands of survival. It's like trying to get the left brain and the right brain to operate freely together. It requires enormous intuition, and at the same time, it requires logical delineation of the task. I try to gather information on both sides of the spectrum, going as deeply as I can into the intuitive aspects of my work and at the same time trying to strengthen those things that require correlation, synthesis, organization, and logic.

My job at the Arena was also difficult because I had around two hundred people working there, and it was hard to keep them functioning as a unit, as a collective consciousness, so that everything adhered to the central vision. It's a hard job synthesizing the individual wills of a lot of creative people without reducing them to a gray neutrality, trying to keep everybody functioning out of their own creative center and at the same time feeding the center of an institution.

What aspect of your work do you find most rewarding?

I guess I find it most rewarding when those two most difficult things happen. I also like my work as a director – when I take a play, investigate that, and bring it to life in theatrical terms. I'm happiest when I'm on the stage and directing.

How do you deal with pressure?

I try to breathe, to get in tune with the pulse, the rhythm of my surroundings, which means I try to see myself in proportion to the universe – that I'm just one of the creatures in it. I try not to think that I'm going to either die or solve the problems of the world by responding to a particular pressure. I try to remember that we are the human animal, which is the playing animal, *homo ludens,* I believe, and that if we aren't playful, we die psychologically. As serious as it seems to reach the goal, one has to have a playful attitude and realize that it isn't life and death. I don't know if I could deal with pressure if I were the president of the United States. I think that I wouldn't sleep very well. But in my job, which is making, thinking about, and paying serious attention to play – because a play is play – I am able to deal with pressure just by breathing.

What do you think accounts for your success?

Oh, dear! First of all, people need the stage. They need a place where they can mark out the stand-ins who act out stories in which they can see themselves, their actions, and their dreams, and learn about themselves in the presence of their neighbors. I think my first reason for success is that theater is necessary for human life. People want it and when it has faded away in certain periods of history, it has been reinvented and will always be reinvented, because how do we know what we are doing until we *see* what we are doing? How do we objectify it unless we have a forum where we can act it out?

Also, I think, I have an endless work capacity. I have been able to sustain my vision of the theater not only in its general outlines but also in its detailed needs. I think that my general philosophy of life is that life is precarious and there really is no safety; therefore, courage is quite natural to it. You can't really control the large issues anyway. You might as well act out your fantasies, impulses, and dreams. This has proved to be a very viable philosophy in creating an institution as an art form. What people describe as my courage to me seems very simple and natural. There isn't any inherent logic in anything, so why not go with a dream?

I also feel that I have a good instinct for people: I hear them; I see them; I can recognize talent; I can empathize with them and release the creativity that is in them. I seem to have that ability, and therefore they give back to me and to the institution. Together, we have this kind of group synergy that seems to keep the institution growing and building. I guess I go back to a certain kind of willfulness. I just *won't* give up! I don't believe that you're through until it's over.

What advice would you give someone interested in pursuing a career as a theater producer or director?

I think you should get a liberal arts education so you know something about the world and want to communicate it in theatrical terms. It's very important. You really need to have a world view. Anything you learn is useful: sociology, psychology, anthropology, mathematics, political science, anything. A liberal arts education is very important. Anything that develops self-awareness, awareness of the human situation, is important. Then you need to get technical craft skills, probably best at a good conservatory where you can learn acting and directing. After that, an apprenticeship period, and then finding a way to get your own work launched, which usually requires a great deal of risk and courage. There are all kinds of theaters where you can apprentice. There are mentorships. There are grants for growing directors. There is a way to block out a career. It isn't easy, but it's possible.

Has it been difficult juggling a career and family?

Very, very difficult – practically impossible! When my children were growing up, my husband and I really did only two things: we worked, and we took care of the children. We had no social life. We had no time to ourselves. I had a housekeeper, who is still with me, but she didn't live in, so while I had continuing support and care for my kids, it wasn't around the clock. My profession is demanding. It isn't nine to five. It is nine to midnight. It's extraordinarily difficult raising children and having a major profession. I think women are thinking more seriously now that you can't have it all. Unfortunately, there is this thing called the mommy track, where you are not expected to put in eighty hours but thirty hours. Therefore, you don't rise to the top of your profession. That is very unsatisfying for women. On the other hand, it is a way to be there for your children and not to get so exhausted that you are on the edge of a nervous breakdown all the time. I don't think women have solved this problem. I think men have solved it better because they have wives, but women haven't found out how to have wives, so the problem remains unresolved.

Growing up, did you always know you were going into the theater?

No, but I always knew I was going to have a career. I always knew I wasn't capable of giving myself only to a home and children. I think I knew that I was restless and creative and needed to work outside the home, and there never was a question whether I was going to have children. It was sort of like my fate from the time I can remember, from the time I was six. I was even more sure about having a profession than I was about having a family. I remember thinking, "Maybe I won't get married," but that washed away as I got older. I knew something would occupy my creativity. It would be very important to me. It would make me very difficult to be married to, and it was going to make my life unconventional.

Who was your role model?

If there was a role model, it was Margo Jones. She was a pioneer in the resident theater movement, and she opened a theater just a few years before we opened ours. Her theater did new plays and classics and had a resident acting company. After we set up our theater, I went to see her, and she was very inspiring. She had this dream that there would someday be forty theaters in America. There are now four hundred, so her dream was overfulfilled! She died when she was forty-two years old and didn't live to see accomplished what she had launched.

As a woman, have you experienced discrimination?

Oh, yes, but only early on. As a freshman in college, I had the highest grade in a chemistry class with five hundred students, and the award was given to a man because the money was left to "the highest ranking man" in freshman chemistry. I'll never forget that! I didn't get a scholarship at Cornell for tuition because they said they needed to give it to a "needy man," because they expected that I would get married and wouldn't use the money. I went all the way to the top over that issue, and I got that scholarship aid.

There has been subtle discrimination. I wanted to be a stage director when I was young, and that was impossible. In the early fifties, nobody would trust a young woman to direct. My personal, very personal, professional ambitions couldn't be satisfied until I had control over my own life. That is why I set up an institution – that, combined with my thinking that people outside of New York should also have a theater. There was discrimination against women artists and particularly women directors who were in charge of money and were powerful in terms of hiring other people and functioning in the world of commercial art. Then, as I got to be good and recognized as being good, there was the kind of discrimination like, "Who *really* runs the theater? I mean, I understand that you are here, but who *really* runs it?" As the years went by, that faded because social expectations and points of view shifted to recognize that I was capable in spite of being a woman. I don't experience any discrimination anymore.

Business
and
Finance

Agi Clark

Profession: Advertising Executive

Currently: Chairman and Chief Creative Officer, Lord, Geller, Federico, Einstein, Inc.

Date of birth: June 21, 1941

Education: B.F.A., Pratt Institute, 1962

$\mathcal{A}$t age fifteen, Agi Clark arrived in New York City from Budapest, Hungary, with the dream of becoming a painter, a writer, and a public servant. Out of necessity, she went into advertising. Today she is chief creative officer of Lord, Geller, Federico, Einstein (LGFE), Inc., a Madison Avenue advertising agency with annual billings of approximately $50 million and more than one hundred employees.

In 1969, N.W. Ayer hired Clark as a creative supervisor to become part of a major effort to transform the agency into a pivotal force in the advertising industry. Nineteen years later, Clark became managing director of creative services and was appointed to the board of directors.

Clark headed up N.W. Ayer's successful pitch for the Diet 7-Up account and went on to direct it. The outcome was a major market share growth for Diet 7-Up. She was equally successful with her pitch for the Howard Johnson account and an award-winning Bahamas campaign. Clark also worked on the Gillette account, introducing Gillette's Mink Difference Hairspray. When AT&T was about to be divested, she headed the creative team that success-fully guided the company through some difficult years. The Cliff Robertson campaign and the "Reach Out & Touch Someone" campaign were instru-mental in maintaining AT&T's market share.

Clark led the creative team that landed the J.C. Penney account and was charged with repositioning the company's fashion image. She met the challenge with the slogan "You're looking smarter than ever. J.C. Penney." In spite of a tight budget, the campaign was a success, winning dozens of awards and resulting in the continued growth of J.C. Penney. When the U.S. Travel & Tourism account was up for bid, Clark made the pitch and won the account with the slogan "America. Catch the Spirit!"

Clark has participated in numerous public service advertising campaigns. For the National Council on Alcoholism, she was involved in the award-winning campaign "Say no. And say yes to your life." She has been a consultant to hunger organizations and donated her considerable talents to other groups.

In 1988, Clark was recruited to join LGFE as chief creative officer and co-head of the agency. Her task was to rebuild the spirit of the agency after the departure of name partners, to keep the old clients, to bring in new ones, and to make the agency among the most creative in New York. A year later, she was appointed chairman of the board.

Agi Clark lives in New York City with her husband, Zsolt Csalog, a sociolo-gist who has published numerous books in Hungary and is currently involved in the political evolution of that country. Her son, Oren, is the designer of a state-of-the-art pocket computer. When not working, Clark enjoys relaxing in her country retreat in upstate New York.

❧

What attracted you to a career in advertising?

Initially, I had absolutely no plans of getting into advertising. I was alone with my little boy, and I had to get into some kind of business and earn some money. It was that pure and simple. I came from art school, and I was going to be a painter. I wasn't really prepared for any kind of commercial venture, but I could draw and just got lucky.

How did you get your first job in advertising?

A friend told me about an art director who was looking for an assistant, and I went up with a portfolio of art school drawings. The art director saw the drawings and said, "Gee, I can't draw. So you can draw my layouts for me, and I'll teach you advertising."

President Franklin Roosevelt said that if he could switch careers, he would go into advertising because that is one field where you can really influence people. Have you found that to be the case?

Oh, my God! He didn't know what he was talking about. (Laughter) Just a few hours ago, I was talking to a friend and colleague after having read an article about an ad agency that had a sign over the door that said, "We create needs. We create desires." I got very upset with it, terribly upset! This whole idea of influencing people, as I am sure you are aware, is a double-edged sword. You have to feel unbelievably responsible – which I do – because whatever we do, we intrude in people's lives through television and other medias. I've always felt very strongly about doing advertising as factually and as respectfully as possible. But whatever we do, we are trying to influence people to buy whatever product we happen to be selling. You can't be ambivalent about that.

What qualities do you think are important for a career in advertising?

You have to love problem solving. My own particular feeling about it is that you have to be a people person because you are always talking to people. You really have to be in touch with people.

Do you think humor is effective in advertising?

Sure it is! Anything that moves you or touches you emotionally is effective. The thing about humor is that some is funny, some is not, and some is disrespectful. I like humor that is really, truly funny, but not when it is at the expense of anybody or any group.

What aspect of your work do you find most challenging?

It is challenging to pinpoint the initial direction, to find the key problem that you are going to try to solve for your client. I find that the most exciting and challenging aspect of my work is seeking out a strategic direction.

What are you most proud of having accomplished in advertising?

First of all, having been able to create an agency where there is zero politics, zero backbiting, and where you have a very positive, loving environment. I am also very proud of having nurtured and helped a lot of people along, encouraging them to produce their best work and reach their potential.

Do you have favorite advertising campaigns?

Not really. If you asked me if I have favorite books, I could tell you. There have been a lot of very good campaigns. I've been around for a long time, so it's hard to pinpoint a favorite. I was initially very charmed with the Eveready battery campaign. I thought it was fresh and different. I really like campaigns that are single-minded, that have one point to tell and tell it in a fresh and memorable way.

What do you think accounts for your success?

Quite a few things. One is I was raised with the feeling that I could be anything and do anything. I didn't grow up in this country. I grew up in Hungary. It never occurred to me I couldn't do anything I wanted to do, so that gave me an edge and a very good base. Beyond that, whatever I do, I throw myself 100 percent into it, and I do it with all my concentration, all my attention and caring. Also, I think I'm pretty damn talented! I've never been afraid to speak up and take a stand and do whatever I think is the right thing.

Do you think that ads grow on you, or is the initial impact more important?

It all depends; it has very much to do with your budget and with the competition. If you don't have a lot of money, then impact becomes crucial because you are not going to be around long enough or often enough to allow your message to grow. On the other hand, if you are doing any kind of brand and image building, then it is much more important to make a long-term connection with the viewer.

Is there any other profession you would rather be pursuing?

There are a lot of things I want to do, but I don't know about another profession. I wish there were a way I could be effective in politics without going into politics. I wish I could earn a living *and* do more public service advertising *and* help the social situation in this country.

What advice would you give someone interested in pursuing a career in advertising?

It is getting very tough to get into advertising because advertising is the mirror of our economic situation, and the economy isn't doing so well. I would advise getting a job in the summer with an agency, even if it is without pay, just to get a sense of the business and to see whether you like it and which departments within the agency interest you.

As a woman, have you experienced discrimination in your profession?

I have, but not so much myself as I have seen it happen to others. I never expected to encounter discrimination. I didn't come with any baggage. I also didn't respond to the expected discrimination the way many women have had to respond. So many women in business for so many years felt that they had to don a man's mantle and become tough. Many times they would lose what is part of their strength, which is their womanliness. It is no big kudo for myself, but much more because of my upbringing, that I didn't fall into that.

Has it been difficult juggling a career and family?

In retrospect, it was very difficult. My son is now twenty-eight. I was a very young mother. I used to be very proud of the fact that I juggled a career and raised a son. I had very little money, and I was on my own. But now as I look back, I was awfully lucky that my son turned out to be so wonderful! I was a single mother, and I couldn't afford a nanny; therefore, he was constantly shuttled from one person and place to another. There are very few things in my life that I would do differently, which I guess is a nice thing, but I do think I would do this differently. If I could have, I would have liked to stay home with my son, at least for his first three or four years.

How do you unwind?

Fifteen years ago, I bought a place in the country, and that's where I go when I am stressed. I just read and cook and forget about it all. But I think in day-to-day situations, the way you do it is to have good relationships. If you have good relationships at your workplace, you can just sit and talk with people and talk out your tensions. For instance, if someone at work is walking around and looks as though he or she has been working hard, one of us will stop and give the person a little back massage. I think being open and allowing yourself to say, "Oh, God! I feel awful," helps, too.

Leslie E. Bains

Profession: Banker

Currently: Managing Director, Citibank, N.A.

Date of birth: July 28, 1943

Education: B.A., American University, 1965 (Spanish and Latin American Affairs)

 $\mathcal{W}$hen asked by *Forbes* magazine why women were making inroads in private banking, Leslie E. Bains responded that clients sometimes prefer women working on their accounts because, as one client explained to her, "Women work twice as hard." Bains has held top executive posts in the private banking divisions of The Chase Manhattan Bank, Manufacturers Hanover Trust Company, and Citibank, which she rejoined in 1991 as managing director of the Private Bank Investment Division. Her range of activities includes product and business management of portfolio management services, trusts, and estates, as well as the sales and marketing of these services worldwide.

If success in private banking depends on one's ability to generate new business, Bains has been very successful. In her former position as senior vice president of The Chase Manhattan Bank and the executive responsible for its U.S. Private Banking Group, her 550-person staff brought in $5 billion to $7 billion in new funds, raising Chase's total private banking assets to more than $30 billion.

A former president of the twenty-five-thousand-member International Financial Women's Association, she has also served as chairwoman of the New York Philharmonic Orchestra's bankers and lawyers advisory committee and chairwoman of the Educational Cable Consortium, a nonprofit New Jersey-based cable company. She serves on the boards of the Private Banking Council of the American Bankers Association and Interplast, a worldwide organization devoted to providing reconstructive surgical services to children.

Leslie Bains is married to Harrison M. Bains, Jr., vice president and treasurer of Bristol-Myers Squibb. They have a teenage son and daughter.

Why did you focus your career on the private banking sector?

The one sector that hired women with a defined career path was the trust area, so I began to build my career in investments. Private banking as we know it today wasn't around in the late sixties and early seventies. The concept began to take hold in the late seventies and eighties. We provided services to wealthy individuals, but we didn't call it private banking. When the concept was born, I was already working in that private banking group.

Is there any special educational track one should pursue for a career in banking?

Having an MBA [Master of Business Administration] or a law degree gives you instant credibility in an organization, and I think having such a degree is prudent. When I was starting in the work force, it wasn't as important, but now I regret not completing my MBA.

What aspect of your work is most challenging?

It sounds trite to say this, but just finding enough time to do everything! I find that as you move ahead in your career, the demands on your time increase substantially. The demands are not only in the area I'm immediately responsible for, which is private banking, but I'm also asked to serve on a number of bank task forces. In addition to that, because of visibility, I am called on to serve on outside committees. The challenging part is setting priorities.

Do you think your job is stressful?

Very much so, but I enjoy stress. I thrive on it. I think I probably do some of my best work when I am under pressure. My style is quick decision making. I was recently interviewed by *Forbes,* and the interviewer asked, "What makes you *you?*" I answered by talking about perseverance and stick-to-itiveness. Later on, when my husband heard the question, he said, "I hope you answered it by saying 'boundless energy and always being optimistic!' "

Besides those qualities, what other qualities are helpful in your profession?

More than anything else, ease in dealing with clients and assuming leadership positions. Whether it is a professional association, a charitable organization, or an organization within the workplace, I tend to be asked to be chairwoman or president, and I enjoy that. But I do not spread myself too thin.

What is the most frequent problem you encounter in your line of work?

I think it's the balance between strategic thinking and the action-oriented, implementation side. Sometimes people err on the implementation side and get caught up in a lot of minutiae. At other times, people are so strategic they forget to implement! I can't tell you how many business plans I've seen where they spend so much time writing beautiful strategic plans and then the implementation falls down. So it's that balance between the strategic thinking and the implementation.

Has it been difficult juggling a career and family?

It's a constant balancing, but what makes it work is an extraordinarily supportive husband and a terrific woman who has helped me take care of the children for over fourteen years. I look at people who don't have that stability in their lives, and I don't know how they do it.

As a woman, have you experienced discrimination in your profession?

Early on, yes. I believe a "glass ceiling" does exist. I like to tell our children never to put a boundary on anything they want to do. Don't ever build a fence. I think you just have to be practical, though, and recognize what some of the fences are along the way. Then you can deal with them. You can't be a Pollyanna and think "If I work really hard, I'm going to be recognized," because it doesn't always happen.

Do you think job discrimination against women is much less noticeable today than when you began your career?

Absolutely! I see that in our hiring practices. Seventy percent of the people entering our training program this year are women. That's quite different from when I began, when there was 1 percent of women at best.

What do you think accounts for your success?

I had a plan; I set specific career goals for myself and then tried to implement those goals. Also, having mentors has been influential. When I may not have been completely ready for the next job, a couple of mentors were willing to take a chance on me. For example, when the question was asked, "Has she ever managed 550 people before this job?" the answer was no. But someone said, "She does it very well with thirty people, why not add a few more?" Also, surrounding myself with people with different points of view. I like to have people who don't just say yes but who work as a team to drive the business ahead. I always want to find bright people who have a different perspective and will challenge each other and me because that's how you build a competent staff.

Who were your role models?

In the first ten years of my career, there weren't many role models. There were very few women who were married and working; there were even fewer who were married, working, and had children; and there were still fewer who were married, working, had children, and had a commuter marriage. My husband, because of his job with R.J.R. Nabisco, had to move to North Carolina for a year and a half, so we had a commuter marriage. There haven't been a lot of role models for that pattern. As far as people who have been influential in my career, there were two or three people at a senior level within the corporation who took an interest in me and gave me exposure to people and situations that helped me grow as an individual.

Barbara Pope

Profession: Certified Public Accountant

Currently: Tax Partner, Price Waterhouse

Date of birth: February 15, 1948

Education: B.B.A., University of Wisconsin, 1970
M.B.A., University of Wisconsin, 1971

$\mathcal{B}$arbara Pope is the partner-in-charge of the Personal Financial Service Group at Price Waterhouse in Chicago. As a tax partner, she specializes in tax and financial planning and is responsible for tax matters concerning her clients.

After working for a year at a small certified public accounting (CPA) firm, Pope joined Price Waterhouse in 1972 and became a partner in 1982. She is a certified financial planner and a member of the advisory board for Price Waterhouse Investment Advisors.

Pope serves as chapter president of Beta Alpha Psi, a national accounting honorary fraternity. She is a frequent speaker on tax and financial planning, the subject of executive seminars she conducts. She also appears regularly on radio and television financial programs, and her opinions on various tax and financial issues often appear in publications such as the *Wall Street Journal, Money, Working Woman, Success Magazine, USA Today,* the *Chicago Tribune,* and the *New York Times.*

Pope's husband, Ed, is vice president of finance at R.H. Misner & Co. They have three children.

What drew you to a career in accounting?

Probably the wrong things. I think in high school and college, you get erroneous impressions about what a particular career is going to be like. I was drawn to accounting for the mathematical and mechanical aspects. I really thought that I would find the logic, the math, and the analytical side of the work most appealing. In retrospect, I find I spend most of my time interacting with people and doing tax research — trying to apply the judgment I've developed throughout my career to complicated questions where there is no black or white answer.

What are you most proud of having achieved in your career?

I would say my partnership with Price Waterhouse. I really consider us to be the premier accounting services firm in the world, and the fact that I have become a partner with this firm has meant a great deal to me.

Are there ever days when you just don't feel like looking at another tax form or keeping abreast of another change in the tax laws?

Of course there are! I think in any profession, you are going to have peaks and valleys. You live for the peaks. You live for the really high points, when you know that you just did something great that has been a bit of a stretch and a challenge for you professionally and that really means a lot for the person you are dealing with. Those are the moments that you should *try* to keep in memory. The ones that you *do* keep in memory are maybe the low points. That's what might cause a person not to want to get up and go to work in the morning.

How do you deal with pressure?

I try to leave the office at the office. I find it very difficult to work at home when I am with my family. I deal with pressure by spending time with my family. I also am able to escape through reading. I read a great deal, often not very selectively. But if I can sit down and dig into a book for an hour or two – whether it's on an airplane or sitting at home at night – that really means a lot to me in terms of rejuvenation.

Could you describe a typical workday?

I spend a lot of time on the phone and in meetings – with people bringing things into my office that they need to discuss or need approval to act on; going to a client's office for a meeting; having a client come to my office; dealing with the Internal Revenue Service; attending community or professional meetings.

Does your work seem to snowball around tax time, or is it well paced year-round?

It used to be that there was a busy season and a slow season. I think there still is a little bit of that skewing for our staff, the ones who are really involved in the detail work of preparing and reviewing tax returns. But by the time you reach the management or especially the partner level, it's really year-round. There might be times of the year when you would anticipate being in the office until nine o'clock every night, but I am not pulling the 2:00 A.M. shots that I used to. It's really pretty constant.

What do you think accounts for your success?

I think a number of things. I was raised and educated to have a fairly high degree of self-discipline and motivation. I think my parents and my schooling – I went through twelve years of Catholic school – gave me the message that I could be successful at almost anything I cared to try. When you have that in mind, it gives you a head start in being successful. You approach things with the thought "How can I make this work?" Rather than "What happens if I fail?" I think to be successful in this business, one needs to be intelligent, not only from an academic standpoint, but one must have common sense and street smarts to be able to deal practically with the kinds of problems and situations that a client brings.

What advice could you give someone interested in pursuing a career in accounting?

I think first of all you need to decide what kind of a career you want in accounting. If you want to go into public accounting and your mission is to become a partner in a firm, you ought to go to one of the schools where the large public accounting firms recruit very heavily. In each part of the country, there are schools known for the strength of their accounting programs. There are also accountants working in a lot of other areas, including govern-ment and industry. The most important thing you can do is to prepare yourself academically. I am not just talking about business and accounting courses. I am talking particularly about developing communication skills, both oral and written. A lot of our work, a lot of our communication with clients, is through letters, memoranda, and formal reports, and we really need to be able to express ourselves in an intelligible way. We also do a lot of public speaking, and we make oral presentations to clients. The ability to communicate effectively and get your message across is essential.

Has it been difficult juggling a career and a family?

I think it's difficult for any professional, male or female, to juggle a career and a family. Everybody needs your time. In a service industry, you have to be accessible to your clients. You also, obviously, have to be accessible to your family. It is not easy. I waited to have a child until I was a partner in the firm. At that point, I had a bit more control over my schedule, but it's still difficult.

As a woman, have you experienced discrimination in your profession?

I honestly can't come up with any [incidents]. In fact, I remember in the mid-seventies, I was reading something in the *Wall Street Journal,* and it said something like two-thirds of all chief executive officers believed in equal pay for equal work. I was absolutely floored because up until then, it hadn't occurred to me that anyone could *not* believe in equal pay for equal work. It was totally foreign to anything I had experienced.

Do you think you would have made partner at Price Waterhouse any earlier had you been a man?

That definitely wouldn't have happened because I made partner in ten years, which equates to twelve years out of undergraduate school. I got my bachelor's degree, then a master's degree twelve months later. Then I worked for a small firm for one year before joining Price Waterhouse. That ten-to-twelve year progression is par for the course.

Who were your role models?

I think most of my professional role models have been male partners in the firm who really took an interest in my career and helped me move forward. There was only one woman partner in the firm for quite a long time when I was coming up through the ranks, and she was in New York. It was maybe five years into my career before I dealt directly with another woman profes-sionally, and she was a client. There just weren't a lot of women in the business world, at least in the financial area.

How many women partners are there today at Price Waterhouse?

I think about thirty-five, or about 4 percent of our total partners. Last year about 15 percent of our new partners were women.

If you unexpectedly had a month off, how would you spend it?

I would spend a great deal of it just interacting with my family. I think it would be one of life's great pleasures to pick my seven-year-old daughter up from school at 2:30 in the afternoon and do some of the things that I've not had the opportunity to do. But after a week or two, I think I would need something a lot more stimulating. The problem with a month is it is too short to really change your life. I know that from my seven-week maternity leave, which really wasn't enough time to get involved in things other than work. You are not going to launch yourself into some sort of a community activity knowing that your available time is going to be curtailed rather abruptly. A month off might be appropriate for some sort of executive-in-residence program at a university, but I really think the best way to spend it would be getting back to basics and spending some concentrated time with your family.

Alice M. Rivlin

Profession: Economist

Currently: Senior Fellow, The Brookings Institution

Date of birth: March 4, 1931

Education: B.A., Bryn Mawr College, 1952 (Economics)
Ph.D., Radcliffe College, 1958 (Economics)

$\mathcal{A}$lice M. Rivlin, first director of the Congressional Budget Office, from 1975 to 1983, is currently a senior fellow in the Economic Studies Program at The Brookings Institution. She has been described in *Current Biography* as "one of the best-informed and most consistently reliable analysts of the American economy and the federal budget."

Rivlin served as assistant secretary for planning and evaluation in the U.S. Department of Health Education and Welfare (HEW) during the Johnson administration. She has written extensively on the U.S. economy and budget and on public decision making. From 1983 to 1987, Rivlin was director of the Economic Studies Program at The Brookings Institution and spent a year as a visiting professor at the Kennedy School of Government at Harvard University. In 1989, the mayor of Washington, D.C., appointed her to head a commission on budget and financial priorities set up to devise solutions to the city's budget deficits.

Rivlin was the recipient of a MacArthur Foundation fellowship in 1983 and in 1986 was the president of the American Economic Association. She currently serves as a director of Unisys Corporation, Union Carbide Corporation, and T.J. International, and she is chairman of the board of The Wilderness Society. She is the editor of *Economic Choices 1984* and coauthor of *Economic Choices 1987*. She continues to write on such varied topics as national health insurance, income distribution, federal taxation, and social experimentation.

Rivlin is married to Sidney G. Winter. She has three children by a previous marriage.

How did you decide to become an economist?

I got interested in economics in college. I started out as a history major but switched to economics because it seemed more definite and, I think, more useful.

In what situations do you think economists make a difference?

Economists make a difference largely where there are hard choices to be made. They show what has to be given up to achieve alternative policy objectives, and they show what the costs are of what the policymaker wants to do.

What is the role of an economist in government policymaking?

To help make the choices clearer, to show what might happen, and to provide alternative thinking.

What aspect of your work do you find most demanding?

Well, most demanding is getting everything done! (Laughter) I'm interested in a lot of different things, and I tend to take on more projects than I can do – but that's not peculiar to me!

What do you enjoy most about your work?

I enjoy communicating, either in writing or orally. I do quite a lot of speaking, and I enjoy that when it works well, when I feel I'm communicating with an audience and they are understanding something that they didn't understand before.

How do you deal with pressure?

I exercise. That helps me a lot. I walk; I hike; I used to do a good deal of running, but I'm doing more walking now. I love to get off in the mountains for an extended hike or trip. That really takes me away from everything, including the pressure. On a more limited basis, I just try to concentrate on something else for a while, like reading a novel.

What would you say is the central theme of your work today?

Reexamining the relationship between the federal government and state and local governments. I think it's time we sorted out those responsibilities in order to have more effective government through all levels.

What issues in our economy and society concern you most?

The two biggest issues are that we're not investing enough in future growth and we're allowing some groups in the population to fall behind, with the distribution of income getting more and more unequal.

Is there any other profession you would rather be pursuing?

I don't think so. I really enjoy what I do. It's a combination of economics and public policy, of writing and speaking, and also being involved in groups that are working on public policy issues. So for me, it's an ideal situation.

As a woman, have you experienced discrimination in your profession?

Yes, but not recently. At the time I was starting out, there was serious discrimination against women. Universities didn't hire women. There were almost no women professors. Economics departments were worse than most because many were in business schools, and business schools were among the last to be conscious of equal opportunity.

Has it been difficult juggling a career and a family?

It was in the beginning. I'm way past the stage at which it's difficult because my children are all grown up. I'm into grandchildren these days! But certainly when they were younger, it was a challenge.

Who were your role models?

Several of the people I worked for early in my career were role models. Joe Pechman, director of economic studies at The Brookings Institution for a long time, was one, and John Gardner, who was secretary of HEW when I was there, was another.

What do you think accounts for your success?

I think some combination of luck, energy, ambition, and a desire to succeed.

What advice would you give someone interested in pursuing a career as an economist?

Well, I would say get the best training you can get. That means more math and more computer science now than in my day. Go to a good graduate school. Then just start working on things that are really interesting to you.

Debbi Fields

Profession: Entrepreneur

Currently: Founder, President, and CEO, Mrs. Fields Cookies, Inc.

Date of birth: September 18, 1956

Education: Los Altos Community College, 1973 to 1975

"There are no limitations other than those we impose on ourselves," Debbi Fields says. "You do not have to be superhuman to do what you believe in." Fields is president and chief executive officer of Mrs. Fields Cookies, one of the world's largest and best-known purveyors of gourmet cookies and other specialty bakery products.

Fields oversees her international network of stores, located in thirty-four states and six foreign countries, from her corporate headquarters in Park City, Utah, with a corporate staff of almost one hundred people. Her stores and businesses employ more than four thousand people and include 466 Mrs. Fields Cookies outlets, 97 La Petite Boulangerie bakeries, 22 Mrs. Fields Bakeries, and 7 Mrs. Fields Marriott Cookie Stores. A computerized information and electronic mail network provides headquarters with real-time linkage to every store. This information network, among the most sophisticated and comprehensive in the industry, was designed by Debbi's husband, Randy.

In launching a career, Fields followed her father's advice: "Whatever you do, do it because you love it, not because of the money." The activity she loved to do and did best was bake cookies. Fields opened her first cookie store in Palo Alto, California, in 1977 with $50,000 from her husband and a banker who believed in her product. Her first day in business began with Randy's bet that she would not sell $50 worth of cookies. Discouraged after several hours went by without a customer, Fields walked into the street with a tray of free samples and returned to the store with a following of cookie lovers. By closing, she had won the bet, registering $75 in sales. Twelve years later, the combined store sales for Mrs. Fields Cookies were $118 million, and the company was registered on London's unlisted securities market.

The company's success is founded on Fields's physical stamina, her spirited "can-do" approach to meeting goals, and her faith in the ability of her team. She travels to each Mrs. Fields store twice yearly, logging more than 350,000 air miles. She believes in having a good time on the job, saying, "Life has to be fun, or else it's just one long dental appointment."

Fields has penned an autobiography entitled *One Smart Cookie,* and has received numerous awards and honorary degrees acknowledging her professional achievements. In 1986, Debbi and Randy Fields established the Mrs. Fields Children's Health Foundation, a philanthropic organization dedicated to research and education in children's health, injury, and rehabilitation. Each year, Mrs. Fields cookie stores and bakeries also contribute more than a million "cookie orphans" (products that are not sold within two hours of being baked) to food banks and other needy groups.

Fields lives with her husband and children in a country home outside Park City, Utah, and enjoys horseback riding and cross-country skiing.

What attracted you to an entrepreneurial career?

I never knew I was going to be an entrepreneur. But I had a dream, and the dream was that I wanted to do something that I loved. I wanted to do something where I felt I could make a genuine contribution.

What aspect of your work do you find most challenging?

Working with people is the most challenging and the most rewarding aspect. People are the core of the business. We are here because of two groups of people – our sales teams and our customers – who interact over Mrs. Fields sales counters every day, all over the world. Meeting the needs of both groups is a great challenge and responsibility, and above all a great satisfaction.

What do you think accounts for your success?

I would say that the success of Mrs. Fields is due primarily to a commitment to quality. We are truly dedicated to quality. I know that people talk about that all the time, but my message to the people I work with is "We are quality." It's the way we do business. It's an expectation. I believe that our focus on quality has allowed us to get where we are. We do make mistakes. The benefits of having a high-quality focus is that, possibly, when a mistake is made, the quality standard is so high that nobody ever notices.

The second thing is that we guarantee our products. We accept that we will make mistakes. We don't want to make them often, but when we do, we want a second chance. We want to make sure that our customers know that we are there for them, no matter what. I think the second part of that message is that the success of Mrs. Fields is the responsibility of the people who work in the organization. They're the ones who have captured the dream – the vision – not only to have great-tasting products, but also to take great care of our customers and to build our business.

A lot of things can go wrong in running a business, especially at the initial stage. What made you persevere?

I don't want everyone to think that every day goes perfectly, that there are no failures, no mistakes. There are days when you simply want to pull out your hair and say, "Why am I doing this?" I think it comes with the territory. When you care as much as I do, it's very frustrating and worrisome when things don't turn out right, whether they are within your control or not. But I always start with this view: I really believe that people are great. Sometimes what we have to do is work more on training, showing, telling, and communicating to get the right results.

The second thing is I am very positive. I think it's critical to be extremely positive, especially when you are building a business, because you've got to show others that they can do it even when you are not so sure yourself.

What do you consider your biggest coup in business?

I think my biggest coup is actually doing it. Taking a dream – a product that I made at home – and having the guts to go out and do it in spite of everybody telling me I couldn't. My second biggest coup was opening my second store, because I certainly didn't have a vision that we could go beyond one. It was really the people I worked with who said we could.

As an entrepreneur, have you experienced discrimination because you are a woman?

Because I am a woman and because I knew there weren't many women when I started, I didn't think of it as discrimination. I thought of it as a challenge, a challenge that at least we have to begin somewhere. I never felt discrimination because I wouldn't let people make me feel that way. But I did feel that people didn't take me seriously. I knew what I was up against, but I wasn't afraid. I was willing to stand my ground. Granted, a lot of people didn't want to talk to me about financial facts; a lot of men assumed I had nothing to say. But I was not willing to give up. Thirteen years ago a woman starting a business was a relatively novel idea. Today, the fastest-growing economic sector for women is small businesses. It's no longer a novel idea.

Has it been difficult juggling a career and family?

Absolutely! I have five daughters, and they worry me. Every time I get a call at the office and they say, "Mom, we just called to say hi" or "We called to say I love you," it's a relief, because I'm afraid they're calling to say they fell off their bike. When the girls are sick, I have to change things; I have to be at home because it's so important for me to be a good mom. It does require a lot of juggling. You have to be very good at setting priorities; you have to be good at time management. The one thing I have done is make sure the kids really understand what Mom does. They are very involved. For the summer, for example, I've given the girls cookie projects to work on. I have created the ideas, but the girls actually work on some of my recipes at home, and they think it's fun! So I'm keeping them busy for the summer, but they also are involved in the business in some small way, which is very important to me.

When you build a business from the ground up, I would imagine it's difficult to delegate authority. How did you learn to do that?

I'm still working on that! That's one of the things that has been very difficult because I want to be involved in *everything.* You have to force yourself to let go. The one thing that led me to delegate is the size to which the business has grown. About three years ago, I realized my job was to build world-class teams. My job is no longer to do it [make cookies] but to show other people how, to allow them to bring their creativity into this business without compromising our values.

When I work with people today, I tell them my philosophy. I don't tell them what to do. I don't tell them how to do it. But I tell them about my values. The second thing I do is sit down and talk with new people in, for example, marketing. I explain how marketing should represent Mrs. Fields. It should not be superglitzy; it should be real. I try to give them a perspective and then allow them to make decisions once they understand the thought process I use. That seems to have worked quite well for me. To build a team, you've got to give people a chance to succeed *and* fail. More importantly, if I tell them up front I'm against an idea but they can proceed anyway, I think they will try even harder to make it work. Being open and honest with people is essential.

Did you have any role models?

I never really had a role model other than my parents, who always told me, "You have to work extremely hard; nothing in life is free; be the best you can be and love what you do."

Laura Waller

Profession: Financial Planner

Currently: President, Laura Waller Advisors, Inc.

Date of birth: July 17, 1945

Education: B.A., Sophie Newcomb College, Tulane University 1966
(Sociology)
M.S.W., Tulane University, 1968 (Clinical Social Work)
C.F.P., College of Financial Planning, Denver, 1982

$\mathcal{A}$ccording to *Money* magazine, Laura Waller, a certified financial planner and former social worker, is "one of the foremost financial planners in the United States." She currently runs her own business, Laura Waller Advisors, in Tampa, Florida.

Waller began her career as a social worker and was a therapist for eleven years. After opening her own therapeutic practice, she decided to launch a career in business. She started out as a stockbroker, then eventually moved into financial planning.

A much sought-after corporate guest speaker and business commentator, Waller also is a licensed insurance agent. She is a member of numerous organizations and was a director on the National Board of the Institute of Certified Financial Planners from 1982 to 1987. She has served as president and chairman of the Tampa Bay Institute of Certified Financial Planners, chairman of the Tampa Bay chapter of the International Association for Financial Planning, and as a director on the Florida West Coast Employee Benefits Council.

Waller's husband, Edward, is an attorney, specializing in business litigation and bankruptcy law. They have three children.

What drew you to a career as a financial planner?

I had originally worked as a therapist at a mental health clinic and in private practice for a total of eleven years, the last three of which I worked as a therapist in my own practice. I liked running my own small business, so I decided to make a career change. I didn't want to go back to school and get another master's degree, so I looked to see what I could change into without getting additional schooling. I was hired as a stockbroker, and then, because of my counseling background, went into financial planning, which really combined both fields.

What do you do as a financial planner?

I help people plan their finances. I work with individuals, small businesses, and families to create a full financial plan. We look at all aspects of their finances, such as cash flow, net worth, their tax situation, retirement planning, and educational planning if there are children involved. We also study where their investments currently are, what their insurance program consists of, and what their estate plan is. Then we tie it all together in a financial plan. I am also licensed in securities and insurance. Some clients come in strictly for the financial advice; other clients choose to do investment transactions or insurance purchases through the firm. Depending on their needs, I can service both.

What aspect of your work do you find most challenging?

I like spending the time and the thought necessary to gain a real understanding of my clients and their desires so that I might make the best recommendations for them. That means not just looking at the quantitative numbers that you can gather from their finances but getting a real feel for what their qualitative needs and desires are.

What problems do you encounter most frequently?

Cash flow is the core of financial planning. It really is the fuel that drives the machine that allows people to meet their financial goals. I deal a lot with what we used to call budgeting, but in this high-tech society, people are much more amenable to doing it if you call it cash flow accounting. I work with people on where they are spending their money. They need to get in touch with these expenses to be able to put money aside to meet the goals they have for their family's finances.

What is the difference between a financial planner and an accountant?

An accountant is basically an expert in the area of tax planning. A financial planner is somewhat of a generalist in a world of specialists. We need to know something about all the areas I mentioned to you that would go into a full financial plan. Some people refer to us as the quarterback of the team, in the sense that we would want our clients to have their tax specialist, their accountant, their lawyer, their estate planning attorney, their banker, and their insurance expert, because the knowledge of all those people are needed to develop and implement a plan that really works for the client.

Are your clients generally people with income they don't know how to invest, or are they on a fixed income trying to make the most of what they have?

My typical client is hard to describe because I consider this a family practice. I meet with executives and heads of companies. I also meet with the college-age children of my clients, partly because that is my future client base but also because I feel that if my client's children are not independent, it is very difficult to plan for the parents to have a comfortable retirement. Sometimes clients come to my firm because they want to focus on one particular area of their finances. In this day and age, it might be someone who has been offered an early retirement package where the company sweetened the benefits the person would get. They might come to discuss whether what they are being offered is a good deal for them. I spend time examining this issue and also work with their accountant to make sure that if they take a distribution from a company's retirement plan on leaving, the way they reposition their money is to their advantage tax-wise.

Aside from a market crash, is your profession a pressured one?

It's a profession that can be as pressured as you make it. You need to put pressure on yourself to be successful because starting in this field, you face a lot of rejection. You begin with a limited knowledge base and have to learn enough to be able to convince people to trust you with something that is very dear to them: their finances. As an independent planner, the only pressure I have is what I decide to put on myself and what my clients might put on me for deadlines. If I were in an office where I had to meet a quota, that would be somewhat uncomfortable for me.

What personal qualities benefit you most as a financial planner?

I think I'm a good listener, I'm a good teacher, and I have patience. I also have a tremendous amount of respect for my clients. I am often asked whether this is a good field for women, and I think it really is. Most women, particularly those my age, in their forties, might have first started in nurturing fields like nursing, teaching, and social work. Those are fields that teach you the traits I just mentioned.

What do you think accounts for your success?

I try to be fair with my clients and myself. The reason I say you have to be fair with yourself is because you have to earn a living to be able to be there to serve your clients. I consider my reputation to be the most important thing. It's now my twelfth year in the industry, and I wasn't a sprinter in the beginning. I slowly built my practice, and now I have very fine clients who refer other people to me.

What are you most proud of having accomplished?

Building a business from scratch and being pleased with the way it has developed. Outside of my profession, being a mother and a wife is really important to me. At this stage, I feel I've been very successful at both!

Has it been difficult juggling a career and a family?

Yes, except I have a really helpful husband. I also have super kids who are supportive of what I do. That's been very helpful. Days when I get really frazzled, when I feel too many things are pulling at me, I usually wind up taking the day off and just getting away by myself to do something relaxing.

As a woman, have you experienced discrimination in your profession?

In some ways, being a woman has been an asset. Many people choose a woman because, right or wrong, they perceive us as being more honest and fair. I've also found that my high-pressured male clients feel more comfortable talking to me about areas of finance that they don't know much about than they might if I were a man. So in that sense, it's been helpful. I wouldn't know if I were discriminated against in my field. People come to my firm because they chose to come here. I am sure there are some people who would never go to a female planner, just like there are some who would never go to a male planner.

Who were your role models?

There were many. I have an aunt who was an attorney before women easily went into that field. She was a real trailblazer, and that was very helpful to me. There was a high school guidance counselor who was very helpful. I skipped my senior year in high school, and everyone at the school was against that except the guidance counselor, who thought it was an excellent idea. She really supported me. I think my mother really encouraged me to go as far as I could in school. Also, in my field, I've received a lot of support from other women in moving into an area that traditionally was thought of as something women didn't get concerned about.

What advice would you give someone interested in pursuing a career as a financial planner?

I think they should start as a stockbroker. That's the best way to learn about investments. Most people who come into this field come from another field. It's not a career to enter right out of high school or college because it helps to have gray hair and wrinkles to be listened to! (Laughter) Coming from a stockbrokerage background is the best way to start.

Before you get into it, you need to be self-motivated. You need to realize there are tremendous ups and downs. It's a cyclical field, a tough field to get started in. It helps if you have a separate source of income while you are building your client list, because your income is going to fluctuate in the initial stages until you really get a client base.

I think you have to be somewhat goal-directed and stubborn. It's tough getting going, but once you have clients who want to work with you, it's a wonderful feeling to be in this business!

Don't burn bridges behind you. Once you lose your reputation, it is very difficult to regain it. If I can give you a rule of thumb, it is be the kind of planner you would send your grandmother to. Of course, I am assuming you love your grandmother!

Olivia Hsu Decker

Profession: Realtor

Currently: Founder, Olivia Hsu Decker, Inc., and Decker Bullock Realty, Inc.

Date of birth: February 20, 1948

Education: B.A., National Chentsu University (Taiwan), 1969 (Cultural Anthropology and Ethnology)

O livia Hsu Decker knows how to break records in real estate sales. In 1987, she was the nation's top realtor, with $37 million in sales. The following year, she sold property worth $46.3 million, equal to the combined total of the other sixty-one real estate agents operating out of Merrill Lynch's southern Marin County, California, office. That year, her earnings from commissions totaled $1.5 million, and she received Merrill Lynch's Associate of the Year Award for taking more listings and selling more properties than any of the fifteen thousand Merrill Lynch agents in the country. Since then, Decker has launched two brokerage firms, Olivia Hsu Decker, Inc., and Decker Bullock Realty, Inc., where she continues to break real estate records.

Decker immigrated to the United States in 1975. The eldest of five children, she was born in Shanghai, China, and forced to flee with her family to Taiwan when the Communists came to power. Regarding that time in her life, she says, "In Shanghai, my parents were well-to-do and well educated. After they left Shanghai as refugees, they were never happy. They lost everything. Not only everything material, but their careers."

As an amateur photographer, Decker takes her own pictures for the advertisements and brochures she creates for her listings. From her days as a cohost of a comedy show, she is able to regale her clients with a steady stream of jokes, which she can relate in English, Japanese, several dialects of Chinese, and Spanish, ensuring a lively drive to and from homes.

Decker credits her success to a combination of sensitivity, patience, hard work, and above all, service. "Sensitivity," she says, "means not pushing people into a transaction, but working for a win-win situation for both buyer and seller." She defines patience as the "ability to really listen to people, to make that extra effort to discover what people need and want, and be willing to show as many houses as it takes to find their dream house."

Decker resides in a Mediterranean-style home on Marin County's affluent Belvedere Island. When she has free time, she enjoys tennis, plays the piano, collects antiques, and listens to classical music.

How did you decide to pursue a career as a realtor?

Prior to coming to California, I lived in Tokyo, Japan. The real estate in Tokyo is very expensive, so when I compared prices, real estate in California seemed like a comparative bargain. Every Sunday I would go out and look at open houses. I've always been curious about what big, beautiful houses look like inside. I love to see how people decorate their homes, what they plant in their gardens.

What do you find most challenging about your profession?

Matching the right property with the right client.

By all accounts, you are a very hard worker. What motivates you to work so hard?

I came to America when I was twenty-eight. I appreciate the opportunity this country has offered me. I thought I would be discriminated against not only as a woman, but as an Oriental woman. Instead, I have found just the opposite. Most of my clients are affluent Americans, and they really appreciate my hard work. It's a pleasure to work hard and know your work is appreciated.

How do you deal with pressure?

I've lived in China, Japan, and Taiwan. I know the Oriental culture very well, and in keeping with that tradition, I am able to create and gain peace from within myself. At the end of a long day, I come home to a totally different environment. My home is like a villa in Italy. The furniture is Italian and French. The music is always opera or classical. It's a very special place for me. As soon as I enter through the door, the pressures of my business are forgotten.

Do you think it is easier or more difficult to sell a house in the million-dollar range than to sell a less expensive house?

It's not easy to get into the higher bracket, but once you are in that bracket, it is easier because clients know what is involved in buying a house. I don't have to walk them through the process, because this is not the first house they've bought. Money is no problem. It is very pleasant to sell in this price range because the clientele is very knowledgeable about real estate, as well as very successful in their own fields.

How would you describe your sales style?

I would describe it as a soft sell. As you know, a lot of realtors are quite pushy – we are accused of that in society. Realtors are very competitive people, especially in the lucrative high-price area. I believe in a more subtle approach. There is a certain subtle way of selling without being pushy. If somebody doesn't want to buy, there is no point in pushing. If they do want to buy, it will happen. I believe in patience. I spend a lot of time with clients who take their time looking for that special dream home. It might take a year before they buy. There is no hurry. My clients know that's the way I do business, and they appreciate it.

You have been quoted as saying, "In the high end, it's all social." Do you consider your work to be your hobby as well?

Yes, in the high end, you almost always blend your social life with your business life. My clients invite me for special occasions and introduce me to their friends and family. When they have a birthday, a dinner party, or a special occasion, they invite me because they want me to be part of it, and that is quite nice.

What advice would you give someone interested in pursuing a career in real estate?

You have to be prepared to devote yourself totally. It's a business that involves evenings and weekends. That's when most people have time to talk to you and look at property. You have to be prepared to sacrifice your family life. People call you at all hours. You have to be prepared for intrusions on your private life. My beeper goes off all the time. I carry my portable phone everywhere, including the ladies' room, movie theaters, and restaurants. The only place I don't take it is to the opera or a concert. If you want to be successful, you have to be accessible.

Do you think it's a man's world?

As much as women have accomplished, the business world is still a man's world. The successful woman is hardly ever recognized by her peers, and, if she is, it takes a lot longer. I remember attending a speech several years ago by Justice Sandra Day O'Connor. She spoke about her position on the highest court. She said that because she was a woman, people were more interested in what she was wearing and what parties she was attending than what she thought about certain Supreme Court decisions. People don't discuss that aspect of a male Supreme Court justice's life, but because she is a woman, they feel they have a right to know more about her personal life.

Another thing that I think is very unfair to women is that when a successful man is out there in the world, nobody is curious about meeting his wife. But if it is a successful woman, everyone is curious to death to know whom she is married to. If they find out that she is married to someone with a questionable past, they will use it against her and attack her for it. Look what happened to Geraldine Ferraro. She is a good and intelligent politician, but they attacked her viciously because of her husband's reputed questionable dealings.

What have you learned that has made your life easier?

I started out with a tough life. I had to leave China with my family as refugees. We lost everything. We left Shanghai in a hurry when the Communists took over. When you start with nothing, everything else is icing on the cake.

As far as business, I think I've learned something about the art of selling, which is not selling. It is a very Oriental notion – very Zen. The funny thing is that when you don't try to sell, you can sell better and more convincingly, especially in the high-end bracket. My clients never feel that I am selling a house to them. I am very subtle. I like to talk to them about life, tell them jokes. Selling, well, that's incidental.

Elizabeth Terry

Profession: Restaurateur/Chef

Currently: Owner and Chef, Elizabeth on 37th

Date of birth: October 9, 1942

Education: B.A., Lake Erie College, 1966 (Psychology)

Craig Claiborne, food critic for the *New York Times,* hailed Elizabeth Terry as "one of a new breed of Southern chefs," praising her "marvelous imagination and sense of invention." This accolade was further confirmed by another food critic, who lauded her "knack for coming up with unusual food combinations that send your taste buds into orbit!" *Time* described her as a "Southern Sensation" and *Town and Country* as "an artist in the kitchen."

In the past ten years, as owner and chef of Elizabeth on 37th in Savannah, Georgia, Elizabeth Terry has developed her own style of southern cooking and, in the process, has entered the ranks of America's great chefs. Her restaurant, dubbed by *Atlanta* magazine as "the best restaurant on the Georgia Coast," is located in Savannah's historic district. Terry describes her style of cooking as "Southern American with a Continental influence." Her goal is to bring a light and modern touch to southern cooking while preserving the old flavors. "Southern food is very nurturing, and that's how I cook," Terry says. "I cooked first as a wife and mother and then as a chef. I feel it's important that you cook with other people in mind."

A perfectionist who believes that if you are going to do something, you should do it well or not at all, Terry, while still in high school, entered a sewing contest and won a trip to France. That would be the first of many trips she would take to Europe. Not having had any formal cooking training, she viewed the trips as on-the-job apprenticeships and was able to meet and observe most of the great chefs of France.

After the birth of their second child, she and her husband, Michael, a Harvard law school graduate who had been practicing law in Atlanta, decided it was time for a new beginning in a new setting. They wanted to find a city where he could have a law practice, she could have a restaurant, and their children could grow up safe and happy. They chose Savannah as their city and an elegant, fourteen-room Victorian mansion on 37th Street as the place to realize their dreams.

Michael volunteered to take a year off from his law practice to help set up the restaurant. When the year was over, he opted to continue to manage the business side of the restaurant and serve as host and wine steward. The Terrys live in spacious quarters above the restaurant.

Julia Child has characterized this time period as a "fear of food" phase. Have you revised your menu or changed your eating habits because of this health revolution?

Nope! My cooking and our menu have always reflected our health and nutrition consciousness. When we first opened, we had four vegetarian dishes on the menu, but they really didn't sell very well. We don't have any right now, but everybody knows we do wonderful vegetarian things. I think there are a couple of problems with food. First, I think that the growers got away from taste in fruits and vegetables like tomatoes, apples, peaches, and pears. They grew them for shape, shipping, and shelf life. People got very bored with basic food.

I think a lot of growers now know people are more concerned about quality, and chefs are now stressing more regional ingredients. People are getting back to appreciating food, and growers are beginning to grow food that tastes wonderful by itself. People are more experimental with lettuces. It's not just an iceberg salad that requires lots of blue cheese, but it's spicy arugula, flavorful basil, lots of thyme, grilled onions and peppers – beautiful colors in the salad. I think people feel better when they eat a variety of foods and when they eat foods in a more natural state. At this restaurant, we pretty much do that. We use some cream and butter, but I don't believe that cream and butter necessarily make everything taste better. They make some things taste better.

We don't really bill ourselves as a health-food restaurant. But, for instance, at first we used to put a kind of mayonnaise and peppercorn on fish before roasting. Now we make a mustard barbecue sauce that has garlic, mustard, thyme, and oil in it. We use only olive oil, canola oil, soya oil or a mixture of those oils and just put a tiny bit of oil on the fish. It gives the fish a lot of flavor without masking its own flavor, but there are no eggs, cream, or butter. I think professional chefs have an obligation to work with people and through some of their food concerns. That's what I do.

How did you become a chef and restaurateur?

I became a chef late in life. I was thirty-seven. I had a degree in psychology. So it was really my passion for cooking that drew me to this career. Also, my husband and I really enjoyed entertaining, and people reinforced this special feeling. They said I was a very good cook. So I had plenty of time to experiment with what I really enjoyed doing by the time I opened the restaurant and went into cooking professionally.

In my case, all I did was open a restaurant and bill myself as the person in charge of the cooking. The restaurant was specifically named Elizabeth on 37th so people would know that there was a person responsible for the cooking and for the restaurant. Naming the restaurant after myself was a conscious effort to make a very personal statement. After several years, our reputation grew, and I must say we were always pretty busy. I had never worked in another restaurant or taken any professional cooking courses, but I'd read practically every cookbook. I made all the classic sauces of the various countries, and I enjoyed cooking international dishes, whether it was mandarin pancakes or truffle soup. Cooking is exciting for me.

What is your idea of a perfect meal?

It depends on whether it is winter or summer. In the winter, a perfect meal is a loaf of freshly baked whole grain bread, some kind of soup, a salad, and fruit. In the summer, I love cold things. I like, for instance, grilled shrimp or some kind of grilled seafood with several cold relishes like cold eggplant, yellow pepper, maybe a cold green salad or a tabouli, and cold slices of tomatoes with dill or basil. Then for dessert, fresh berries or a fresh berry pie.

What aspect of your work do you find most challenging?

Creating new dishes is a very exciting part of my job. The restaurant has a southern framework. Therefore, I try to keep all of my creativity within that framework. That is very challenging.

Are you eager to get up and go to work in the morning?

Yes, and we've had this restaurant now for ten years. What's exciting is I can always change the menu if I want to. As a matter of fact, I am encouraged to do that by the customers. We always have new things for them. We keep a few of the old familiar things as well. So it's a very creative, very exciting job. Now, it's not for anyone who likes a quiet day, because the restaurant business is a small manufacturing business. Everything that comes into the restaurant must be changed before it goes back out: it must be washed, cut to size, cooked, put on a plate, and served with some special sauce or garnish.

Do you consider your job to be a pressured one?

Yes, because each day we must feed the people who come. It's not a business where you can put something off until tomorrow. In our situation, if key people are ill or someone is new, other people have to fill in. The show must go on. And it must be perfect, because your reputation is on the line each night. A restaurant is like a theater. Once the curtain goes up, there is no stopping the play.

How do you deal with pressure?

Well, immediate pressure is getting things done for that night. If I sense that everybody is not working quite up to par – we have new people, or we are running really close to a deadline and might not make it – I just start to work a little earlier or stay a little later the night before. I also am a great fan of hot baths! (Laughter) We are not open for lunch any longer, which is wonderful. We live twenty minutes from the beach, so I go to the beach, take a swim, read a book for an hour, and come back and work with the rest of the staff. That's one way of getting totally away from the business. We also have an herb garden, and I really like to work in the garden.

What do you think accounts for your success?

I think my passion for food and cooking has generated incredible interest in the restaurant. I would rather cook than do anything else. I really love it. You have to have a very high level of energy to be a chef and to be in a professional kitchen. So I think it all boils down to my high level of energy and also my passion for food and cooking.

As a woman, have you ever felt you were discriminated against in your work?

I'm not certain I would recognize it. I have a pretty positive outlook on life. I think sometimes people take negative things too seriously. I have had women in my kitchen whom I would never hire again – not because they were women, but because they were crabby and incompetent. I have had men in my kitchen who had similar negative attitudes. If someone says, "You can't do that because you are a woman," I think you should do it and show them "Ha! I can do it better!" There is great fun in that.

Has it been difficult juggling a career and a family?

No, because we set it up exactly the way we wanted. When we moved to Atlanta, where my husband practiced law, I didn't work full-time because we were planning to start a family. That was our second year of marriage. So I worked part-time in a wine and cheese shop because I really liked to cook and we enjoyed drinking wine. I gave lectures on herbs, wine, and cheese.

After seven years, I finally became pregnant, and then I stayed home for a couple of years and threw myself into being a mother. We both threw ourselves into being parents because it was a real blessing, a real treat. We were just so delighted.

After several years of this, my husband said, "This is getting boring." (Laughter) It just so happened the little wine and cheese shop where I used to work part-time wasn't doing well, and the owner suggested I take the deli space and give him 10 percent of whatever I grossed. I would be my own boss. I could close the store if I needed to, and I could take my child with me to work whenever I wanted.

More and more women are finding they like to call the shots when they have children. I think it's not just women either. I think husbands and wives should have ongoing talks – ideally before they have children – about what is and isn't working. My husband and I rearrange our focus all the time. We talk about our goals with our children and with each other. I think that's what keeps our family working. Also, I haven't worked for anybody in the past ten years. Neither has my husband. We always remember that you earn money for a life-style. Sometimes you have to say, "I don't want that money because I won't give up this part of my life-style to earn it." Now, I don't know if it works on all levels. We have a successful business, so we've always had enough money. Therefore, saying we don't want that money doesn't really interfere with our being able to do pretty much whatever we want.

Who were your role models?

Certainly, Julia Child. When we were in Boston, we watched her on television and thought she was wonderful. She has a marvelous exuberance for food and has done wonderful things making people aware of how much fun it is to entertain, how easy it is, and how appreciative your friends are of that personal effort. I admire her a lot. Also, Alice Waters, because she did what she wanted. She defined the philosophy that came to be known as California cuisine. People liked it, and she didn't change. She just kept growing within a certain structure. Another role model is Deborah Madison. She was at Greens, a vegetarian restaurant in San Francisco. Although I've not spent a lot of time with them personally, they come across as women who enjoy being women and working in the food business. I like that combination.

If you had a month off, how would you spend it?

I'd go to the beach and have dinner parties for friends. I really enjoy talking with people, but the best part of cooking is I have a good excuse to stand up and walk around. (Laughter) I think that's why I'm always cooking, because I love to have people around. Also, I like doing something with my hands while I'm talking.

What advice would you give someone interested in pursuing a career as a chef?

I wouldn't recommend they do what I did, because most people can't wait until they are thirty-seven to begin earning money in a chosen career. So I think going to one of the culinary schools is really the most expedient way. Most of the culinary schools do have a requirement that you apprentice in a restaurant kitchen for a year or two before you go to school. I think it's very important to know the basics. Secondly, save your money so that you can have your own restaurant. And most importantly – this applies to any job or profession – if it doesn't get you excited, keep looking.

Communications
and
the Media

Maria Shriver

Profession: Broadcast Journalist

Currently: NBC News Correspondent and Host of "First Person with Maria Shriver"

Date of birth: November 6, 1955

Education: B.A., Georgetown University, 1977 (American Studies)

$\mathcal{M}$aria Shriver, a fourteen-year veteran of television news, embodies the charisma, energy, and public-spiritedness associated with the Kennedy clan of which she is a member. Her arduous globe-trotting schedule as an NBC news correspondent prompted her mother to observe, "You take planes the way other people take taxis."

Shriver began her career in 1977 as a newswriter/producer for KYW-TV in Philadelphia. The following year, she moved to WJZ-TV in Baltimore as a writer/producer on the station's "Evening Magazine," where she produced reports on public affairs, sports, and local news.

Before joining NBC News in 1986, Shriver served as coanchor of the "CBS Morning News"; was a reporter for CBS News, based in Los Angeles; was a national correspondent for Group W's "PM Magazine"; and coanchored two special projects for WTBS in Atlanta – the award-winning "Out Here on My Own," a program about the Winter Special Olympics, and the station's live coverage of the 104th running of the Kentucky Derby.

Shriver is currently hosting "First Person with Maria Shriver," a series of prime-time specials. Previously, she coanchored NBC's "Sunday Today"; anchored weekend editions of "NBC Nightly News"; and substituted on a number of other NBC News programs, including "NBC News at Sunrise," "Today," and "NBC Nightly News with Tom Brokaw."

Shriver has said that because she grew up with a lot of opportunities, it was important to be goal-oriented. "It can be hard to focus if you think, 'Well, I'll go on this vacation over Christmas and then go away with my family over Easter, and then take a few weeks to go to the Cape.' So when someone would say, 'We're going to such and such a place; you must come,' I wouldn't even listen." This single-mindedness has contributed to her success in coping with the rigors of network news.

Shriver is married to actor Arnold Schwarzenegger. They live in Pacific Palisades, California, in a Mediterranean-style house. The couple has two daughters and enjoys tennis, horseback riding, visiting art galleries, and traveling.

What drew you to a career in broadcast journalism?

The opportunity to be challenged and tested on a daily basis, and the chance to learn something new every day. I also was intrigued by the overwhelming influence television was having on people's lives, and I assumed it would only grow.

Your husband has said, "Maria cares very much about her work. I don't think she could do it so well if she were not by nature very curious, very

eager to learn about the world's people and share with others what she learns." What do you consider to be your greatest asset as a journalist?

I am very curious, and I really like to learn. I find it fascinating at the end of the day to talk about what I've learned, to think about what I've learned, and to try to use what I've learned for the next day. My parents always taught me the importance of listening, so I try to listen to other people, because that's the way you learn.

What do you find most challenging about your work?

The day-to-day uncertainties of it. You are confronted with different issues, different subjects on a day-to-day basis. You never really know what each day is going to bring, what story you're going to be assigned to or what you can think up. You find yourself learning about the court system, international politics, law, inner-city schools – it could be that wide-ranging in a given week. I find it challenging to keep learning, to be well read and *au courant* on a variety of subjects.

Could you describe a typical workday?

No. That's what I like about television. No one day is like the other. One day it's maybe fifteen hours; one day it's twelve hours; one day you are traveling to the Middle East; one day you are in Maine; one day you are in Los Angeles. It depends on the story. Every day is different. It can be a little frustrating because it's hard to plan your life, but I've also found it exciting.

Do you ever have prebroadcast jitters?

I think it's good to have a little adrenaline flowing. You don't want to sleepwalk through your job. Once in a while, I have jitters – when I'm anchoring a summit, covering an election, or in a live situation. I remember I was covering the announcement of the new Supreme Court justice, and we were all sitting around. It was 4:30 or 4:45 in the afternoon, and all of a sudden Bush was about to announce David Souter as his new appointment to the Supreme Court. I was the anchor of the nightly news, substituting for Brokaw. All of a sudden, I found myself having to vamp about a man nobody knew anything about. It had taken everybody by surprise. At that point, your heart does start to beat faster and you start to wish you had read a little bit more about the Supreme Court. But most of the time, if I'm just anchoring the nightly news or doing "Sunday Today" or my own show, I don't have broadcast jitters.

How do you deal with pressure?

I try to take it one day at a time, one assignment at a time. If one day is especially tense, sometimes I'll just get up, walk around the block to clear my mind, and try to convince myself that by tomorrow it will be better.

Being a broadcast journalist and a newsmaker in your own right, you have a unique perspective regarding the media. How has that influenced your work?

It probably has made me reticent about asking well-known people about their personal lives. I think that's probably the big thing I feel uncomfortable with, because I don't like to be asked personal questions myself. I think it has made me sensitive. It has made me make sure I get the story straight, because I've seen stories done on my own family that have been inaccurate and totally without reason or merit. So I always try to make sure that I've uncovered every stone, that I come in with a fair and objective viewpoint, and that I'm really sure what I'm doing is right. I don't want people I do stories on to say they were misquoted or I misled them and the story wasn't what I said it was going to be.

Your coworkers say that you are a very hard worker. What motivates you to work so hard?

I respect people who work hard. I think that no matter what field it is, people who succeed all work really hard. I figure you spend so much of your life at work, why not do it well? Why not learn as much as you possibly can and be as good as you can be? I try to do that in everything I do, whether it is my work, sports, or raising a child. To be the best you can be, you have to work hard.

How do you decide whom you are going to interview for your show?

I try to talk to a lot of people. I try to find people in different fields who are having an impact on society, who are pushing the outer edge of the envelope. The idea behind the series is to interview people from different walks of life and put them all on the same show. For instance, instead of doing a traditional businessman, we did Richard Branson, a billionaire businessman who has a unique business philosophy. I'm interviewing Anita Roddick, a businesswoman who started The Body Shop, which is an avant-garde cosmetic company. She has an interesting philosophy about coupling social activism with business. I try to find people who are different from the majority of people in their field.

As a television journalist, what part of your work do you enjoy most—anchoring, reporting, or interviewing?

I actually enjoy reporting. I like to be out in the field. I like to meet people. I like to find out about their stories. I like to assemble the stories. I like to write them, create them, and figure out how they will flow together. That's really what I find the most challenging. I think that's also the most difficult part.

Is it essential to be a polished ad-libber to be an effective television journalist?

I don't think so, but it helps. I think it depends on the job in television. If you want to anchor a morning show, it helps to be interested in a lot of different subjects. If you are going to be in economics or a [Capitol] Hill reporter, then it's important to be well versed in that subject. I've never tried to pick a particular subject to focus on. I wanted to be what I call an all-purpose reporter so I could cover politics, medicine, features, anything I wanted. To do that, I've tried to develop a little bit of an interest in a lot of different subjects. It always helps to ad-lib, because if you are in a live situation and all of a sudden there is no tape and you've got to talk for five minutes, you have to think on your feet.

Women television correspondents often are criticized for things that have nothing to do with their job, such as their appearance. How do you deal with such criticism?

I don't pay attention to it. I don't call it criticism. I call it an observation. People make observations about other people all the time. This is a physical society we live in. People make judgments about appearance. Women make observations about men who are good-looking, overweight, or whatever. Television is a visual medium. You are criticized for looking too good, and then you are criticized for not looking good enough. So I think you find what works for you. You find a style. You never want to overpower the story or overpower the subject. I just try to dress and groom myself as I do in everyday life. If some people don't like it, that's just tough luck.

Have you ever felt that you were discriminated against in your profession because you are a woman?

I try not to worry about that so much. I think this is still a very male-dominated business. It's changed a lot since I first started. I think a whole wave of women who went before me and are now in their forties helped women like myself, who are in their thirties, to be able to get jobs like anchoring the weekend nightly news, substituting for Tom Brokaw, and anchoring their own prime-time show. I don't think that would be possible had it not been for women like Barbara Walters, Cathy Mackin, Linda Ellerbee, and that whole generation of women who went before us.

I think it's the responsibility of women in my generation to try to pave the way so that women can work in this business in prime time at night and also still have children. When I was starting out in broadcast journalism, there were no women reporters or women working in the networks who had kids. The only job you could have at the network and have a child was a morning show because you didn't travel. In the past year or so, several women have said, "I want to stay at the network. I've paid my dues. I've been here fourteen years. I've shown that I'm good and I'm a marketable commodity." The networks have to make some sort of adjustment. Women like myself, who are in their childbearing years and want to continue working, need to be creative and work out some kind of system that works for the company and for women.

What aspect of your work do you find most demanding?

The incessant travel — never knowing where I might be on any given day — the constant separation from my family.

How do you deal with the opposite pulls of a demanding career and a growing family?

It's tough. But I think it's tough for everybody. I try to take each day as it comes. I always put my family first. That's the most important thing to me. I'm sure, in the long run, my career, to a degree, will suffer because of that.

But that's okay. If I'm good enough, talented enough, and work hard enough, maybe I'm not going to be the most talked-about woman in television journalism for the next five or ten years, but I'll be working. My hope is that I'll be respected, and when I look back, I'll have had a good, solid career.

Television is a changing business. It's changed dramatically in the time I've been in it. It's nothing to get too carried away with. Your family is a lot more important and a lot more worth spending your time on.

Has motherhood changed you?

Yes, it has. I think I was, by everyone's account but not my own (laughter), a workaholic before I had a child. I think now I have a lot more balance in my life. Everything isn't work. Before, I looked at work as the most important and fun thing that I did. Motherhood has given me a different perspective.

What advice would you give someone interested in pursuing a career in broadcast journalism?

I would advise them to start in a small town and do as many different things as they can in the business to gain experience. I also would advise them to learn how to write well and be prepared and willing to work their can off!

What person or persons have made a difference in your life?

My parents certainly have made the biggest difference in my life. I admire them individually and as a couple more than any two people on the face of the earth. They've made my family the most important thing in my life. My husband, certainly, has made a huge difference in my life. I met him when I was a month or two out of college. I was twenty-one. So I've spent basically all of my adult life with him. He's very disciplined – a visionary – and he's taught me the importance of hard work and setting goals. And my daughters have certainly made a big difference in my life. They have taught me that being a mother is an admirable and incredibly gratifying and fulfilling role. They've also taught me how deep love can be. I think all the people who have made a difference are family people. They are the most important people in my life.

What lesson have you learned that has made a difference in your life?

I always tell young people that failure is an important part of succeeding and nobody ever taught me that at school. You were always taught it's such a horrible thing to have a failure. In fact, if you look at anybody who has succeeded, they've also failed. I think it's important for people, especially young people, to know that they are going to fail at some point along the way and that they should use the lessons of that failure to keep going. It's worth taking risks because failure isn't a bad thing as long as you learn from it and use it as a step toward eventual success.

Paige Rense

Profession: Editor

Currently: Editor in Chief, **Architectural Digest**

Date of birth: May 4, 1934

Education: B.A., California State University–Los Angeles, 1954 (English)

$\mathcal{W}$hen asked to describe an interior designer acquaintance, Paige Rense, without a pause, responded, "Beautiful, colorful, successful, and you will like her." With those words, she could easily have been describing herself. As editor in chief of *Architectural Digest,* Rense has made that magazine the undisputed leader among home design publications. Due to her efforts, *Architectural Digest* now boasts a circulation of 625,000 and, at $46 million a year, among the highest advertising revenues in the business.

When Rense joined *Architectural Digest* in 1970, it had a circulation of 50,000 and was a lackluster magazine featuring mainly black-and-white photographs of homes. Within six years, she transformed it into an exclusive showcase of architecture and design. Many designers now measure their professional standing by the number of times their work has appeared in the magazine. The ultimate dream guide for those who aspire to the "good life," the magazine routinely features the residences of presidents, royalty, movie stars, executives, and celebrated literary, diplomatic, and social figures.

In her own words, Rense was a late bloomer, having spent the first fifteen years of her career moving from writing positions at a water-sport magazine and a teen magazine to a series of jobs in advertising and public relations. Not until she was thirty-six, did she find her niche at *Architectural Digest.* When Knapp Communications Corporation, the parent company of *Architectural Digest,* acquired *Bon Appetit* in 1975, Rense became that magazine's founding editor. Under her direction, *Bon Appetit* became the leader among culinary publications. *Geo,* another Knapp acquisition that she edited concurrently, along with *Bon Appetit* and *Architectural Digest,* did not fare as well. With her characteristic aplomb, Rense is quoted as saying, "Editing *Geo* was like banging my head with a hammer. I was so glad it stopped."

Rense is one of the most widely traveled editors in the world today. She has appeared on national talk shows and has received numerous awards. Her husband, Arthur, a former public relations executive, died in 1990. She lives in Santa Barbara and commutes daily in a chauffeured limousine to her Los Angeles office high above Wilshire Boulevard.

What drew you to magazine editing?

It was an accident. I was told that a magazine called *Architectural Digest,* which I'd never heard of, was looking for a writer. I mentioned to the journalist friend who told me about their search that I didn't know anything about architecture. He said, "That doesn't matter; wait till you see the magazine." So I did. I talked with the publisher. I saw the magazine, which was less than wonderful. It was very regional and filled with lots of white shag rugs and gold-veined mirrors, and the text was dreadful.

When I joined the magazine as a writer, it bore little resemblance to the magazine you see today. I was the fourth person on the so-called editorial staff. A full-time art director joined the magazine the same day I did. With a small staff, you have grand titles, and a few months later, I became editor.

When the publisher asked me what I thought of the magazine, I told him very candidly. But I also told him what I thought the magazine could become. At the time, there were many beautiful European magazines. I thought, "Why not have a beautiful magazine based on interior design: the relationship between interior designer and client and how it all happens, or the rare individual who can successfully do his or her own home in a way that is interesting enough for other people to want to see?"

The big problem in all of this was that the magazine was struggling. There was no photography budget. I had to mount a campaign with the top designers in the country, promising them that I would change the magazine as I said I would and convince them to give me their material before any other magazine. Then I had to tell them that I didn't have the money to pay for photography and that *they* would have to commission the photographer. That was the beginning; it was about five or six years before the magazine was at least close to what I had hoped it would become.

What aspect of your work do you find most demanding?

If you mean what do I like least, then it has to do with the business and corporate end of the magazine. I am a senior vice president and on the board of directors, so I have to go over budgets. I have to have business meetings. I'm not a businesswoman, and I don't really like that aspect of my work much at all. The most intense work and the work I like best is the orchestration of the magazine. The creative work of the magazine – gathering the material and putting it all together in a harmonious and exciting fashion that I hope our readers will respond to in a very positive way.

What are you most proud of having accomplished as a magazine editor?

Oh, that's very simple. I've made *Architectural Digest* perhaps the best magazine in the world. I also turned around *Bon Appetit.* I took that from a circulation of 150,000 to 1.3 million, and I took *Architectural Digest* from 50,000 to about 625,000.

Did your being a late bloomer have an effect on your career or your outlook?

Well, it wasn't a career until I bloomed (laughter), so I don't know quite how to answer that. If this wonderful recognition that I've received because of the magazine had happened years ago when I was younger, perhaps I might have been an idiot about it and started to take myself seriously. But I don't.

How do you deal with pressure and deadlines?

Largely by ignoring them.

You ignore deadlines in the magazine business?

Yes, absolutely! After all, by this time, I do know what I am doing. I try to create an atmosphere of reasonable calm. To be chaotic and run around and yell and wave your hands is not productive. I have a fabulous staff. Everyone knows what he or she has to do, and they all do it brilliantly. Our deadlines just keep coming. We work six months in advance, so it's not like we put out one magazine and then start another. We have six issues in the works at all times, and then we have another two or three issues that we are working on in a very preliminary way. Every day is a deadline, and you know that, so you just accept it and do as much as you can one step at a time. There isn't any other way.

Is there any other profession you would rather be pursuing?

I think my one regret is that I was never a newspaperwoman, and I always thought it would have been wonderful fun to be a screenwriter in Hollywood in the thirties. But in terms of today, there is no other magazine in the world that I would want to do, and I can't think of anything else I would rather do.

Has it been difficult juggling a career and a family?

Yes, I think that is always difficult. The work is very intense. The work takes a great deal of focus and concentration, and when you are so involved in your work, you can't just turn it off and stop thinking about it. I would say it was difficult in the first few years. Even without a family, I think it is difficult in terms of your personal life. It's a bit disappointing sometimes to find out someone has been your supposed friend and that he or she has really been seeing you as the magazine. I think probably the other thing that is a little difficult is simply finding time for personal things. When I travel, I always feel that I have to be working every minute, so there is a lot I don't do, like taking time to go to museums, seeing whatever the city may offer, or going out into the countryside. But there isn't anything I regret, and I wouldn't trade my work with *Architectural Digest* for anything.

Have you experienced discrimination in your profession because you are a woman?

I'm sure I have. I don't know if it is truly discrimination, but women are treated differently, and we are different. When I am in a room filled with men, I am conscious that I am a woman and I know they are conscious that I am a woman. I know that their conversation would probably be quite different if a woman were not present. And yes, I do notice a tendency in some men to regard women as not their intellectual equal. And yet I notice a tendency in other men to absolutely delight when a woman says something wonderful. They are both forms of discrimination.

Who were your role models?

The only role models I had were Ginger Rogers and Rosalind Russell. (Laughter) They were always playing magazine editors, newspaperwomen, or career women. That was all we had. I felt that people were probably always terribly disappointed in me because they expected me to be six feet tall, have a feathered boa, and walk with a brace of wolfhounds!

What advice would you give someone interested in becoming a magazine editor?

Well, I always thought that my greatest advantage was my ignorance, so I would remind that person that editors are usually generalists and it might be best not to know too much. The other thing is when I do the magazine, I think only of the reader. I don't think of other magazines and what they will think. I don't think of advertisers. I don't think of anything except the reader. Now that seems like an obvious thing to say, but I think in some cases, magazine editors worry a little too much about what other editors are doing.

What do you think accounts for your success?

I don't really know. I think my timing with *Architectural Digest* in terms of the kind of magazine it has become was a wonderful and happy accident. It was not planned. We just did the best we could, and the recognition, success, and place in publishing that *Architectural Digest* has achieved have happened as a result of that work, not as a result of an attempt for success. I love magazines, and I love *Architectural Digest.* The wonderful things that happened have come from that passion for magazines.

William Huber

Ellen Goodman

Profession: Journalist

Currently: Associate Editor and Columnist, the **Boston Globe**

Date of birth: April 11, 1941

Education: B.A., Radcliffe College, 1963 (History)

Ellen Goodman's Pulitzer Prize-winning column is described in *Time* magazine as "a cool stream of sanity flowing through a minefield of public and private quandaries." Goodman has said, "It is my job and my predilection to try and put the scattered items from the daily newspaper scrapbook into context." Her column appears in more than 440 newspapers across the country and is noted for its insight, humor, and sensitivity. In many ways, she personifies the ideal that the heart of the columnist is the heart of journalism.

Goodman's column, which generally appears on the op-ed page, has expanded the range of topics considered worthy of editorial comment. She has an uncanny ability to go straight to the heart of issues people care most about. "Goodman writes about more than recent legislation, new taxes, elected officials," William Dickinson, her syndicate editor says. "Her work touches readers' lives and hearts, as she examines values, relationships, middle age, women's rights, families," and a plethora of other issues. Following brief stints at *Newsweek* and the *Detroit Free Press,* Goodman joined the *Boston Globe* in 1967. Her column, syndicated by the Washington Post Writers Group, received the Pulitzer Prize for Distinguished Commentary in 1980. She is the author of *Turning Points,* a book on social change. Four collections of her columns – *Close to Home, At Large, Keeping in Touch,* and *Making Sense* – also have been published.

Goodman lives in Brookline, Massachusetts, with her husband, Bob Levey, restaurant critic for the *Boston Globe.* She has one daughter, Katie.

What drew you to a career in journalism?

I can't say that I had a very organized career plan. When I graduated from college, I was looking for work in New York. I applied for all kinds of jobs. I found that *Time* and *Newsweek* both hired young women for fairly crummy jobs, but it sounded interesting, and my sister was working for a newspaper, so I had some idea that it was a good thing to do. But to be honest, I had no goal or particular plan. I kind of shuffled into it.

What was your first job?

I got started by being a researcher-in-training, which is a glorified name for a horrible job at *Newsweek* in the days when all the women were researchers and all the men were reporters. This was in 1963. I was a fact checker for a while. Then I started doing free-lance work in and around New York so that I could write, since they literally didn't let women write for the magazine. And it took.

What do you find most challenging about your work?

Thinking — I mean that literally — and producing. Getting it right is hard. Rewriting is hard. The thing about journalism is that it's not like writing poetry. It's not like doing creative work. You have deadlines. You have to get up in the morning, do your job, and get it in the paper. Newspaper journalism is showing up. You've got to do it again and again and again. I write two columns a week, and I've been doing so for close to twenty years. That requires quite a bit of endurance.

When you make your living telling people what you think, you have to spend a lot of time thinking. Some days it's easier than others, but it's always challenging. I have written in every environment, from an airplane full of journalists on a campaign trail to a hotel room, a quiet office, and a porch — the great world of portable computers. It's also hard being responsible. When you write what you think, people tell you what they think of what you think. You have to learn, slowly, to stand up to that. If you can't stand the heat. . . .

Are you eager to get up and go to work in the morning?

I don't bounce out of bed in the morning eager to seize the day and the next issue. If you know anybody who does, check their urine! But I find that my work energizes my life, engages me in the wider world, and is often as interesting as it is hard.

How do you deal with writer's block?

I don't get writer's block. Journalists aren't allowed to. We can be good or bad, but we can't be late. That's the difference between being a journalist and being a creative writer. You don't wait for the muse in my business. Deadline is an accurate and threatening word.

Is it difficult to come up with topics to write about?

Not so much. People seem to think that's the hardest part. I'm often juggling things. It's hard, sometimes, to make a decision about what I *want* to write about. But I never feel totally empty.

How do you deal with the pressure of deadlines?

I have a pretty high tolerance for pressure, or else I would have gotten out of this business. It's literally a job requirement. You can't freak out under pressure and be a journalist. People who do just don't last.

What traits do you think are important in your profession?

The capacity to listen. You have to be able to listen and understand what people are saying and then be able to get it through your own brain and communicate it again. A certain amount of understanding and energy is required. Also, I think, you have to have some interest in playing with words.

What do you enjoy more, rewriting or the initial challenge of putting it together?

There are days when you fly through it. You are in a rhythm, you feel good about it, and it's easy to communicate. It's fun just to write right through it. But it varies tremendously. Even though I'm doing the same thing on one level, which is writing 75 lines twice a week, on another level, it's not the same at all because sometimes – this happened to me just yesterday – you have so much material to squeeze into the seventy-five lines. It's like standing in the middle of a room with everything you own on the floor and trying to get it all into one suitcase.

Other days, it's like you have a little idea and you're just winging it, expanding it, and playing with it. It's not that one [writing or rewriting] is more fun than the other, or one is more challenging or more interesting than the other, but every day is different, even though it appears to be the same.

Could you describe a typical workday?

There are days when I have more meetings than others. But on a writing day, I read a great deal before I write. I have this rule that at a certain time, I've just got to start writing – period. This is a journalistic rule called "You have to go with what you've got." There's a point at which you have to stop reporting and start writing.

What do you think accounts for your success?

I think I started out trying to articulate things, write about things, that people were thinking about – social change in particular. At the time I started writing, there was almost nothing written in op-ed pages about family, about children, about relationships, or about the women's movement. Those were relegated to other parts of the paper. It's not something that's easy to judge about yourself, but I'm often told by people, "You write just what I'm thinking." That's not quite accurate – that's my job! People get up in the morning, hear something on the news, and think about it. But it's not their job to think about it. They go to work and do whatever they do. But it's my job to go to work and think about it. So a lot of times what I have written seems to resonate people's thoughts. I think, also, I'm trying to work out for myself and others some of the very complicated things we're seeing in society, whether it's questions about bioethics or questions about family.

If you unexpectedly had a month off, how would you spend it?

I would spend it up in Maine, in my house, on the porch, reading; maybe doing a little notebook writing; playing tennis; having wonderful meals with friends; being happily indolent.

Are there ever days you wish you were in another profession?

Sure. There are days when I would rather be hitting rocks with hammers. I think it's true for every writer. I think it's Pete Hamill who said, "It's the hardest work in the world that doesn't involve heavy lifting." There are days when it's very hard. And there are days when it's a real luxury to be paid to tell people what you think.

Has it been difficult juggling a career and a family?

At the moment, it isn't. Of course it was. It's difficult for everybody. It just plain is.

As a woman, have you experienced discrimination in your profession?

Sure. I don't think there is any woman who hasn't – certainly no woman of my generation. When I went to *Newsweek,* it was prior to the Civil Rights Act of 1964. It was legal to discriminate against women. People forget. They know it happened, but they forget that it was also legal. *Newsweek* had a two-tier system: the *girls* did research, and the *men* did reporting. There was nothing you could do about that. I was part of that system until I left. The system didn't change until women, a few years later, sat in. *Newsweek* was one of the great journalistic sex discrimination cases. When I worked at the *Detroit Free Press,* I was the second or third woman in the city room. Women previously had been pretty much kept out by the managing editor who left just before I got there.

Did you have a role model?

In my generation, in particular, there weren't a lot of women role models. I mean, who were they? Where were they? There were just a few women ahead of us, really, and I didn't think of them as role models. By the time I got to the *Globe,* I had a friend and a supporter in the editor. He was somebody who wrote me notes – "Great stuff! What a beaut! A real corker!" – and said I was doing a good job, and that was very important. But I didn't have a mentor guiding my career.

What advice would you give someone interested in pursuing a career in journalism?

Do it. It's a hard profession. But it's also one of the few places where you can express yourself within, explore anything that you are interested in, and make that your day's work; where you're in real contact with this society; where you are both creative, to a certain extent, and involved with others, as opposed to being creative in a more isolated fashion. And it's both an individual pursuit and a group pursuit. It balances a lot of interests, and it's fun. I had an editor who used to walk through the city room saying to people, "Are you having any fun?" Well, it *is* fun!

Jean V. Naggar

Profession: Literary Agent

Currently: Head, Jean V. Naggar Literary Agency

Date of birth: December 5, 1938

Education: B.A., London University, 1960 (English)

$\mathcal{J}$ ean Naggar, one of the literary world's premier power brokers, has built a multimillion-dollar literary agency with her keen literary judgment, unerring tact, and well-honed negotiating skills. She launched the Jean V. Naggar Literary Agency in 1978 from her living room with a client list of ten unpublished authors. Today Naggar represents many of the most successful writers in the business.

"Jean's very tough. She's as tough as every big gun you could name," says Nansey Neiman, publisher of Warner Books. "The only reason you don't slam the phone down in frustration sometimes is because she's very nice. But at the end of any of my dealings with her, I've never felt it was a bad situation. Whether or not I feel I've paid more than I wanted to, I always feel satisfied."

A year after opening her own agency, Naggar negotiated an extraordinary deal for first-time novelist Jean Auel, who had completed *The Clan of the Cave Bear,* the first of six novels in her very successful "Earth's Children" series. Crown Publishing Group paid an advance of $130,000, the largest advance ever paid to a first-time novelist. Naggar has subsequently negotiated countless record-breaking contracts. She landed author Karleen Koen a $350,000 advance for her historical novel *Through a Glass Darkly.* She negotiated a $250,000 movie option for author Tony Kenrick's suspense thriller *Neon Tough.*

Naggar, the daughter of British and Italian parents, grew up in Cairo, Egypt, and was educated in England. She moved to New York in 1962 and, while raising three children, free-lanced for many years as an editor, proofreader, and copy editor for numerous major publishing houses. During this period, she also did some free-lance writing and reviewing for *Publishers Weekly,* the *Village Voice,* and the *New York Times,* as well as translating several books from French and articles from Italian, languages she speaks fluently. It was while at Liveright Publishers and Norton that she received the publishing education that would prepare her for running her own agency.

Naggar manages her agency with the assistance of several staffers. Among their responsibilities is handling subsidiary rights – including magazines, films, television, and foreign translations – and coordinating the activities of fourteen foreign agents. Naggar's list consists of approximately two-thirds fiction and one-third nonfiction. About 15 percent of her titles are children's books. The agency receives more than five thousand queries annually, and Naggar estimates she reads three hundred manuscripts a year.

As a literary agent, Naggar sees herself as the writer's business partner. She does not sign up a writer unless she admires his or her work. This passion for the writers she represents and a willingness to go the distance for them make her a tough negotiator. Naggar is described by her friend and client Jean Auel as "the iron fist in the velvet glove."

What do you look for in a book manuscript you agree to agent?

I look particularly for a distinctive voice, for something that tells me this person is the only person who could have written this particular work of fiction or even nonfiction. No matter how much background research anchors it, it comes from a very personal source and puts the reader into a unique world that only this writer could have created.

What qualities do you think are important for a literary agent?

I think one has to have something that you could call gut feel, an intuitive marker, a sense of what is going to work. You have to have good interpersonal skills. You have to be able to work with a lot of different people, take a lot of aggravation, and be able to negotiate. I think one of the most important qualities for a literary agent is to be well organized. The reading and selecting of material is a very small part of it. The rest involves tracking, following, and dealing with a million details.

When reading a manuscript, do you immediately know whether you want to agent it?

I like to take the time to think it through, but actually after I've read a chapter I very often know. I still take the time to think about it. I ask other people in my office to read it. We discuss it. But there's no question that I very often know, almost immediately, that it is or isn't going to work for me.

Does the manuscript stand on its own, or do you generally like to meet the author before you make a decision to agent?

The manuscript stands on its own, but I always like to have a long conversation with the author before we make that final commitment to work together. It's very important to establish a philosophy of working together that's going to work out. I don't have to meet the author face-to-face. I have learned to eliminate potential troublemakers from my life that way. They are not worth it.

Can you pick out a best-seller?

I have been able to pick out novels that have become best-sellers. I knew they would. But I think, more than that, it's a question of being drawn very strongly to the work of that writer. It's a very subjective thing, with fiction particularly. What would work for me would not necessarily work for every agent. I believe that what we call intuition is a large mix of instinctual feel combined with a tremendously strong subconscious feed-in of experience accumulated over many years.

How do you deal with job stress?

I try to take it one step at a time. I try to step back from it. Sometimes I have a whole lot of appointments and somebody calls up with a major problem that wasn't anticipated and the day looks as if it is going to just disintegrate into a tremendous pressure. At that point, I find it helpful just to look at the calendar and say to myself, "Really, I don't need to do this today. I can actually do it in two weeks." Sometimes just a little phone call will make a huge amount of difference in the way I feel. I find that if you do reschedule, as long as you don't do it at the very last minute, the other person frequently welcomes the relief, particularly if you are not canceling completely but merely rescheduling because your calendar is full.

If you were a writer trying to select a literary agent, what would you want to know about that agent?

Well, I would want to know if the agent was able to navigate successfully and comfortably in the world of publishing; if the agent had the right contacts; if the agent was somebody I could trust, whose opinion I cared about; and if the agent had a reputation for being honest and trustworthy.

What do you think accounts for your success?

That's a very difficult question! I really don't know. I think it may have something to do with the fact that I like people and I respect the people I work with – both the people I work with who are my clients and the people I work with in the publishing industry.

I think, also, that I am fortunate in having a very strong sense of priorities, detail, and organization. You can't just be an erratic genius to be a good literary agent. You really are a traffic center for many, many things, and you have to keep on top of a huge amount of detail. Unless you can organize yourself initially, and then yourself and the staff, so that you have materials immediately accessible and professionally handled, I think you can founder very easily and possibly drown. In answering your question, I am trying desperately to avoid saying "luck" because I have a husband who refuses to accept that. I don't consider myself to be a genius, either. I think this is the kind of question that probably should be asked of other people about me rather than of me.

What advice would you give someone interested in pursuing a career as a literary agent?

Well, I would certainly advise them to start out within the traditional publishing framework to get some sense of who is who and what kinds of books different publishers publish before trying to embark on selling, because those contacts and that network are absolutely invaluable.

Is there anything you've learned in your profession that, had you known earlier, would have made your life easier?

One of the things I've learned is that a lot of the things that you dread and believe you can't do you *can* do, that a lot of the fear one feels is invisible to the world and sometimes serves to sharpen one's own reactions and ways of dealing with things. I've also learned that when the pressure builds to the point of discomfort, it's always possible to lessen it by shifting appointments, taking less work, deciding to let go of somebody who has been creating tremendous problems and anxieties. I've come to understand that these are not the kinds of irrevocable things that will cause disaster. I think early on in one's career, one feels that is the case, that if you don't hang on by your fingernails to every opportunity, everything will somehow disappear. I have learned that it doesn't disappear.

What aspect of your work do you find most demanding?

I think one of the things that is particularly demanding, and that most people are not aware of, is that I'm not only a literary agent, I am also a small business owner. Not only do I attend to the needs of my clients, make deals, negotiate, deal with the occasional person who is having a fit of momentary craziness, and read a great many manuscripts and certainly a huge volume of correspondence, but I am also running a business. I deal with a staff. I deal with hiring and firing. I deal with all personnel matters. Also, if we need equipment, I have to do the research and make those decisions. When we moved our offices, all of that was my responsibility, too. I think essentially the hardest part of what I do is organizing it.

Has it been difficult juggling a career and a family?

Very difficult. No matter what you do, you always feel that somehow you haven't quite done it right. I have a wonderful family. I have a very supportive husband. I have terrific children, who are now adults. I did what I thought was right all the way through. I tried not to shortchange anyone at any point and did what I felt was best for everybody, but I look back now and regret a lot of the time I wish I could have spent with my children when they were younger. My career choice was really not made on the basis of self-fulfillment. It was a question of finance, among other things. There was no other choice for me, but looking back, now that the children are all grown and have left home, I regret that I didn't have more time. I know that people who do have more time also have regrets, so I think it is just part of being at that stage in life. It was very difficult.

When I started out, I was working in a corner of my living room, and I always tried to involve my children as much as possible. My daughter read manuscripts for children's books and gave me a report. My children used to take the manuscripts to the post office in a shopping cart. They knew what work I was doing and what was going on. One night, at the dinner table, my son David mentioned something to do with a triumph that he had at school a year ago, and I said, "I didn't know that!" And one of the other children said, "Oh, you must have told Mommy before six o'clock. You *know* she never hears anything we say before six o'clock." I think that was a significant part of making it all work. I was able to put myself in a work bubble, but the children knew that after six o'clock in the evening, I was theirs.

As a woman, have you experienced discrimination in your profession?

It isn't as clear-cut as that. I would say not so much discrimination as a tendency to give recognition to a certain type of ... male bluster. I think that men have an easier time blowing their own horn, and as a result, because I don't have a very aggressive stance in the way I speak, there has been a tendency to see me as a nurturing, mothering kind of agent, and it is only recently that the deal-making element – the financial strength and the negotiating strength – have begun to come out. It isn't overt discrimination. It's much more subtle. It's a tendency to see me as – I hate to say this – "that nice woman" rather than as "that tough literary agent." It is just a difference in style. I am very tough for my clients. I have probably made the best deals in publishing history, but it has taken longer for that to be recognized than it would have had I been a man.

Who was your role model?

I haven't had a specific role model in my profession. In my life, my role model has been my mother who, although she has never been a professional woman, is a woman of great strength, energy, determination, and optimism. I have never seen her sit down under adversity; she always finds a way to do something, to be active.

Diana Walker

Profession: Photojournalist

Currently: White House Photographer for **Time**

Date of birth: January 20, 1942

Education: Foxcroft School, 1959
               A.A.S., Briarcliff College, 1961 (Drama)

$\mathcal{A}$s White House photographer for *Time* magazine, Diana Walker has traveled the world recording important events and photographing some of the most influential people of our times. Her assignments have included covering Presidents Bush and Gorbachev at the signing of an historic arms agreement in Malta, accompanying Rosalynn Carter on a visit to a Cambodian refugee camp, and photographing President Bush with the troops in Saudi Arabia.

After several years in the retail dress business, Walker transformed her photography hobby into a career. In 1972, she joined the *Washington Monthly* as an in-house photographer, and via free-lance work, accumulated an impressive portfolio of political portraits that brought her to *Time* magazine in 1979.

Walker grew up in Washington, D.C. where she lives with her husband Mallory, who works in real estate and mortgage banking. They have two adult sons.

How did you launch a career in photography?

I didn't do it right out of college. I had a mid-career change, if you will. When I first married and moved back to Washington, D.C., I was in the retail dress business. Photography started out as a hobby for me. I had a darkroom in my house when I was young, and I asked for my first camera when I was in the sixth grade. What was a hobby just grew, and I started taking pictures of friends and family and doing Christmas cards. I was interested in politics, and when you live in Washington, it's very easy to get involved in what makes this city tick.

I had a friend who said, "Listen, why don't you go into business and take pictures for a living?" So my friend and I started a business called "I Am a Camera." We photographed anything and everything we could, from weddings to bar mitzvahs to parties. I had been doing some free-lance work for Charlie Peters, who runs the *Washington Monthly,* which is a small political magazine, and he asked me to come on board and be a sort of in-house researcher/photographer. I jumped at the chance! The pay was low, but the job offered me the possibility of getting my [Capitol] Hill and White House credentials, and his staff was wonderful to work with.

I started to work for the *Monthly* and to free-lance for a lot of other magazines and newspapers. I worked on my portfolio. I'd take a look at the mastheads of magazines, particularly in New York, and call up and make appointments and go to see them. They would either hire me or they wouldn't. That's how I got started.

As a photographer, are you basically self-taught?

Yes, totally. Except when I was in high school, there was a math teacher who was interested in photography, and he taught us how to use the darkroom. That was very helpful and wonderful fun. But my skills were limited.

Do you do your own developing and printing now?

Not at all. I never have except when I first started. I did my own black-and-white work when I was working for the *Monthly* and the *Village Voice* and a few publications like that. First, there isn't time. Secondly, I'm working mostly in color now, and it is processed professionally by either the Time-Life lab or by the lab of the magazine's choice.

What aspect of your work do you find most challenging?

Well, there are two aspects. Physically, you have to be on your toes. You have to be up and ready to move any minute, and you have to be professionally proficient. You have to know what your camera can do and what it can't. You have to know which film is good for which situation. You have to know lenses. You have to know what you are capable of doing to make quality pictures. I'm not talking about making a lasting image. I'm talking about making an image that is properly exposed, that has quality – technically speaking.

Next, you have to convey to whomever is looking at the picture a real sense of what happened – beyond the physical aspect of the photograph and beyond what is happening on the surface. There must be a dimension to that picture that really tells you more. It's difficult to do especially in the confines, for instance, of the White House. There is so much going on there, but you are allowed only certain access. The familiarity of the scene is very redundant. Somehow you have to get under the skin to show what really is happening, and that's a very difficult job.

What type of assignments do you enjoy most?

I'm covering the White House for *Time* every other month which is a wonderful assignment. I love it. I share it with Dirck Halstead. It's really ideal because after a month in the White House, you are ready to do other kinds of assignments. It can be tedious, and it can be exciting. Having us divide it the way we do is ideal. I am very interested in watching the President of the United States and all the players. It is fascinating. So that assignment is wonderful, and I don't tire of it.

During the month that you are working at the White House, are you on call twenty-four hours a day?

Basically, yes. The White House is mine to cover, and I have to make sure I'm there when something is happening. It's my responsibility to be there between 8:30 and 9:00 every morning and stay until there is what is called a lid, which means there won't be anything else happening. If something happens, they would call us up in the middle of the night and tell us to get down there.

What do you look for when you shoot pictures in the White House?

I shoot pictures, always keeping in mind what I know about that week's magazine. I'll shoot not only the President but also the other players and the interaction between them. If I go to the Oval Office for a picture of the President with the Easter Seal poster child, I will look around the room and see who else is there, what's going on. If [Secretary of State] James Baker is whispering to Scowcroft, that might fit into our story. If we are doing something on how the President makes his decisions, I'll make sure I have a lot of tight head shots. If I see something in his eyes that says to me this man is distracted or he is thinking of something else, I've got to think about how to show that.

How do you deal with pressure?

You deal! I think it's very much like an actor. Don't tell me that an actor doesn't get butterflies before he or she goes onstage. I think it's exactly the same thing. I think photographers get very anxious. I could be traveling somewhere photographing the President, and it could be an extremely important event – a meeting – and Time could be holding space for a picture on Saturday. I have to make a picture that is good. It has to be processed and transmitted by satellite to fill that hole in the magazine. Think how that makes me feel! It makes me scared to death! (Laughter) You deal with it by talking yourself into being calm. But still, you get clammy hands and butter-flies and all those things that come along with fright and the anxiety of deadlines.

Do you ever feel frustrated that you are missing an important event in history because you are too busy literally focusing your camera trying to capture it?

No, I don't find that frustrating in the least. You think about it later. On board the ship in Malta, you are perfectly aware that what's going on between Gorbachev and Bush is terribly important, but you don't think about it at that time. What you think about is getting the picture that tells the people what you are seeing. History is made all the time in these events.

There is an enormous difference between the kinds of situations I see and a Washington Post street photographer, who sees extraordinary action in front of him or her. He can see a horrible accident or something that is very emotionally gripping. For that kind of thing, you steel your mind against your human feelings. You have the camera between you and the subject, and you are filing it all away. You can't help it when something moves you terribly. It's etched in your mind forever, but you are able to continue working. Your concentration is so acute that the anguish you may feel over what you are photographing is accepted. What's foremost in your mind is being able to capture it on film. But I think your sympathy, your understanding, may make you "see" better.

What qualities are you most often called upon to use in your profession?

I think it is important to know what is going on, to listen, to be aware of more than meets the eye in terms of understanding what you are seeing and hearing. I think the ability to get along with people is very, very important, especially if you are going to be alone with someone and spend time with him or her.

I went to do Corazon Aquino for "Woman of the Year" in 1986 for *Time*. It was important that I get along with her. It was important that I be able to put myself into her life without being obtrusive. I wanted to be a fly on the wall in her office. I wanted her to give me access she had never given anybody before. So I think being able to deal with people – make people at ease with you, make them understand what you're after, make them trust you to a certain extent, and make them comfortable with you – is very, very important.

Is it still thrilling to see your pictures published?

Yes, I love seeing my pictures in print. Sometimes you have no idea you shot a particular picture, and you get a great surprise. All of a sudden there it is – big – and it's wonderful fun! I get very upset sometimes when we work intensely for a week and they don't use anything. But it has to do with so many different factors: whether they are interested in the President that week; whether they decide to use drawings, cartoons, or maps.

When does your day end?

When the President goes "home" at about 6:30 P.M. If he has a dinner to attend or an event in the evening and I'm in the [press] pool, I have to follow him.

If I'm traveling with the President, my days are extremely long. If the President is on a campaign swing in November through seven states in six days, or seven states in three days, which is more like George Bush (laughter), your days are endless. You get no sleep whatsoever.

Has it been difficult juggling a career and a family?

Yes, it is difficult, but I happen to have a family that has been very excited and enthusiastic about my career. My husband has been extraordinarily elastic in not having a set pattern of life that would be difficult to intrude upon. He's always been willing to accommodate my peculiar travel schedule.

I came home one night several years ago, and I said, "I know Thanksgiving is next Thursday, and I know that we have twenty-two people coming here for Thanksgiving lunch. I can't tell you where I'm going, but *Time* is sending me someplace, and it's extremely exciting. It's a big deal, and I hope you don't mind cooking the turkey." And he didn't. I went to the Philippines to photograph Corazon Aquino for the M.O.Y. [Man of the Year/Woman of the Year], and I couldn't tell him where I was going!

As a woman, have you experienced discrimination in your profession?

I have always felt that being a woman works both ways. Sometimes it's an advantage, and other times it's not. It was hard when I first started working in the mid-seventies for *Time, People, Fortune, Business Week, New York Magazine*. It's the same thing in anything. There are some people who are difficult to deal with and are going to give you a hard time. I have run into the old-boy network over the years, but times have changed so much. I was lucky because when I came along, *Time* was looking for a woman. Sure, there have been difficult moments. Once in a while, you run into somebody who can't deal with you or can't take you seriously because you are a woman. So move on. No big deal.

Who were your role models?

People ask me all the time if Margaret Bourke-White was my role model. I've always felt that she and certain other photographers were part of another stratosphere. It never occurred to me to try to emulate them. What I wanted to do was take pictures. I love looking at other people's work. I am so unabashedly admiring of so many photographers' work. I just love looking at photographs. I collect photographs. I'm passionate about photography. I've admired so many photographers, but I never wanted to be like anyone.

What advice would you give someone interested in pursuing a career in photography or photojournalism?

Go to museums and look at pictures. Don't look necessarily at photographs; look at paintings as well. Keep your eyes open all the time. Color, design, shape – all of that is very important. If you want a career in photography, you ought to become technically proficient. Save yourself an awful lot of time by getting a degree in photojournalism or by taking some courses in photography.

I am a believer in a liberal arts education. I also believe in specializing in photography as early as possible because there are so many people who will be competing with you. For instance, I don't take assignments I don't know much about. If I get a call from a book publisher to take pictures of some buildings, I'll say no. There are so many good people who photograph buildings and interiors and know how to do it well. Sure, I could learn to do it. But I couldn't do it like the good ones. I do what I do best, and what I do best is people. It's important to focus. If you are interested in photojournalism, go and do a story. Show that you know what it means to do a picture story, that you can get the action and bring it home. I suggest people not sit around waiting for the phone to ring. It's not going to ring. The best thing you can do is join a newspaper and do the whole thing inside out from the darkroom to the front page.

Anna Perez

Profession: Press Secretary

Currently: Press Secretary to First Lady Barbara Bush

Date of birth: June 13, 1951

Education: Hunter College, 1970- 1972 (Journalism)

$\mathcal{A}$nna Perez has a wonderful sense of humor and is known for her quick repartee. She is described by First Lady Mrs. Barbara Bush as having "good sense, great instincts, and terrific judgment" – all essential qualities for a press secretary. According to Perez, her biggest job is keeping up with and responding to the daily avalanche of mail Mrs. Bush receives.

When her husband, a broadcasting engineer, was recruited by Howard University to run the university's television station, they moved to Washington, D.C. from Tacoma, Washington where they had owned and run the *Tacoma Facts,* a weekly newspaper. Subsequently, Perez found a job in Congress and worked her way up to press secretary to U.S. Congressman John Miller (R-Washington). During the 1988 presidential campaign, she also served as regional press secretary for George Bush at the Republican National Convention in New Orleans. After the election, Barbara Bush invited her to interview for the position of press secretary, and the two women hit it off. Perez has said that she has learned a lot from Mrs. Bush, particularly that "you treat people the way you want to be treated" and "it's hard to dislike somebody who likes you."

As press secretary to a popular and active first lady, Perez is constantly on the go, attending campaign events, commencement exercises, social engagements, and literary events. On one such trip, she spent Thanksgiving in Saudi Arabia; rode a camel to the Sphinx in Cairo, Egypt, at four o'clock in the morning; and shortly thereafter was in a confetti-covered motorcade in Monterrey, Mexico, on the way to the governor's palace.

Perez is married to Theophilus Sims, with whom she has two children. Barbara Bush has said of her press secretary, "When people talk about the modern woman, who manages to balance her job, her marriage, her home life and children, I think Anna is the perfect model. And I think it's unusual to be so successful at it. You know how I can tell she's a success? From her kids. You've never met such friendly, smart, sweet children."

What drew you to your job as a press secretary?

My husband and I owned a small newspaper in Washington State. I've always been a news junkie. Actually, I remember reading the *Long Island Press* going up to Queens when I was still in grade school. Knowing a little bit about a lot of things is a prerequisite for the job, and I like doing different things all the time, which is another huge part of this job. I guess my job and I are a good match! I did some marketing work before going into politics. I never wanted to grow up to be a press secretary (laughter), but once I got into it ... well, I just really like what I do.

What did you want to grow up to be when you were a child?

At various times I wanted to be a writer. When I was very young, I wanted to be an actress, but I quickly grew out of that.

What aspect of your work do you find most challenging?

There is always something new to learn. You never stop learning. Politics is not a science; it is an art.

What is the difference between working as a press secretary to the First Lady and working as a press secretary to, say, a corporate head?

Well, I've never been a press secretary to a corporate head. I've only worked for politicians. I was press secretary to a senator and a member of the House, and there is a difference there, particularly in the types of things you talk about. It is a heck of a lot harder to get a member of Congress in the papers than it is Mrs. Bush! (Laughter) But the basics are the same. You have to be scrupulously honest, straightforward, and never afraid of saying, "I don't know, I'll have to get back to you."

What is your primary function as press secretary to Mrs. Bush?

All aspects of Mrs. Bush's press relations. My office is responsible for setting up what is called press availability – out-of-town events, as well as arrangements for the out-of-town press – and we do some research for speeches.

Do you find yourself constantly clarifying issues, or is that not necessary with Mrs. Bush?

(Laughter) Mrs. Bush is very clear about who she is and what she means.

How do you keep your perspective?

I read a lot – that's the way I relax. My husband and children are very good at perspective (laughter) and letting me know that there is life outside the White House. This is not my life; this is my job.

What problems do you encounter most frequently in your line of work?

I don't want to seem like Pollyanna, but what some people may view as problems we simply view as arrangements that are part of getting the job done. I have a great staff, and we all work well together. To tell you the truth, I just don't have that many problems.

Could you describe a typical workday?

A workday may include spending two-thirds of it on the phone and the rest of it signing letters or setting up three or four interviews, a roundtable interview with eight reporters, television interviews, and the press arrangements for a state dinner. I may be at the White House from 8:30 in the morning until 6:30 or 7:00 in the evening or from 6:00 in the morning until midnight. There are no typical days.

What are you most proud of having achieved?

A happy marriage and two children who haven't driven me to distraction – yet.

Has it been difficult juggling a career and a family?

In some ways, yes, because you always have feelings of guilt when you are away from your family, particularly in this job because there is a lot of travel involved. But I can imagine circumstances where it would be much more difficult – if I were a single parent or if I weren't married to a wonderful man or if my sister-in-law didn't live with us. There are actually three adults in our family. That is important when two adults work outside the home. This doesn't work for everybody, but it works for us.

Is it difficult juggling? Not nearly as difficult as it was for my mother, who was a single parent and worked almost the entire time outside the home when I was growing up. And not nearly as difficult as it is for millions of other parents.

As a woman, have you experienced discrimination in your career?

If I have, I don't know about it. Truly, I may have, but I just don't know. Maybe I just didn't recognize it. Maybe that's the best way to deal with it. I just barrel on. I'm more self-absorbed than I'd like to be. I just do whatever I'm doing, and if people have a problem with that, I figure it's their problem, not mine.

Who were your role models?

My mom. I also had a teacher in the fourth and fifth grades who was superb. Her name is Joy Berry. She is chairman of the Georgia Human Rights Commission now. But she was probably my most influential role model outside of the home.

Terrie Williams

Profession: Public Relations Executive

Currently: President, The Terrie Williams Agency

Date of birth: May 12, 1954

Education: B.A., Brandeis University, 1975 (Psychology)
M.S., Columbia University, 1977 (Social Work)

"J am a very spiritual person, and I really do believe in destiny and that my purpose here is to build a major institution," says Terrie Williams, president of one of the fastest-growing public relations firms in the entertainment industry. Williams founded The Terrie Williams Agency in 1987 with the signing of her first client, actor/comedian Eddie Murphy. She says of her field, "I like the challenge of turning people on to something new and different."

The agency specializes in publicity, media relations, and events planning for entertainment, sports, and corporate clients. It represents some of the best-known entertainers and sports figures in America.

A native of Mount Vernon, New York, Williams was a medical social worker at New York Hospital before opting for a career in public relations. Her communications career began at the New York radio station WWRL, where she was an associate producer for the public affairs department. In 1980, she joined the Black Filmmaker Foundation and a year later was named the first executive director of the Communications Alliance, a trade association of media owners. Williams has served as executive director of the World Institute of Black Communications and producer of the annual Communications Excellence to Black Audiences (CEBA) Awards. She also was responsible for organizing the public relations department at Essence Communications, Inc.

Williams has received numerous awards for her work in the communications industry and was described in *Newsmaker* as "an extraordinary giver of time and talent." She says she learned from her parents how to say thank you: "It pays to be nice to people. I treat everyone the same way. I don't differentiate." When the late jazz great Miles Davis was asked why he retained her agency, he responded, "She treats me like a brother."

Williams resides in New York City. When not commuting between her New York and Los Angeles offices, she travels around the country encouraging young people to live their dreams and reminding them that "one dream leads to another."

What drew you into the field of public relations?

I saw an article one day in the *Amsterdam News*. It was just a little item that said that a public relations course was being taught at the "Y," and it sounded interesting. The man who taught the course wasn't particularly inspiring, but he had a number of guest lecturers. There was a fellow who had his own public relations firm, and he whet my appetite for the business. From there I took another course, and then I just started doing a lot of volunteer work. I was really disenchanted with the social work field, so I started thinking about other things. I think it was destiny, because I didn't know anyone in the public relations field and to pick up the paper one day and see a little item about a public relations course being taught . . . for that to catch my eye just made me think I was expected to do it.

What aspect of your work do you find most demanding?

The need to respond quickly to so many different issues. We get calls requesting a client's viewpoint on certain things. A reporter doing a story might call and ask if we have any clients we would like to get involved in X, Y, and Z. We go through our roster to check who might be the best person to respond, and then we help develop our client's position. We come up with a statement for the client, get the client's approval, and then get back to the media person in time to meet the deadline.

What are you most proud of having accomplished as a public relations executive?

Starting the company and having developed the kind of reputation that we have to represent the caliber of people that we do. Eddie Murphy was the first client I signed, and we were retained by American Express to handle the New York host committee for the 1991 Grammy Awards, which was a major coup. Most of our clients are either black entertainers or corporations that have community relations components that largely have to do with the black community. The American Express account was probably the first piece of business that we have gotten where we competed against other firms that specialize in music and have absolutely nothing to do with color. It is a step in the right direction in terms of breaking out of being viewed as a black public relations firm. Handling Mr. Mandela's visit to New York is also something that I am very, very proud of having done.

Are you selective in whom you will represent?

Yes, I have to believe in the person or the project I am representing. I have to have a passion about the project or person to get competitive ideas for that editorial space in a magazine, newspaper, or television or radio show. You have to have a passion about the project, because if you get told no as many times as you will, you have to be able to go back in there and say, "Now wait a minute! You really need to take another look at this."

What do you think accounts for your success?

A really strong sense of professionalism. I genuinely care about people. I mean, it's not superficial. In terms of the people I represent, I genuinely care about them as people. If they lost what they have today, I would still be in their lives, and I can't say that about a lot of people who are in this business.

We also pay attention to detail, and if there is something we can't do, then we'll pick up the phone and say, "Look, we're not going to meet this particular deadline, but this is when we'll have it done." Just paying attention to detail and doing what you say you're going to do are important. Then again, if you can't, you should pick up the phone and say so.

Is there any other profession you would rather be pursuing?

I have a fantasy about being a toll collector. (Laughter) That is my recurring fantasy because I like meeting people. I'd smile and say hello and take their money and give them their change, and I don't believe I would have to take work home with me at the end of the day. I would do that, or I would run a country store. Something peaceful and quiet, because this business is very draining. Entertainment P.R. is especially draining because you work all day, then when you have clients who are performing late at night, you are out with them until twelve, one, two o'clock in the morning. Then you hit the ground running the next day like you had a good night's sleep. It can be very, very draining.

As a woman, have you experienced discrimination in your profession?

Sure. But that only gives you inspiration and the fuel to go out and do what you set out to do. I am representing three people today who at one time did not want to give me the time of day. So that gives me a little charge. I don't hold any grudges. I smile and think, "I know you'll be back. That's okay. You'll be back."

Has it been difficult juggling a career and a personal life?

Yes, it is a challenge to juggle my friends, my family, and my business. I'm not married. I lived with someone for about a year, and then we started to work together, and the living and the working together was a little too much. So now we just work together. But, yes, it is a challenge – there is no question! I don't know how people come home at the end of the day and prepare dinner for their husband and children or lunch for the kids for the next day. I think that's truly extraordinary. I am able to do what I do because I don't have a husband and kids. I think the really extraordinary people are those who accomplish great things in business and also juggle a family.

Who was your role model?

I would say a lot of people. But it starts from home. My mother was the only one of nine children who graduated from high school and then went on to college and graduate school. When I was, I guess, about sixteen years old, the trucking company my father worked for went out of business, and I remember thinking that we were going to starve to death. But somehow my father got us together and started a business. I think just having my parents as examples did a great deal for me. I also draw a lot from successful people. I read stories about how people do what they do, and I draw a lot from that.

What advice would you give someone interested in pursuing a career in public relations?

Read everything you can get your hands on. We skim eight to ten newspapers a day in our office; forty to fifty magazines on a monthly basis. Read, read, read! Meet and talk with as many people as possible. Understand trends. See who is doing what with whom. That's important. Read the society pages and find out who is marrying whom. That's how you find out a whole lot of stuff. Persevere and never take no for an answer.

Cathleen Black

Profession: Newspaper Publisher

Currently: President – CEO, American Newspaper Publishers Association

Date of birth: April 26, 1944

Education: B.A., Trinity College (Washington, D.C.), 1966 (English)

When asked what qualities were intrinsic to a good boss, Cathleen Black could easily have been describing herself when she responded, "Self-confidence, ability to share glory, a caring personality, decisiveness, commitment to colleagues and projects, and enthusiasm." As an ex-publisher of *USA Today,* Black is one of the most visible publishers in the United States. On Madison Avenue, she is regarded as one of the best marketers in the publishing business.

Black began her career on the advertising sales staffs of *Holiday, Travel & Leisure,* and *New York.* She joined *Ms.* magazine in 1972 as its first advertising manager, performing the Herculean task of convincing corporate America to advertise in a new women's magazine that was progressive, innovative, even radical.

Black rejoined *New York* magazine in 1977 as associate publisher during a period when the magazine was foundering financially. Within two years, she had turned the magazine around and had become the first woman publisher of a weekly consumer magazine. In 1983, she joined Gannett as president of *USA Today* and one year later was promoted to publisher.

"It's very important to define success for yourself," Black says. "If you really want to reach for the brass ring, just remember that there are sacrifices that go along." Black lives in Washington, D.C. with her husband, Tom Harvey, an attorney, and their young son, Duffy. She resigned her position with *USA Today* to assume her prestigious and challenging new position with the American Newspaper Publishers Association shortly after this interview was conducted.

Is it much different being the publisher of a newspaper as opposed to being the publisher of a magazine?

The major difference is that you are dealing with a daily news product. Your sensitivity and sensibility about what is going on in the world is much sharper. If some news is breaking, you are thinking, "That will be in the paper tomorrow. How are we going to treat it?" So on one level, that is a major difference. On another level, I think, the difference between being a magazine publisher and the publisher of *USA Today* was that *USA Today* was a start-up. It was an enormous undertaking. I really can't compare it to an ongoing newspaper that has been in business for a long time. Plus, it's a unique paper, since it is the country's first national general-interest newspaper.

How would you describe your leadership style?

I think I am a strong, decisive, involved leader who has the ability to focus on both the long and short term. I am definitely hands-on, I think that the people who report to me appreciate my involvement. But I do not micromanage. I have very strong and capable division managers who know what they are doing.

You have a remarkable track record of turning publications around. What do you think accounts for this?

I have often said that my interest in start-ups must be from a deviant gene! (Laughter) A real sense of challenge and excitement comes with working on something that is new, that is big, and that I find interesting. It certainly happened when I was the first advertising manager of *Ms.* magazine. It was a thrilling experience to be a voice for the women's movement. It also was very difficult to convince companies to advertise in the magazine because the women's movement was so misunderstood in the early seventies and so misrepresented by the media. It was an enormous challenge and something that I found personally fulfilling.

When Rupert Murdoch purchased *New York* magazine, we had to rebuild the editorial credibility. We also had to rebuild a lot of the infrastructure because a lot of people had left the magazine. I find that situation very challenging and in keeping with what I like to do. I have a good sense of what needs to be done. I can lay out a game plan and figure out how to get from point A to point B. With *USA Today,* it was much the same experience, although on a much larger scale.

Do you think that a woman has to "act like a man" to succeed in the corporate world today?

I have a lot of trouble with that concept. I think that a woman has to be incredibly capable – to some extent even more capable than a man – because our society has not yet reached a point where women are judged equally. I think a woman still has to be a notch or two better than a man occupying the same job, which means she has to work harder and be better prepared. Gloria Steinem once said that she would know that the women's movement had been successful when women could be mediocre and get promoted just like men have been doing for years!

I don't think women should try to be men. I think that women should be who they are. Some women are tough and aggressive; other women don't have that in their makeup, just as some men don't. I think we tend to imagine that all men are the same; they are not. I know guys who swear at meetings and guys who don't, I've seen men cry, and I've seen women cry. I think we need to get beyond labels in trying to define the attributes for success. If a person wants to be in the top echelon of a company, whether it is a man or a woman, he or she has to sacrifice a lot along the way. A CEO running a huge Fortune 500 company by and large puts that job first and foremost in his or her life. As women get into that ring, we may be able to humanize things more. Studies show that the few women who are in the upper echelon are single or divorced and don't have children. I think as the next wave of women moves up, more of these women are going to be married and have children. I think that they will attempt to make more reasonable the life and the life-style of a CEO. But the truth is, it is an all-encompassing job.

In becoming publisher of *USA Today*, did you feel that you had to give up anything that a man would not have had to?

No, not at all. In the Gannett Company, people are judged on results. It is not a sexist company. I put in an enormous amount of work but no more than would have been expected of a man.

What do you think accounts for your success?

I believe that my success comes from being very interested in the work I do, feeling challenged by it, wanting to succeed, and being determined to accomplish that. Also, a very strong self-confidence, a good sense of humor, and good judgement.

What does power mean to you in your career?

It means a sense of responsibility and being able to make decisions, to have control and be decisive. It does not mean being able to make a phone call and have people be terrified at the other end of the phone or some of those other ridiculous things that have been attributed to power over the years.

What are you most proud of having accomplished?

Combining a successful career with a family.

How have you managed to do that?

Well, my flip answer to that is that some days are better than others. But that really is true. There are some days when I feel conflicted, but I have not yet had to miss anything important in my son's life. He is three-and-a-half years old. I am sure that at some point, I will not be able to attend a school play. But I look at my calendar and try to work it out as best I can. Also, very importantly, I have a wonderfully supportive husband who met me when I was an accomplished professional. So none of this is a change in his life. We also have a great nanny, a young woman who has been with us for three years.

Have you ever felt that you were treated differently or were discriminated against in your profession because of your gender?

I have been, certainly, but not in a long time.

Did you have any role models?

I had many role models, but the one who made the greatest impression was Patricia Carbine, the publisher and editor in chief of *Ms.* She gave me the confidence to make mistakes and encouraged me to dream a very large dream. She showed me that if I were really dedicated and worked hard, I could be a publisher. Pat is a very warm and nurturing person. She, more than anyone, was a mentor. I have had a lot of good male friends who have helped me along the way, but no one who stands out as a mentor as much as Pat.

What advice would you give someone interested in pursuing a career in newspaper or magazine publishing?

Well, first of all, study the publishing world. People, when they think of publishing, think of being a writer, a reporter, an editor, a columnist. But there are a wealth of other opportunities ranging from advertising, marketing, and sales to design, photography, art, and finance. Even if you are not interested in the creative side of the product, it is interesting to be involved with something in the news, information, or communications business.

Especially if you are a woman, you want to be in a company where women have opportunities. I have always believed that the tone is set at the very top. If a CEO wants a company to reflect diversity, he or she will make it happen. Everything else is lip service.

What is the most important lesson you've learned that, had you known it earlier, could have made your life easier?

I don't know about making my life easier, but I do think that a balance between your professional life and your personal life is really important. I have been very fortunate in the jobs I've had. They have been fun, interesting, exciting, and challenging. I have been exposed to a world of different people in a way that I could never have hoped or imagined when I was growing up. Although this is not original, I remember reading a long time ago that as much as you love your job, your job is not going to love you back. I think that is really important to keep in mind.

Chriss Hurst Winston

Profession: Speech Writer

Currently: Deputy Assistant for Communications to the President of the
United States, Director of Speech Writing at the White House*

Date of birth: November 24, 1948

Education: B.A., University of Iowa, 1971 (Journalism)

---

*Ms. Winston has left this position since the interview.

Chriss Hurst Winston, director of speech writing at the White House, has the final word on all presidential speeches, from the State of the Union Address to toasts made by President Bush at state dinners. A consummate communications professional with twenty years of experience, Winston is known for running a tight ship and demanding nothing short of the best from her staff. She is described by a colleague as "probably one of the most diligent and hardworking people I've ever known at the White House, and this is not a nine-to-five job. It's a pitch-until-you-win job."

Winston began her political career in 1973 as news and research director of the Republican State Central Committee in Des Moines, Iowa. Two years later, she moved to Washington, D.C., as special assistant to the Republican National Committee and has worked in Washington ever since, holding such jobs as press secretary to Representative Jim Leach, vice president of a political consulting firm, and deputy director of public affairs at the Bush Presidential Transition Office.

When Winston is not traveling with the President or working late into the night on speeches, she spends time with her husband, David, director of strategic information for the Republican National Committee, and their young son, Ian.

How did you become a speech writer?

Once upon a time, I thought I was going to be a newspaper reporter, and then I got interested in politics. My background is a journalism degree. My second real job was in politics, and I've been there ever since. I started out as a press secretary in a number of different reincarnations starting in Iowa and then ending up in Washington. My background is a combination of press work, which included a lot of writing and communication, and a general campaign background.

Three years ago, I decided I had never done any government work and had no experience in that area, so I became press secretary for the Occupational Safety and Health Administration and later deputy secretary of labor for public affairs and information. All of those jobs involved a lot of writing and political background and editing. I ended up in my present job by being the Bush/Quayle deputy director of communications, which I thought at the time was going to be mainly public affairs and media relations with some speech writing. Well, I ended up being director of speech writing!

What do you do as director of speech writing at the White House?

I work with speech writers on a speech in the same way as a chief editor on a paper would work with a reporter on a story. I take assignments, develop the theme, and assign it to a writer. The first draft comes to me, and I either do the rewrite or send it back to the writer with rewrite instructions. Then the speech is staffed for clearance around the White House, comments come back to me, and I decide which of the comments to take. I sometimes play the compromiser when we have two different entities in the White House and each wants a change to occur in a different way. Sometimes people want to make policy changes, but their suggested language is not rhetorically very good, so I rewrite their changes and call them and work out the language. Then the final draft goes to the President. It's a long and involved process. I generally don't wake up in the morning and come in and sit down and write a speech from scratch. I have done it when we were pressed, but I generally don't have time to do it.

Are the seven White House speech writers generalists, or do they each have an area of expertise?

They are generalists, but each of them has an expertise that I sometimes lean toward. I have one writer who is particularly interested in the environment, and he has written a lot about it. When we have the clean air bill signing, he will be assigned to write that speech. I have one writer who is an assistant U.S. attorney from Manhattan on loan to us from the Justice Department. He writes a lot of the speeches on crime and drugs and anything having a legal overture, such as Supreme Court justice David Souter's swearing-in remarks. But they each write on almost any topic you can imagine. We don't have the luxury of having so many speech writers we can put them in certain boxes and let them write only on one subject. The President does too many speeches to be able to do that.

What aspect of your work do you find most challenging?

It's the wide range of topics: you go from writing about Little League baseball to writing about a particular policy to writing about trees. I usually have to deal with three or four speeches every day. The challenge is trying to be knowledgeable on the subject so that when I am reading the speech, I have some concept of whether it is correct, whether it adheres to administration policy as well as to the President's style. If we wrote about the crime bill last week and two weeks later we write about the crime bill again, I have to make sure nothing has changed, and that is not always easy to do.

I've always been pretty good at keeping many balls in the air. When we have fifteen speeches going on at the same time, it's like cooking a very complicated dinner. You want to make sure that the roast comes out at the right time, the rolls are done on time, and the dessert doesn't melt before you get to it. The President's remarks can't wait. They have to be done right and on time. I've always been good in situations where the pressure is on, the pace is very fast, and you have to react quickly and get everything done.

How do you prepare for a major speech?

It is very much an input-intensive operation when you are dealing with a big speech. They are always harder, because not only is there more media attention focused on them, but there is a lot more attention focused on them in the White House, as well. So you have more people who weigh in, more people who feel strongly about it, and more people who want to leave an imprint.

Of course, it depends on the speech. If it is a foreign policy speech, we will meet with General [Brent] Scowcroft [assistant to the President for national security affairs] and the National Security Council staff and discuss what the speech ought to say. Obviously, the speech writer also does some reading on the subject. The State Department usually weighs in with a draft, a bulletin, or just informational materials. Basically, we get a lot of input, and then the speech writer sits down and writes it. That's usually how it works. If it is a really big speech, we frequently will meet with the President. Sometimes we will do a draft and discuss it with him. Other times we will meet with him before we even put fingers to computer keys.

State of the Union is a little bit different in the sense that it is such a big speech. Not only is there so much media attention on it for starters, but there is also a lot of attention within the administration. All the agencies want something in the State of the Union about their shop, and understandably so. Unfortunately, if you put a blurb in from every single agency, you would have a terrible speech. Looking at State of the Unions over the decades, I don't think they have ever been overly great speeches for exactly that reason. There is so much stuff that has to be crammed in that you run the risk of a speech being nothing but a laundry list. The alternative is a very broad, visionary, general kind of speech. Then you are criticized for not having any specifics. So I'm not sure that you ever win!

What are the most frequent problems you have to deal with in speech writing?

One of the problems is trying to keep on top of what is going on so the speeches are as up-to-date as possible. Also, President Bush is a very active president, and so despite the fact that we have what seems to be a lot of speech writers, we reach points where they are all very busy! Everything is moving at a fast pace. I think almost any writer would like more time, rather than less, to put something together.

How do you deal with pressure?

My son's nanny asked me that same question last night. I walked through the door, and she said, "I don't know how you do this!" And she's only been with me two weeks! I've always had jobs that tended to be high pressured. I'm used to it. It generally doesn't bother me. I do think that I can keep a lot of balls in the air—up to a point. This morning was a prime example. I realized that the dog and the cat both have fleas and I wanted to take them to have them dipped. The guy at the kennel wouldn't keep them because he said they didn't have the right shots to stay overnight. I said, "I can't get back before six o'clock to pick them up. Can you wash them first and I'll wait?" He said, "Nope, I can't do that." I was sitting in my bedroom this morning at seven o'clock wondering what I was going to do with these animals! I have to go to Saudi Arabia with the President in two days, and I've got fleas in my house! This job requires long hours, and things happen that you don't expect. You just have to be flexible enough to deal with them.

Is there any other profession you would like to pursue?

I'd like to write novels. We bought a house in the country about a year ago. When this is all over, I'd love to sit out in the country, look out my window, see the deer in the backyard, muse about life, and write a book or two!

What are you most proud of having achieved?

I think the team of speech writers that we've put together is a very solid group of writers who have molded into a really good team. As a group, we are very supportive of one another, and I am proud we've been able to create a kind of family atmosphere among the speech writers, researchers, and everyone working on the team. We have long hours, and people have to believe in what they are doing to do a good job and to last. All the speech writers are the same ones we started with, and I think, as a group, we've been very unified. I'm proud of that from a management perspective.

I'm also proud of a number of the President's remarks. They were extraordinary moments, and I think the remarks met the moment, and that was very rewarding to me. They are the President's speeches, and we are merely footnotes on the pages of history. But I'm proud to be a footnote.

Has it been difficult combining a career and a family?

It isn't easy at all. You do feel guilty. It wasn't hard when it was just my husband and me. He's in politics, too, so he understands, and his hours are about as bad as mine. David and I have never had a problem on that side of things because we understand what each of us does, but once a baby enters the picture, that really changes your life. That's been the hardest part, because I'd like to spend a lot more time with my little boy than I do. I try to do that on the weekends, and he stays up so I can see him at night. But it isn't easy.

As a woman, have you experienced discrimination in your profession?

Not recently, but I did when I first started in politics. It was pretty pervasive on both sides of the aisle — Republican and Democrat. When I came to Washington and started moving up in my career in politics, there were a lot of women my age. All of us were in the same boat. We were bobbing along. We came to Washington during a time when it was really male dominated. I came as a result of Mary Louise Smith becoming Republican national chairman. She was an ardent feminist. It was a real break for me. It was my opportunity to do my own thing, to shine, and to be given real responsibility. If she hadn't been elected national chairman, who knows where I'd be today! But that's how I got from Iowa to Washington.

There were six of us women in the Republican National Committee, and we all became very good friends. We really just decided to stick it out, and by and large most of us have been pretty successful in terms of what we wanted to do way back then in 1975. It's not like I had some grandiose game plan. I just rolled with the punches and ended up here. The point is I was given increasing responsibility.

Who were your role models?

Mary Louise Smith was my role model back in the early seventies. She was a very strong woman who had been in politics for a long time and was very well respected. She taught me a great deal, and she had a big impact on me early on in my career. There have been people I worked for and people I've admired a great deal, but I don't know if I've thought of them as role models. I think some of the former presidential speech writers, like Bill Safire, are excellent writers. I've always admired Safire's work a great deal.

A turning point in my young life and the reason I went to journalism school was because at age twelve I saw Roger Mudd. He came to my hometown when Richard Nixon was campaigning. My parents were very active in politics, and they took me along with them. I remember not being all that excited about seeing Richard Nixon, but I stood right next to Roger Mudd, who was on CBS all the time. I remember, there and then, deciding I was going to be a journalist like Roger Mudd. It's funny; I've gone through all these years and dealt with the press in so many different aspects, but I've never met Roger Mudd. Someday I will, and I'll tell him the tremendous impact he had on my life!

To some degree my mother was a role model. She had five children and was very active in Republican politics and child abuse programs. I wasn't quite sure how she juggled all those things, but she did. Now that I'm a mother, what I'm most proud of is my little boy. In that context, my mother would definitely be a role model.

Chris Evert

Profession: Sports Commentator/Athlete

Currently: Sports Commentator for NBC

Date of birth: December 21, 1954

Education: St. Thomas Aquinas High School, 1972

Chris Evert epitomizes the true champion. A fierce competitor, Evert held the number one world computer tennis ranking five times and was ranked in the top four women's tennis players for eighteen consecutive years – a feat unsurpassed by any player in the history of the game.

With her disarming blend of grit, grace, and glamour, Evert popularized women's tennis around the world. She captured eighteen Grand Slam singles titles and won more singles matches than any other player since the Open era began in 1968. Evert is most noted for her mental toughness and her two-handed backhand, which has become an integral part of women's tennis. The late Ted Tinling, an aficionado of women's tennis for more than six decades, said of Evert, "She is a great role model for the image she projects."

Evert did not turn professional until her eighteenth birthday because her father, James Evert, a tennis pro who was also her coach, insisted that she finish high school first. Since turning professional in 1972, Evert has earned more than $9 million in prize money and several times that amount in endorsements.

As a tribute to her enduring popularity, on the eve of her last U.S. Open in 1989, Evert was elected for an unprecedented eighth term as president of the Women's Tennis Association. Billie Jean King describes Evert as "calculated . . . she says and does the right thing, regardless of how she really feels."

Although Evert retired from competition in 1989, she is still very much a part of women's tennis. She is a commentator for NBC and spokesperson for more than a dozen companies. Married to former Olympic skier Andy Mill, she divides her time between residences in Boca Raton, Florida, and Aspen, Colorado, and gave birth to their first child in October, 1991.

Were you unusually athletic as a child?

In school, I was always one of the better athletes, but I certainly wasn't like a Martina Navratilova or a Steffi Graf as far as being exceptional. My mental capabilities were exceptional, and that's what got me as far as I went. Later on, the more I started playing tennis and winning junior tournaments, the more I began to enjoy tennis. I also saw that it was pleasing my father, whom I really looked up to. It brought me out of my shell. Tennis was a way of expression for me. Then we started traveling to the national tournaments, and I liked getting away from my hometown. It just snowballed. I realized that with hard work, the world was your oyster. You could do anything you wanted to do. I learned that at a young age.

Do you think you would have done well in any other sport?

Sometimes I wonder why I became such a great tennis player. I don't think that I would have been the best runner or the best basketball player, but anything else like ballet, ice skating, or anything that stresses grace, timing, and balance, I think I would have been good at.

Besides your mental toughness, what do you think gave you that extra edge?

I was very competitive. I had that killer instinct. I hated to lose. I always got upset when I lost, and I had that drive to be the best.

I believe that you can judge a person's character by their conduct on a tennis court. With all your experience with tennis players, do you agree with that?

I think the real "you" comes out in certain intense and pressured situations. I also think your style of play can indicate what kind of a person you are: whether you are very aggressive or more passive. I think you can tell a lot about a person by the way he or she plays tennis and acts on the court.

What do you think accounts for the fact that you persevered in tennis for so many years?

First of all, I never would have done it by myself. My father was the one who pushed me into the game. I remember I was a little upset with him because I was used to going over to my girlfriend's house and having barbecues and going swimming. All of a sudden my father took me away from that way of life. He started taking me over to the public tennis courts and throwing me tennis balls from a shopping cart. I remember feeling resentment. I wanted to go and play with my friends. I was definitely pushed into tennis at a young age.

Did you feel you were pushed into retirement by the media?

It's almost like once you've won all the Grand Slam tournaments, you've been number one, and all of a sudden it's, "Well, how much longer are you going to play?" Then it's, "When are you going to retire?" And then it's, "Why are you still playing?" (Laughter)

I think that I played as long as I could have played at a top level. I would say the last two to three years I really did level off and even started to get distracted. I met my second husband, I enjoyed my homes a lot more, and I didn't really like the traveling and the life-style. My last year, I ended up number four in the world, but if I had continued another year, I might have slipped to five or six. I think I realized that I was never going to be number one again. I was enjoying playing half of the time, but the other half I didn't want to be on the court.

Looking back, was all the practice, and the travel, and pressure worthwhile?

Oh, absolutely! It was a great life. It was wonderful. There is such a high when you win a tournament. I also enjoyed the challenge of working out, the competition, and the pressure. Monetary-wise, it was wonderful. It set me up for life. Also, any kind of exercise is great in the sense that it is a physical, emotional, and mental outlet. Every time I stepped away from the court, I felt like I had just been through therapy!

What is your sweetest memory of the game?

I really feel that my last two Grand Slam wins at the French Open in '85 and '86 meant the most to me because I was in my early thirties. The older you get, the sweeter victory gets, because you understand what it takes and time is no longer on your side.

I really enjoyed team events such as the Federation Cup. I played for the United States on the same team as Martina Navratilova and Billie Jean King. There were so few times that we got to play together as a team instead of playing against one another. Playing for my country also was very meaningful to me.

Have you ever thought about coaching?

No, because to be a proper coach, you have to travel and go to the tournaments. As a player it was wonderful, but I think it would be a real letdown for me to go and coach.

How did you deal with pressure and stress between matches in a tournament?

I handled pressure well. I was pretty calm. I could turn it on and off pretty easily. After my match, I would get a lot of massages, and I'd usually be with my family and just have quiet time. I'd read, watch television, or go to the movies. I'd try to get away from the thought of playing another match tomorrow. When I didn't play, I could get away from it completely. If I had a week off, I'd go to the beach and just not think about it. Then I'd get excited when I had to resume my tennis.

How has being a professional tennis player influenced your tennis commentary?

I've played most of the women players, so when I'm talking about Martina Navratilova or Steffi Graf or Pam Shriver, I have firsthand knowledge of them. I know them professionally as well as personally, having been in the locker room with them after a match when the cameras aren't rolling. On the other side of the coin, it gets tough sometimes because I don't want to cross the line where their privacy is concerned.

I am constantly made aware of their sensitivity to my criticism, so I have to balance those factors in my commentary. It always gets back to me when they feel I've been a little bit critical of them. I'm learning more and more that if I want to do a good job as a broadcaster, I have to be honest because that's my responsibility as a journalist. The first year after I retired, I was more concerned with the players' feelings, but now I call it as I see it.

As a tennis player, did you ever feel discriminated against because you are a woman?

No, I was always made to feel very special. I really feel that as long as I've been in the game – thanks to Billie Jean King, who paved the way for all of us – women's tennis has been placed on a pedestal. I never felt discriminated against. If anything, I felt we were the premier women's sport. I always felt the spectators enjoyed and appreciated our brand of tennis because they could relate to it more than the wham-bam power game of the men.

Did the disparity in prize money bother you?

Well, it's not that much. In Grand Slam tournaments – the U.S. Open, the Australian Open – it's equal prize money, and it's only a little bit different in Europe. The women get about 90 percent of what the men get. The disparity never bothered me because I was always thrilled with the fact that women were earning a lot of money, period. As much as the top women are just as entertaining as the top men to watch, I could always see the other side: men play three out of five sets, they are on the court a lot longer, they have more depth, and they have better television ratings.

Who was your role model in tennis?

I never really thought of emulating anyone as far as my game was concerned. My father pretty much taught me the basics. He taught me my style of play. But as far as leadership, qualities of greatness, I always looked up to Billie Jean. She has a lot of wisdom and intelligence about the game. She is very smart about tennis.

You have focused such energy and drive on tennis. Do you envision doing the same thing in another field of endeavor?

If I could find something that I wanted to sink my teeth into, I would. It's hard for me now because I haven't been retired two years yet. The first year after I retired, I dabbled in broadcasting and in a couple of things, but I just wanted to take a break from all the intensity. Hopefully, motherhood will replace much of the energy and fulfillment I received from tennis. Maybe it's time to relax and think about family and marriage. My first marriage took a backseat to my tennis. Now my marriage is more important.

What lessons have you learned that have made a difference in your life?

That it all comes down to appreciating the simple things in life. I guess I've learned a lot about fame and its dangers. (Laughter) It's not all it's cracked up to be. You can be number one in the world, but you have to have your feet planted firmly on the ground. You have to be well grounded because it can all be taken away. You have to have something else to back it up. That is where family comes in – your home and just having roots – because, especially at a young age, it is so easy to get carried away with all the money and fame and everything that goes along with being a premier athlete.

Education
and
Social Sciences

Laura Nader

Profession: Anthropologist

Currently: Professor of Anthropology, University of California–Berkeley

Date of birth: September 30, 1930

Education: B.A., Wells College, 1952 (Latin American Studies)
El Colgio de Mexico (Smith College), 1950-51
Linguistic Institute, University of Michigan, 1955
Ph.D., Radcliffe College, 1961 (Anthropology)

$\mathcal{J}$n the style of her family, Laura Nader is a "public citizen" who holds intense social convictions. As professor of anthropology at the University of California-Berkeley, Laura Nader has sought to deal with problems in law, energy, and public health. In recent years, she has focused on the American legal system, following in-depth studies of the complaint and redress systems of other societies, particularly those of the Zapotec Indians of Mexico.

Nader's civic consciousness was instilled by her parents, who, in animated family discussions, expounded on the duties of citizenship in a democracy. As an associate of her younger brother, Ralph, once said, "When the Naders sat around the dinner table growing up, it was like the Kennedys. Except that the subject was not power but justice."

Nader has been a professor of anthropology at Berkeley since 1960. In addition, she has taught at Yale and Stanford law schools and Wellesley College. She has done fieldwork in Mexico, Lebanon, and Morocco, as well as in New England and on the culture of professionals. Nader has been the recipient of numerous research grants from the National Science Foundation, the Carnegie Corporation of New York, the American Philosophical Association, the Milton Fund at Harvard, and the Mexican government. She was elected to the American Academy of Arts and Sciences.

Nader has written several books, including *Law in Culture and Society; No Access to Law: Alternatives to the American Judicial System;* and, most recently, *Harmony Ideology.* She also has written numerous articles and reviews. She is married to Norman Milleron. They have three children.

How did you decide to become an anthropologist?

Throughout my educational career, I carried points of view that usually clashed enough with the general ideas around me as to make me feel different. While feeling different was not always comfortable, the contradictions that I experienced always helped to sharpen questions of value that underlie the directions I have explored in anthropology.

I majored in Romance languages at Wells College. As a senior, I wrote an honors thesis, "The Concept of Leadership in Mexican Revolutionary Novels." While such an endeavor might sound mundane enough today, in the early 1950s, I was informed by the chairwoman of the department that what I had written did not deal literally with literature nor was it literature in any way; it was sociology, and as such she could not award me a degree in Romance languages – even though the thesis was also written in Spanish. In a rather dazed state, I was sent to the sociology department, where I was informed that while my thesis dealt with interesting sociological questions, they could not award me my B.A. in sociology because I had never taken a course in sociology.

The president of the college had to settle the matter by awarding me a degree in Latin American studies. In the process, the president apologized for the rigidity of the departments. Nevertheless, I left his office bewildered.

As a high school student, I had no idea what I wanted to be. I had no idea what I wanted to be even through college, nor did I know what I wanted to do, though I knew I wanted to do and be something. I wrote my story about my honors thesis in a letter to my older brother, then an anthropology student at the University of Toronto. In answer, he sent me a copy of Clyde Kluckhohn's book *Mirror for Man*. As I read this prize-winning book, I remember saying to myself, "I am an anthropologist."

What do you find challenging about anthropology?

Anthropology offers a wide-angle view of what's going on in the world. Its perspective is not narrow and technical. It allows you to follow and explore a question in its many aspects. If I were in economics, I would have to look very narrowly at certain economic questions that had already been cited and were within the range of economics. The same applies to law. But in anthropology, you can follow your nose. You may start in religion and end in law or vice versa, as I did. I started in family law, and I ended by looking at Christian missionaries and their construction of indigenous law. Anthropology offers a relative absence of hampering paradigms – important when trying to understand something as complex as human society. You can't possibly just look from one angle. That's the first reason I find anthropology challenging.

Secondly, the range of human variation in the world is so great. How many disciplines allow you the comparative perspective that anthropology does? Very few. Perhaps only ecology is comparable in its scope. I think in the twenty-first century, we need desperately to enlarge our scope from the narrow and technical. That doesn't mean we should eliminate the technical or the narrow kind of knowledge, but it must be put in a larger perspective to understand what we're looking at. There are so many people today doing research on subjects who know nothing about the wider significance of their own work. I think that's criminal and can be hampering to creativity. It has been hampering in developing the kind of world we need to have to survive. Anthropologists look at the consequences of things; they follow things out. We need consequence thinkers to trace out the results of planned action and behavior. I think anthropology provides us the best potential for understanding something about humanity through time and space.

Can you describe a typical workday in the field?

I lived with a family. To get a feeling for the rhythm of their life, I got up with them at the beginning of the day and followed them till the end of the day. When they went to bed, I went to my typewriter. So I would go through the day's cycle with them and focus on different parts. If I were focusing on men in the agriculture cycle, I would go to the fields with them. If I were interested in women's work, I would be at the well. If I wished to understand the court system, I'd be at court. Essentially, I spent the day participating and interviewing – direct and indirect. It's almost like what a child does to learn about the culture he or she is born into. Some anthropologists use a more narrow kind of technique for fieldwork. They depend primarily on listening and less on what we call participant observation. The styles differ, but across the board, anthropologists are pretty much the same because they stay a long time.

In general, do you do the bulk of your research in the field or in the library?

When I was developing my theory of harmony ideology, I was dependent on my own skills among the Zapotec as well as work done in the United States. But to prove the notion that the harmony ideology model of law was linked to Christian missionizing, I had to look worldwide, and in that case, certainly, I had to depend on the library and the work of others. So I believe in a combination of approaches, and the particular combination will depend on the question you have at hand.

Not too long ago, I heard an American diplomat suggest to an African official that a team of anthropologists visit his country. The African official's response was "Do you think you are dealing with primitive people?" Do you think anthropology needs to be redefined to avoid such a perception?

I think the notion that anthropology is the study of primitive people needs to be changed. It never was so originally. People who took anthropology at Harvard in the thirties and forties didn't think of it as the study of primitive people. They studied European and American societies as well. I think it's the British and colonizers more generally who brought the notion that anthropology is the study of primitive peoples. So the Africans think of it that way, and once they realize that anthropologists are studying European cultures as well, then I suppose the notion will emerge that anthropology is the study of human societies, wherever. In the meantime, however, it is a stigmatized word in Africa, and some people, when they do anthropology in Africa, use the word *sociology*. I would rather reintroduce the notion of anthropology as the study of human societies – all human societies on this planet – rather than try to hide behind a notion like sociology in order not to be stigmatized.

You once said that your brother, Ralph Nader, "is so committed to his work and so enjoys what he is doing that he can work nonstop." Do you feel the same way about your work?

I have the same attitude when I'm doing anthropology. It's not work. It's pursuing my curiosity about the world, and I'm lucky I'm paid to do it. I'd do it even if I weren't paid!

How have you been able to juggle a demanding career and a family?

I guess I was able to do it because I had a good income and a supportive family. My parents, my siblings, my kids, and my spouse were all supportive in different ways. Without a supportive family, I don't know that I could have done it because I don't think our society is supportive of families. I had three children at this university [Berkeley] with no maternity leave. This was at the same time when women professors in Morocco, a Moslem country, were getting maternity leave.

In the United States, if you were going to have a family and a career, you had to do it in spite of everything. You had to do it "like a man," as someone said to me. How do I juggle? In the first place, my family became my dessert. When I came home, that was the fun time. I had what my mother calls "Operation Cooperation," where ideally everyone in the family pitched in. I think, however, if you were to look at women who have had careers in this country, it probably has affected their health because they are juggling two jobs with inadequate support. The double shift really affects all women, not just career and professional women. But if you add to that the need that some of us have to contribute to public debate then that's a triple shift.

Have you ever felt that you were treated differently or were discriminated against in your profession because you are a woman?

Oh, there is no doubt. You have to be naive not to see discrimination. I was treated the same in some ways: I didn't have maternity leave, but neither did the guys. I was treated differently in terms of promotion and pay. I never dwelt on it, though, until it became obscene. I have been very active in opening doors for women all through my career. I chaired the National Institute of Mental Health at a time when women were trying to get rid of the discrimination against granting women equal opportunity to do research on all kinds of questions, including the study of women.

Would you call it discrimination if everywhere I went, I was the only woman on the committee? That's kind of a lonely position to be in. I have brothers, and I get along well with men, but I would say there are two kinds of discrimination that I have lived through. I have lived through an older-generation chauvinism, which is paternalistic, and same-age chauvinism, which is competitive and often hostile. If I had to choose one chauvinism over the other, I prefer the older, paternalistic one because at least the men are polite and sociable.

What is the single most important lesson you've learned that, had you known earlier, would have made your life easier?

The first thing is to guard good health. That means you have to draw the line at how much you give. Women tend to be altruistic, often to their own detriment. Sometimes the best kind of altruism is self-care, unless you have the physical stamina for double and triple shifts.

What advice would you give someone interested in pursuing a career in anthropology?

Not to call it a career! It's a passion; it's not a career. You have to be interested in how human beings have come to be what they are. You have to be interested in the subject matter first. You have to have an overriding passion for understanding this long history of human evolution and existence.

What person or persons have made the greatest difference in your life?

My parents have made the greatest difference. My mother had been a teacher and throughout our time as youngsters regaled us with exciting stories of her teaching career in a large Lebanese village. Fieldwork as anthropology was simply the modern version of her career. My parents' recent book, *It Happened in the Kitchen,* describes how they raised us to be of healthy mind and body, independent, intensely democratic and egalitarian, nonideological, and very altruistic in terms of social consciousness. They taught us to know who we were so we weren't searching for ourselves all our lives.

In anthropology, I would say the most important influence on my life was Clyde Kluckhohn, an anthropologist I studied with at Harvard. In American history, I would say the person who has had an influence on me is Thomas Jefferson. On the future, the most important influence are my children. Of course, the best lessons are derived from the integrative study of human beings.

Linda Wilson

Profession: Educator

Currently: President, Radcliffe College

Date of birth: November 10, 1936

Education: B.A., Sophie-Newcomb College, Tulane University, 1957
(Chemistry)
Ph.D., University of Wisconsin-Madison, 1962 (Chemistry)

$\mathcal{L}$inda Smith Wilson is described by Harold Shapiro, president of Princeton University, as "an inspiration to those needing to be inspired; and a calming, nurturing vision to those needing reassurance." An academic trailblazer, Radcliffe's seventh president says, "I felt a keen sense of responsibility to those who would come after me. I didn't want any inadequacy of mine to diminish opportunities for others."

As the first woman to serve as a vice president at the University of Michigan, Wilson is credited with enhancing the reputation of that university as one of the foremost research institutions in the nation. During her tenure, she increased research support from $159.3 million in 1985 to $260 million in 1989 and created innovative programs to bolster the standing of women and minorities.

Married at the age of twenty, she attended graduate school with her husband at the University of Wisconsin, where she was awarded a fellowship and was one of two women in the chemistry department. Wilson completed her doctoral studies in four years and gave birth to a daughter, Helen, while in graduate school. When her husband completed his graduate work, the family moved to the University of Maryland. Although Wilson held a Ph.D., the chairman of the chemistry department at the University of Maryland did not believe women were qualified to teach chemistry. When a faculty member died, Wilson took over his classes and proved the chairman wrong.

After her divorce in 1967, her career took on new meaning as she became a single parent. That same year she applied for a teaching position at one college and was told: "Your experience and credentials qualify you for an associate professorship, but we don't want to hire women."

Wilson is an elected member of the National Academy of Sciences and an elected fellow of the American Association for the Advancement of Science. In addition to her responsibilities as president of Radcliffe, she is a senior lecturer in the areas of administration, planning, and social policy at the Harvard Graduate School of Education.

In 1970, she married Paul Wilson, a minister, who is currently pursuing a second career in social work. Avid sailors, the Wilsons built a thirty-six-foot sailboat that they enjoy sailing when time permits.

What drew you to your profession as an educator?

Perhaps the single greatest factor in my choosing to be an educator was the presence of strong role models – some marvelous women teachers in elementary and secondary school and in college. My choice of chemistry was triggered by an enthusiastic and effective man, a teacher in high school;

nurtured by exceptional women chemistry faculty in college; and strengthened by an unusually good mentor/adviser in graduate school. I enjoyed learning, and these mentors responded with encouragement and, at the upper levels, genuine friendship.

My move into academic research administration was incremental rather than sudden. I found I enjoyed the interactions with people, the nature of the feedback cycle, the puzzle solving, the future orientation, and the opportunity to facilitate important work. Role models from my father to colleagues and superiors were important here as well. I have learned much from my coworkers and leaders.

As president of Radcliffe College, what is your long-term objective?

To develop a vision for the institution – a vision that embodies three mutually reinforcing objectives: to educate and inspire women for full participation in all aspects of society; to build a major center for research by and about women; and to engage women in deepening the public discourse on important societal issues.

What aspect of your work do you find most demanding?

Making decisions with less than full information, taking clear and wise actions while still learning about the nature and context of problems, and leading within a context of ambiguity and rapid change.

How do you deal with pressure?

I cope with pressure by injecting humor, by acknowledging explicitly that the pressures are sometimes unreasonable, and by anticipating when the load will be especially heavy. I make lists of what must be done to externalize the pressure. I focus some attention on specific subtasks to recognize small accomplishments within larger projects. I continually keep the larger goals in mind.

What do you think accounts for your success?

A combination of factors. First, wise, encouraging, and loving parents who counseled me to work hard and to take responsibility for my education and life choices were central. Second, good teachers and especially a strong liberal arts education at a women's college, where no limits were set on my aspirations, were very important. Graduate study at a distinguished university with a good mentor positioned me to begin a career as a chemist at a time when women were not very welcome in that field. Commitment, diligence, and persistence, plus recognizing and responding to opportunities along the way, also were important. Lots of hard work and long hours were involved, but I have found much joy in that effort. Self-reflection and honest self-appraisal have kept me focused on continuing to learn. In fact, I should admit that I am addicted to learning.

What is the purpose of a formal education at the undergraduate level?

In regard to a liberal arts education, I think it's a time of great cognitive, emotional, and social development. It is a time when exposure to a wide range of styles of learning and concepts, along with examples of great literature in many different fields, will essentially fill a reservoir and provide a way of approaching learning. I believe a liberal arts education, if it is designed well, engages students in critical thinking and in learning how to learn. That is probably the most important element of such an education, other than encouraging people to love learning.

Is society making progress in eliminating discrimination against women?

Our society has not yet fully accommodated women, taken advantage of their potential, recognized their talents, or valued their contributions. But that is changing. It's changing more rapidly than it did in many years past but still quite slowly. The slowness is difficult for young people and those making their way in the early parts of their careers.

Do you think we place enough emphasis on the value of diversity in our educational system?

Probably not. I think we are having a hard time developing a community with our great heterogeneity. It is an important issue in the world, especially as the population is changing in its diversity. I think the educational system is a good place for overcoming some of those problems and creating a community out of that difference.

Mary Catherine Bateson

Profession: Professor/Writer/Ethnographer

Currently: Clarence Robinson Professor of Anthropology and English, George Mason University

Date of birth: December 8, 1939

Education: B.A., Radcliffe College, 1960 (Semitic Languages)
Ph.D., Harvard University, 1963 (Linguistics and Middle Eastern Studies)

$\mathcal{M}$ary Catherine Bateson, a Renaissance woman in our increasingly specialized world, holds a chair that melds cultural anthropology and English at George Mason University in Fairfax, Virginia. A former dean of the faculty at Amherst College, she is the daughter of Margaret Mead and Gregory Bateson, two individuals whose names are synonymous with the discipline of anthropology. About her work she has written, "The work I do . . . expresses a belief that multiple small spheres of personal experience both echo and enable events shared more widely, expressions of moment in a world in which we now recognize that no microcosm is completely separate, no tide pool, no forest, no family, no nation."

Margaret Mead observed upon the completion of her daughter's doctoral studies, "A Ph.D. is a certification of the capacity for study and original inquiry, not a narrow, professional label." Bateson's scholarly pursuits are anything but narrow. She has taught Arabic and sociolinguistics at Harvard University and anthropology and linguistics at Ateneo de Manila University in the Philippines. She has been a senior research fellow in psychology and philosophy at Brandeis University, and a professor of anthropology at Northeastern University, Damavand College in Iran, University of Northern Iran, and Amherst College.

In her most recent book, *Composing a Life,* Bateson explores "the relationship between work and personal life, not as competing preoccupations but as expressions of the same personal styles and commitments." She believes that the efforts involved in resolving these conflicts form a creative process and "could provide important resources in addressing problems we face in society."

Bateson is also the author of *With a Daughter's Eye: a Memoir of Margaret Mead and Gregory Bateson.* Of her parents she wrote, "They thought of worlds and drew me into them. There were worlds to be built and worlds to be imagined, worlds to be held and cherished in two hands and worlds of abstract argument, in spherical tautology." A valued collaborator in her parents' work, she took a leave of absence from teaching to complete *Angels Fear: Towards an Epistemology of the Sacred,* a book her father was unable to finish before his death. She has said, "I feel strongly that the work I did in relation to my parents and their intellectual legacies has full theoretical continuity with the other kinds of things I have done." She is the coauthor of *Thinking AIDS,* which uses the epidemic to explore the interface of culture and biology.

Bateson divides her time between Virginia, New Hampshire, and Massachusetts. She is married to J. Barkev Kassarjian. They have one daughter.

What drew you to teaching and to the world of ideas?

Both my parents taught, although neither was a full-time, tenured professor. They both taught in combination with other things, which is what I like to do also. I remember when my daughter was little, she was quite clear in her mind that everybody had a school. She had a school, her daddy had a school, her mommy had a school, and her granddad had a school. (Laughter) Her grandma... well, her grandma had a museum, because she remembered visiting my mother at the American Museum of Natural History rather than at Columbia University. From her point of view, "normal" people had schools.

You had such a cosmopolitan upbringing. How did that upbringing influence your outlook and your decision to study linguistics?

First of all, I grew up as an observer. If something annoys me, I try to understand it. That's very important. I also grew up knowing there was more than one way of doing things, that the way I've always done things was not necessarily set up by God at the time of the creation. That applies to linguistics as well as anthropology. A lot of people, when they learn another language, approach that language with the idea that their language is "natural." But the words and grammatical forms we use are as arbitrary as any other.

What would you say is the central theme of your work today?

I guess it's the relationship between our personal lives and our professional work. My concern has been to look at persons in context so that action can be seen as participation and knowledge as identification. Working in various genres, I have been trying to find ways to talk about ethical questions based on empathy and experience. Increasingly, I am focusing on how people act through time and on the contrast between responsiveness and purposiveness, as hopes, fears, and visions inform decisions taken in the present. I have been especially interested for a number of years in the way the patterns visible in the fine grain of human experience – the day-to-day details of home and childhood – affect all other spheres of activity and imagination.

You've written such timely and fascinating books. In what section of a bookstore would you expect to find them?

There has always been a question of where my work belongs in a bookstore. I have tried to work toward a blend of social science and art, an aspiration reminiscent, perhaps, of the paintings of Audubon, whose portraiture of birds was also natural history. Even in my specifically anthropological work, I have been interested in the ways in which self-observation informs the observing eye. It was Carl Rogers, I believe, who once said, "The most personal is the most universal." But other people like to divide things up and keep them separate.

In your dual role as a writer and a teacher, what aspects of your work do you find most exciting and challenging?

For me, the process of writing is the process of discovery. It's not a matter of getting on paper something I have already thought through and know. The thinking process is part of the writing process, so I learn from myself as I write. On the other hand, sometimes I get bored with my ideas if I sit all alone working on them, writing them down. It's very important to me to have the chance to teach, to see other people learning something new. It gives me confidence that what I have to say has value, and all my pleasure in thinking new thoughts comes to life again.

What do you think accounts for your success as a teacher and a writer?

I think it's the fact that I'm an inveterate learner. I don't go into my classes thinking I know everything; rather, I'm involving other people in my learning process.

What is your day like when you are teaching?

Academics who teach at the college level spend only a portion of their time in the classroom. The rest of their time is spent developing material to use in their teaching, keeping up with their field, meeting with students, and correcting papers. They spend time meeting with colleagues to discuss developments in the university where they teach, being on committees, and developing curricula or policies. They're also expected to contribute to their fields outside the university.

I teach long evening classes, three hours at a time, because I get a more interesting mix of students that way. The students who can come in three days a week at ten in the morning are "traditional," full-time students who just graduated from high school. I like to have a mixture of people in my classroom, including those with jobs. I like to do my teaching in a seminar format. I think it makes the class a lot more interesting.

When I have a seminar in the late afternoon, I try to keep the entire day clear to review the material that's going to be discussed in class, so it will be as fresh as possible. I hide out – quite often I work at home – until early afternoon. Then I go to campus and meet with students before class begins, to talk about their independent research projects, their papers, sometimes about their plans, what's happening in their lives, and whatever they want to talk about. Generally, about once a week, I go to some other campus to give a talk or attend a conference.

What advice would you give someone interested in pursuing a career in academia?

The key is to be very interested in your field. My advice is to think less about career strategies and more about finding something you care passionately about doing. You become a teacher when you discover that sharing the thing you have a passion for is in itself deeply rewarding.

We need more people to become researchers and teachers in the sense that academics are teachers who do original research and combine it with teaching. It's a very exciting kind of life that allows you to find a balance between pursuing your own interests and curiosity and having the satisfaction of passing that knowledge on. It's hard to think of a more satisfying balance.

What do you think is the key component of creativity?

An openness to noticing things – curiosity.

What is the driving force in your life?

There are two answers to that. One is that I like what I'm doing and I go on doing it. But it is also true that as time goes on, I get more involved with social issues, particularly the need to give people a better understanding of the importance of cultural diversity, partly because I see some kinds of prejudice coming back – things that we thought we had made a lot of progress on. I don't think we can count on that progress holding. I'm very concerned that the position of women should continue to improve and not deteriorate, that racism should not have a resurgence in this country, and that a value for human differences should become more and more deeply embedded in the educational system.

Do you look forward to change?

Yes. A lot of the changes I've dealt with in my life have been forced on me. They weren't my choice, but I've become so used to adapting to change that my tolerance for doing the same things again and again is very low. So I keep pushing myself into new areas. I usually don't teach the same course for more than a couple of years. I modify it a great deal as I go because I know I do things better if they're fresh.

Have you ever felt that you were treated differently or were discriminated against in your profession because of your gender?

I haven't felt that as an anthropologist, but I have felt discriminated against when I've been an administrator. I was a dean for a while in an institution that was not a comfortable place for any woman, and I felt being a woman made doing my job a great deal more difficult.

What lessons have you learned that might have made a difference in your professional life?

Women often don't get mentoring; they don't get guidance – the same kind of guidance from senior people in their field that young men get. They sometimes get caught believing the official myths about how things work. In every system, there is an official way that things work and then there is a good deal of informal negotiating going on: people doing favors for each other, old-boy-network things that are *sous-entendu* in the way people support each other. I think women have to watch for that. Women sometimes have the problem of underestimating the strength of that system. We rely too heavily on other people's honesty and principles, when that's only part of how they make their decisions. I think I would have benefitted from a healthy dose of cynicism early in my life. I think a certain amount of cynicism is an important defense. People complain that sometimes women who go into the business world or into the competitive environment of academia are naive about how things really work and how people really treat each other.

What about the saying "Ignorance is bliss?"

I think that the way people behave is less upsetting if you're prepared for it. One prefers to be let down slowly. You don't have to compromise your principles, but you're less vulnerable if you know how things really work.

How do you juggle a career and family?

I try to avoid the metaphor of juggling. I've developed a different metaphor, "composing" – to put together all the different things that I do in interlocking ways and come out with a harmony that I find satisfying.

I believe we have suffered from a series of mistaken phrasings. First women were told they had to choose between home and career, then they were told they should try to have it all – home plus career. But the possibility of doing more than one thing depends on the congruence between different kinds of activities and the metaphors with which a given individual approaches each. We are all doing much the same thing in more than one context, and that makes the transfer of learning possible.

What person or persons have had the greatest impact on your life?

My parents and my husband.

What do you miss most about your parents?

Their conversational style. Although they were very different, their idea of what to do when they were with other people was the same, and that was to talk about ideas *all* the time.

What are you most proud of having achieved?

I think that what one achieves is a matter of one's *whole* life, not a particular milestone. I think if you're preoccupied with achievement in the sense of milestones, it's likely to make your life lopsided. It may work against you in putting your whole picture together.

Marva N. Collins

Profession: Teacher

Currently: Founder, Westside Preparatory School

Date of birth: August 31, 1936

Education: B.A., Clark College, 1957 (Secretarial Science)

$\mathcal{M}$ arva Collins and Westside Preparatory School are a beacon of hope and a source of pride for the city of Chicago. In an atmosphere of discipline and love, Collins transforms children who have been labeled "unteachable" into high academic achievers.

While teaching second grade in the Chicago inner-city school system in 1961, Collins became dissatisfied with the quality of education available, not only to her students, but to her own children. She withdrew $5,000 from her retirement fund and, in 1975, founded Westside Preparatory School. The school began with four students including her daughter. Today, Westside Preparatory encompasses two buildings with an enrollment of 125 students (kindergarten through grade eight), a teaching staff of six, and a burgeoning waiting list of about 500. As an affirmation of Collins' outstanding teaching abilities, the entire Oklahoma school system has adopted her teaching methods. There is also a Marva Collins School in Cincinnati.

Collins, often described by the media as a "superteacher" and a "miracle worker," has turned down offers to become U.S. secretary of education (during the Reagan administration), county superintendent of the Los Angeles school district, and member of the Chicago school board. Her honors include thirty-eight honorary degrees, numerous awards including several educator-of-the-year awards, and the prestigious Jefferson Award for helping the disadvantaged. At the invitation of President Bush, Collins serves on the Points of Light Foundation and meets monthly with the President.

A sought-after lecturer whose scheduling calendar is booked three years in advance, Collins was portrayed in a television film "The Marva Collins Story." In addition to her book *Marva Collins' Way,* she has written numerous articles on education and has conducted teaching seminars throughout the United States and Europe.

Collins' husband, Clarence, a draftsman at the Sunbeam Corporation, retired in 1978 to assist his wife in running her school. Their three adult children have also elected to teach and work at Westside Preparatory. For recreation, Collins enjoys reading, gardening, and listening to music.

What drew you to a career in teaching?

I've always been somewhat of a teacher. When I was as young as nine or ten, growing up in a small town in Alabama where most of the population had been denied the right to a good education, I would go from one home to another on certain days after school. I would write letters for people who didn't know how to read or write. Fridays and Saturdays, I would help with Sunday school lessons.

How do you feel each September when the new school year begins?

I always feel it's a new adventure. I have the same passion now that I ever had for teaching. I always say that each year is going to be better. In spite of all the accolades the school has received and the thousands of people from all over the world who come to visit us, I always feel there are many areas that still need improvement. So each year begins with the determination that this year is going to be our best.

What is it about teaching that excites and challenges you?

The mere fact that it makes you feel Pygmalion-like. You have the ability to mold and sculpt the child into whoever you want him or her to become. It's a fascinating endeavor! Being a part of somebody's life, a part of the process that makes a child all that he or she can be. I always tell the children in my school, "I know I'm going to live forever through you."

How would you describe your teaching style?

The enthusiasm that people had for learning during the Renaissance is the kind of enthusiasm I try to kindle in the classroom – the kind of enthusiasm that makes children's eyes hold wonder like a cup. We do a lot of memory work, read great poetry, old classics, and the works of great philosophers. That's very nontraditional compared to what is taught in today's school curriculum. We have six- and seven-year-olds who are students at Northwestern University's gifted program. I think it's fascinating to be here in the inner city and hear all the doomsday cries about things that are wrong with our society. Yet, we are one of the first places to which foreign dignitaries and visitors to Chicago are sent by the Visitor's Bureau. There was an article last Sunday in the *Chicago Tribune* where I was mentioned as one of the people who make Chicago a world-class city! I think it says a lot when black children are considered world class, especially in view of all the negative things highlighted in newspapers and the media regarding minorities and inner-city schools.

What is your educational philosophy?

My motto to my students is "I will not let you fail." I think all children can achieve if they are not taught that they can't. I often tell my students if you give a man a fish he will eat for a day, but if you teach him how to fish he will eat for a lifetime – that is my goal as an educator. I am not only interested in teaching the three R's, but how to live, how to have a positive self-image, how to give back to one's community. For example, we had a student who came here who was labeled a learning disabled child. This same student went on to college and majored in cybernetics and has been accepted at Stanford University's graduate school. He wants to come back and establish his own cybernetics business here.

It all boils down to my belief in expectations: If you expect a child to excel, he will; if you expect him to fail, more than likely he won't disappoint you. My challenge is "Give me any child for one month, and I'll give you back a different child."

You tell your students, "If you can't make a mistake, you can't make anything." I think that is wonderful for a teacher to say.

Far too many people go through life with a sense of chagrin. You always hear people talking about their most embarrassing moments. I think we all, at one time or another, say or do something that is rather stupid or considered not to be traditional. When that occurs, I look at it as just my time to look ridiculous. We all have our turn. I think that's one of the worst things we teach children – that you have to be perfect at all times. I'm not perfect, but I strive for excellence. That's an attitude I try to instill in my students.

Have you found discipline to be a problem in the classroom?

I've never had discipline problems with children. First of all, I get my students to love and respect me. Once they fall in love with you, they'll do anything to please you. If you truly love them and have a sense of humor, you won't have discipline problems.

What about tough kids, how do you deal with them?

I respect children. I don't talk down to them. I don't yell at them or insult them. If a child is constantly in trouble and is in an altercation, I don't jump to the conclusion, "Yes, it's your fault because you are always in trouble." I'll wait to hear the child out. On occasion, the worst devil in the world can be blameless. Your terminology "tough kid" is not accurate. I don't see kids as being tough. Every – what you call – tough kid is a child who is hurting deeply inside. I call them abused children. It's a matter of semantics. I never use the word tough or bad – those words are not part of my vocabulary when describing children.

What advice would you give someone interested in becoming a teacher?

I think it's the most fascinating career in the world. Teachers influence how an entire nation evolves. Unfortunately, the teaching profession is not held in high esteem. Compared to other professionals, teachers are not taken very seriously. We jut out our chests when we are bankers, developers, financiers, lawyers, doctors, engineers, but we should never forget that it all began with a teacher. If you want to become a teacher, you must.

What is the most important thing you've learned about teaching?

That you learn something new every day; you learn from children. Their proximity is a catharsis for me. I'm excited and fascinated by what I do. I've been teaching for almost thirty years and the wonder is still there.

If you had a month off to do anything you wanted, how would you spend it?

I'd go to an island and I would take about three hundred children along with me and several dozen books from our school's reading list. I would take the kids away from society and their parents and then at the end of the month I would bring them back. They would be different children, believe me.

Do you think our educational system places enough emphasis on the value of human differences?

I think everybody wants to be like everybody else. It's less demanding being like everybody else as opposed to being yourself. The hardest thing in the world is to be "me," to be true to one's self. We are constantly influenced to conform to standards set by society, the media, advertisements. If you're not pleased with your nose, you go to a surgeon and pick a new one from a catalog. I think learning to like and respect who we are should be emphasized. Our imperfections make us unique.

Why did you turn down the opportunity to become secretary of education in the Reagan administration?

I don't think most people realize that you are guided by a script handed to you by the White House. You can't go against public policy in such a post. I would have had to renege on my own views to make the White House views palatable to the public. I don't believe you can change anything, no matter what office you hold, if you can't voice your concerns about what is wrong.

You felt you would be more effective outside the administration?

I've reached more than three or four million children in this country through training programs and workshops for teachers, principals, and superintendents. I am training teachers and redoing the entire school system in the state of Oklahoma. I think I've reached a good many children without having to relinquish my beliefs.

What is your greatest concern about our educational system?

I'm very frightened because no nation can afford to be powerful and illiterate at the same time. It's not just what my concern is, it should be the concern of every parent. Every time I hear the word reform, I want to scream. Reforming the educational system we now have is folly at most. We must start from scratch. No more of this easy-to-teach, easy-to-learn, school should be "fun" business that permeates our schools. We must get back to basics. We must once again teach our children the values that made this nation great. We talk about school reforms, but no one talks about the curriculum. We need to emphasize values such as determination, perseverance, honesty, and integrity. We need to set up a mandate stipulating what children should know in kindergarten, first grade, second grade, and so on. There must be a system to verify that a child has the requisite knowledge for his or her grade level. We keep testing, but no one is teaching. We should teach skills for life, skills that every literate citizen should know.

Engineering
and
Technology

Millie J. Kronfly

Profession: Aerospace Engineer

Currently: Director, Flight Systems Design, Performance, and Mission
Operations, Rockwell International, Space Systems Division

Date of birth: June 18, 1950

Education: B.A., Whittier College, 1972 (Mathematics)
Graduate Work in Engineering, Engineering Management,
and Business Management, California State University –
Long Beach, West Coast College, and University of Southern
California

$\mathcal{M}$illie Kronfly has devoted her entire career as a scientist to work on the space shuttle program. As director of flight systems at Rockwell International, she is responsible for managing more than three hundred aerospace engineers who support the National Aeronautics and Space Administration (NASA) shuttle missions. Kronfly has experienced a wide range of emotions on the job: the thrill of assisting in successful missions and the horror and despair of *Challenger.* Of the latter, she recalls, "I saw it fly once over Houston, and something happened inside of me. There was just something about that bird." Yet, in spite of the lingering sadness she still feels over the loss of *Challenger* and its crew in 1986, Kronfly is as excited about the space program as when she first began at Rockwell in 1973 as a member of the technical staff.

When she assumed her current position, some members of her staff were skeptical about her managerial skills because of her relative youth, but it did not take long for her to prove that she was made of "the right stuff." Kronfly has been praised by her superiors for her calm determination, command of details, enthusiasm, and ability to lead by example. She is described by Robert Glaysher, vice president of engineering at Rockwell, as a "dedicated and well-trained engineer who has tremendous organizational and management skills and is able to mobilize large groups of people to make things happen."

Kronfly's area of responsibility encompasses future engineering endeavors, including a lunar planetary flight scheduled for the year 2010, an outpost on Mars scheduled for the year 2020, and a "hyperspace" plane with the capability to take off from a standard runway and head straight into space.

Her husband, Bud, works in engineering, planning, and support services at Rockwell. When they have time, they enjoy going to their cabin in the mountains.

How did you decide to become an aerospace engineer?

When I graduated from college in 1972 with a degree in math education, I had plans to become a high school teacher. At that time, there was a glut of baby-boomer teachers, and since I had not yet completed my certification program, I came to a crossroads-type decision point: should I complete the fifth year required to teach in California, or should I look for something else? I made halfhearted attempts to find work at several of the aerospace firms in the L.A. basin and then learned that Rockwell had recently won the space shuttle contract. I applied during a major staffing period and have been happily associated with the company, the program, and the aerospace business ever since. My good fortune was in part due to my willingness to redirect my career focus based on the real opportunities at the time.

When you see the space shuttle take off, what thoughts go through your mind?

What goes through my mind is the thousands of people who work on it and the fact that it is an extremely complex vehicle — probably the hardest thing we've got operating as far as an aerospace craft is concerned because it has to go through all environments. It's got to launch like a rocket, float around like a satellite, and come back like an airplane. The brainpower that went into devising that vehicle at the outset and causing it to come together, and the amount of effort and the coordination and integration that were required, are mind-boggling! When you actually look at the vehicle and see what its complexities are, it's an ugly duck, but it's something you cannot help but be proud of.

What aspect of your work do you find most demanding?

In most career fields, each individual can master the technical aspects of the job through formal training, education, and on-the-job training. However, the real challenges come in dealing with people. In a place like Rockwell, where we are well known for our part in putting a man on the moon and for designing and integrating a reusable spacecraft, the diversity in skills, experience, styles, personalities, and egos is quite demanding. This is especially true when the primary objective of management is to get such a group to form a well-focused, efficient team. The most demanding aspect of my job as director of some 360 engineers and support personnel is to lead by example, develop people without doing their jobs for them, and ensure that all members feel accountable and are pulling together as a team.

Could you describe a typical workday when there is a NASA shuttle mission in progress?

Quite frankly, we like them to be boring. (Laughter) On a shuttle mission, what we do is support whatever the planned mission is. On the last mission, we had a DOD [Department of Defense] payload. The DOD had a very grueling schedule for the crew. The crew was up twenty-four hours a day. They had a six-man crew, and they split the shifts; some of them were up twelve hours, and some were up the other twelve. We were there to monitor the performance of the vehicle.

If something goes wrong with the vehicle, we work on a "work-around" to allow the mission to continue safely. For example, if one of the little jets that maneuvers the vehicle on orbit has a failure, we come up with different ways to continue the flight. There's enough redundancy that all they have to do is declare what the jet's position is and we take it from there.

How do you deal with pressure?

When I cause the pressure – for example, if I neglected to work on something that suddenly becomes due – I usually can get focused and accomplish the task readily. In fact, I surprise myself with my own efficiency under pressure! When pressure or stress comes from outside sources, and especially when it has to do with personality conflicts, I often have to psyche myself up to deal with it. Whenever the situation is more than I can or am willing to deal with, I ask for help from my subordinates, peers, and/or boss. I also get a great deal of therapy from gardening and fitness workouts, which I try to do daily during the week. It's amazing how much a diversion can help.

What do you think accounts for your success?

Basically, I'm a very open person, a team player, and a good soldier. I have never been afraid to say, "I'll get you the answer," when I don't know the answer at the time. I have always asked questions, and as one progresses into management, being able to question what and why things are done is critical to the success of the program. As a manager, I defend my people ardently, challenge them tactfully, and try to lead with energy and enthusiasm. I have been given some interesting assignments that got me management attention and visibility fairly early in my career. And I have been blessed with mentors who were genuinely interested in my career development. I firmly believe that success is a personal thing, very much dependent on how each person deals with and approaches both opportunities and crises.

As a woman, have you ever experienced discrimination in your profession?

I can honestly say that I have not ever experienced any serious discrimination. I attribute that to the good fortune of working for enlightened management and to the fact that I never let that be a factor in my assessment of my successes or failures. I have had my share of teasing, mostly based on my age rather than gender. I have considered taking some assertiveness management training to help me develop a thicker skin. The sooner we can get comfortable with ourselves, the better able we are to deal with setbacks, be they from unenlightened employers or coworkers, differences of opinions, or business-related disappointments or crises.

What do you find challenging about your work?

Dealing with change, which we at Space Systems Division are doing; changing our management approach and our business strategies. It's challenging because it's such a departure from what we've been doing. What we're asking is how do we change our management style, how do we change the way we do business, how do we get into a more product/team orientation, how do we empower the people. Trying to work your way through a change in tradition and organizational structure understandably causes all kinds of unsettled feelings for people. Dealing with that is a challenge. Right now we're also trying to deal with layoffs. It's agonizing having to look somebody in the face and say we can no longer support your services because of funding levels. That's really tough.

What qualities do you think are necessary to succeed as an aerospace engineer?

Well, aerospace is an up and down business. You've got to be able to deal with that. You've got to be innovative and have some flexibility in the way you do your business. The other thing – it's critical – is to have good communication skills. A lot of the kids think that if they master a course in aerodynamics, physics, or whatever, that will get them in. If they cannot communicate their findings, if they cannot coordinate their results with other people, then they're not going to succeed. Communication skills, both written and oral, are extremely critical.

The other thing is you've got to be able to deal with the ups and downs, not just in the business, but in the environment we work in. One minute you're the hero, and the next minute you're the goat. Folks who have careers in this business have got to be able to deal with congressional advocacy versus opposition, a successful test followed by a failure. Staying interested, even though you have those adversities, is a critical asset and capability.

Currently, do you do much engineering and design work?

Very rarely do I do any really detailed engineering work. I review the engineers' results and try to ask the right questions about their findings. The big thing for me is to make sure they coordinate their story correctly, they've considered all the technical aspects, and they've talked to everybody. That's the role I play. It's really more management-type work than engineering.

What are you most proud of having achieved?

That's a hard one. I guess for one thing, to be in the position I'm in, which is rare in this division. It's not rare in our company, necessarily, but to be in engineering and the manager of 360 people is an achievement. The other thing is just working on the shuttle program. It is still a major asset to the country. That gives me a great deal of satisfaction. As I watch the vehicle operate, I can look at it and think, "I wrote some of the requirements for that capability."

What advice would you give someone interested in pursuing a career as an aerospace engineer?

My advice would be to get exposure to hardware, be it avionics packages or propulsion systems. Also, anybody who wants to pursue a career in this area need not get locked into a particular specialty. Organizations of the future are going to be flatter and have fewer management levels. People need to be able to move laterally into other things. You need to have some hardware exposure because of the kind of business this is. Our big business is building vehicles. We want to design, integrate, and fly them.

Joan E. Goody

Profession: Architect

Currently: Partner, Goody, Clancy & Associates

Date of birth: December 1, 1935

Education: Academy of Fine Arts, Copenhagen, 1962
Institut Des Sciences Politiques, Paris, 1954- 1955
B.A., Cornell University, 1956 (History)
M.Arch., Harvard Graduate School of Design, 1960

"*Functional*, practical, and inviting, conveying an aura of the traditional, Joan Goody's work adapts to modern society and supports the diversity of the community at large." That's how architectural critic Carolyn Cole described Goody's contribution to architecture. Goody, the first woman architect to have designed office buildings in downtown Boston, is a partner in the fifty-member Boston architectural firm of Goody, Clancy & Associates, founded in 1956 by her late husband, Marvin Goody.

As an only child, she was encouraged by her father, an engineer, to pursue her interests in architecture. At Cornell, she took a studio architecture course that prompted her to apply to the Harvard Graduate School of Design. Soon after graduating from Harvard, she married fellow architect Marvin Goody and immediately went to work for his newly established firm. Beginning in a low-paying drafting job, she became an associate within eight years and later became a principal. "You can never build a perfect building because you never build the same building twice," she says. "But the next time you build, you can really draw on what you have learned."

Goody is very active in her community, serving on the boards of Boston's prestigious Friends of the Public Garden and Landmarks Commission. "Keeping Boston looking like itself is a very important goal for us," she says.

Goody's work includes Harbor Point Housing, a 1,280-unit residential community; the Faneuil Hall/Old State House renovation and restoration; renovations and additions at Brown University; a sports facility at Simmons College; two twenty-story office buildings in downtown Boston, including the Paine Webber Building; and the Village at Fawcett's Pond in Hyannis, Massachusetts. Other major projects in which her firm has been engaged include Tent City Housing and the Transportation Building in Boston. "The organization of space to provide a place where the community may meet and gather," she says, "remains a goal in all of our projects."

Goody is married to Peter Davison, a poet and editor. During the week, they reside in her Beacon Hill carriage house in Boston. They spend weekends at his Gloucester farm, where she enjoys gardening.

What drew you to your profession?

A desire to shape the environment, to make things on a large scale.

What do you consider the most important element in design?

I think creativity and the sense of understanding a problem so well and so deeply that you can propose a structure to meet all its needs and then go beyond what anybody ever imagined. To fulfill all the functional requirements and then also create something of beauty and joy – that takes a fair amount of creativity.

As an architect, what do you look for in a building?

I look for how it fulfills the task I just described. Clearly, the first thing that hits me – and probably hits other people, too – is whether it is a joy to behold. Whether it is special, beautiful, uplifting in some way, and depending on where it is and what it is, how it fits in with it's surroundings. Whether it makes the place where it is located a better place and more exciting by something it does. I always look at the quality of the space and the details; the way other people have solved problems that I've tried to solve. I admire ingenious and creative ways of dealing with issues that I've been struggling with.

What is the most frequent challenge you encounter when designing a building?

The single biggest challenge is to make sure that what you are designing will be a positive addition to its environment and the lives of the people who use it. It's an awesome responsibility when you make something that is supposed to last many years and will definitely have a strong effect on many people's lives. Also, it has to be original, since the point of hiring an architect is to create something that has never existed before. Therefore, you have to predict what it will look like, how it will function, how it will wear over time – and that is based on experience. It's always a challenge to anticipate all of those concerns and how they act upon each other in advance. It's a heavy responsibility.

Do you think you encounter a different set of challenges as a female architect?

I think so. There still are a fair number of people who are reluctant to give responsibility to a woman because they have limited experience or they are prejudiced or just don't think that a woman can handle it. That, of course, is ridiculous. But it doesn't help if someone who thinks that happens to be your client or your potential client. So I think as a woman, one has to be all the more thoughtful, strong, and careful, and to project such an image. That is just one additional burden in a profession that has many.

Which is the greatest burden?

Continuing to have creative energy while spending considerable time and effort managing people, pursuing projects, and doing the many other jobs that architecture entails.

What do you think accounts for your success?

A combination of naivete and tough skin. I don't think I saw or acknowledged what in retrospect I'd call put-downs. I pushed ahead expecting to succeed and often did.

What qualities do you think are necessary to be a successful architect?

You have to enjoy working with people because, despite the image of someone sitting alone at a drafting board, architecture is really very much a team profession. If you work with buildings of any size, you work with other architects. You always have clients, and sometimes on larger projects it's a multiple client that includes a public agency, the actual users of the building, and maybe somebody who owns it. I think to be successful and to enjoy architecture, it's critical to be comfortable working with groups of people.

Could you describe a typical workday?

Hectic! The days are long and varied. There is a fair amount of physical movement, whether it is out and around a site or moving around the office talking to different people. It's never boring! There is always more than one project going on at the same time, so you have to switch back and forth thinking about one project and then the other. My day includes running in and out of the office to see clients, visiting a project under construction, taking phone calls, walking around the office and talking to people, seeing how their work is coming along, and teaching some of the younger architects. As you rise in the profession, you find that your drawing and design are often done in airplanes and on weekends and in quiet moments stolen at dawn or dusk. Then there is a certain amount of time spent designing, but much less than one thinks.

If I were a client and I invited you to build any type of structure you wanted—money was no object—what would you build?

What a fascinating question! I'd like to do a village or a community. What interests me are places where people gather, where there is a real sense of community. I'd do something that would have public, residential, and work buildings. As long as you are asking, I'd like to do a whole new town. (Laughter) Or I'd restore an old and somewhat faltering town. But I am as interested in the streets, the squares, and the outside spaces that buildings create as what is inside them.

Has it been difficult juggling a career and a family?

Yes—and I never had children. But a husband, parents, and stepchildren are demanding, rewarding parts of life, and I'd be sadder without the struggle.

Irene C. Peden

Profession: Electrical Engineer

Currently: On leave from the University of Washington to serve as Director of the Division of Electrical and Communications Systems, National Science Foundation

Date of birth: September 25, 1925

Education: B.S., University of Colorado, 1947 (Electrical Engineering)
M.S., Stanford University, 1958 (Electrical Engineering)
Ph.D., Stanford University, 1962 (Electrical Engineering)

$\mathcal{J}$rene C. Peden is professor of electrical engineering at the University of Washington-Seattle, where she has served as associate dean of the College of Engineering and associate chair of the Department of Electrical Engineering. Her colleague Sinclair Yee describes her as "a very skillful administrator and a scholarly engineer." She is currently on a leave of absence from the University of Washington to head up the Division of Electrical and Communications Systems at the National Science Foundation (NSF) in Washington, D.C.

Research she conducted in wave propagation and scattering contributed to her selection as the first American woman engineer to be stationed in the Antarctic interior, where she successfully completed ionospheric experiments, providing important information about radio propagation and the polar ionosphere. This research led to her election as fellow of the prestigious Explorers Club.

Peden has developed courses in electromagnetic theory, radio science, and microwave techniques. Her research interests are in geophysical subsurface remote sensing, radio science, and antennas and propagation. She has published a number of papers in these fields.

Peden has lectured widely, encouraging women to pursue careers in engineering. She was the subject of a profile in *Spectrum* magazine titled "A Few Uncommon Engineers" and of an article in *American Scientist* titled "Seventy-Five Reasons to Become a Scientist." She enjoys swimming and boating with her husband, Leo, in Puget Sound. Peden has two stepdaughters.

What drew you to a career in electrical engineering?

I think it was evolutionary. When I was in high school, I was interested in chemistry. When I started college, I thought I would be a chemistry major. I took physics, which is always recommended for chemistry majors, and I liked it better. I thought maybe I would be in physics, but then I found out that you had to get a Ph.D. to be a physicist of any real viability, and in those days, there was nothing to do with a Ph.D. but teach. I didn't want to do that. I was just a teenager, and I didn't have such long-range goals. So I abandoned that idea, and in the course of taking physics, I found I liked the electricity and magnetism part best. Somehow I found out you could take a four-year curriculum that focused on that area and you could get a bachelor's degree and do something "real" with it.

What do you find most demanding about your work?

Academia is demanding in its own way. We are responsible for teaching, research, scholarly production, grant production, and service. The farther you go and the better known you become, the more demands there are on your time.

What aspect of your work do you find most satisfying?

Probably the same things that satisfied me in graduate school. It was terribly hard. If I worked hard and really dug for it, I always got it. There was tremendous satisfaction in feeling you had worked your way through some-thing hard – a difficult concept or a problem to solve – and had come out understanding it. That personal experience led me to place a high value on teaching and working with graduate students on research projects. It's fun to have a hand in guiding them into getting it, too. It was also a source of tremendous satisfaction for someone, who had played only with dolls as a child and had no exposure to tools or mechanical things, to learn how to build an electrical circuit or a simple device that would work when you turned it on. These experiences have been part of the motivation for my professional life.

How do you deal with pressure?

First, it takes a lot for me to perceive it as pressure because I am used to having a lot going on. I take a regular aerobics class in the late afternoon. I think I probably work some stress off that way. I have excellent health, and I think that is a factor, too.

What do you think accounts for your success?

In academia, of course, it takes a Ph.D. But beyond that, I would say sheer persistence had a lot to do with it. In my generation, it was pretty difficult for a woman to sustain a career. There weren't very many women who dared to try. Of those who did, most of them found one reason or another to bail out. Those of us who were left had a high tolerance for discriminatory attitudes, isolation, and all those things that you read about as being typical of pioneer women's lives and careers. Given that my success has been in electrical engineering, I would say the fact that I was born with an analytical mind has been important. I feel sure I would register as "strongly introverted" on one of those extrovert-introvert scales. The introvert quality is certainly not a requirement, but it would not surprise me to find that the majority of my colleagues fall on that side of the balance point. There must be a connection!

Is there any other profession you would rather be pursuing?

Not really. But I'll tell you, my research interests have always been at the interface of electrical engineering and geophysics. I wouldn't rather be a pure geophysicist, but I think if I had known that earlier, I might have done more specific studies in geophysics.

As a woman, have you experienced discrimination in your profession?

Much! The older I get, the more I would say there is discrimination.

Who were your role models?

In her own way, probably my mother. There certainly weren't any women electrical engineers for me to relate to in the forties, which was when I was an undergraduate. My mother, who is now ninety-four, had been a math major in college and had taught high school math. To do that, she had to go out and teach country school. She couldn't get a teaching job in the city. Women just didn't qualify in those days for anything that grand. So I grew up knowing that if you wanted something, you could do it.

What advice would you give someone interested in pursuing a career in electrical engineering?

That question can be answered at several levels. In terms of probability for academic and technical success, I would strongly advise a realistic assessment of interest patterns and aptitudes. It is very important to like what you do. Once you make a career choice and get well into it, it's difficult to change without loss of time and other resources. If you like math and math-based sciences, your chances of liking electrical engineering are good. If you also find these subjects relatively easy, the probability of career enjoyment and success is even higher. It would be pretty discouraging to find yourself always running behind and trying to catch up with your colleagues. When it comes to careers, as life itself, you have to decide what your priorities are. When you know that, you can make your decisions accordingly and then just go for it!

Jeana Yeager

Profession: Test Pilot

Currently: Head, Voyager Enterprises, Inc.

Date of birth: May 18, 1952

Education: High School, 1970, Mesquite, Texas

$\mathcal{A}$s a child growing up in Texas, Jeana Yeager's first love was riding and training horses. She trained the "untrainable," displaying the fearlessness that she would later show as a test pilot and earn her the sobriquet, "the gutsy little Texan."

On the morning of December 23, 1986, at age thirty-four, Yeager secured a permanent place in aviation history when she and Dick Rutan completed their world flight in the *Voyager* aircraft. They flew the maximum circumference of the globe — nonstop, without refueling, in nine days, three minutes, and forty-four seconds. The flight represented not only a first in aviation but an heroic achievement in physical and psychological endurance. "I was never terrified," Yeager recalled later, "until after the worst moments were behind us."

Voyager, designed by Rutan's brother, Burt, and described in *Newsweek* as "a fuel tank that flies," weighed 1,858 pounds empty and carried 1,489 gallons (8,934 pounds) of fuel. Along with the grinding fatigue, the roaring of the engine, and the constant bruising caused by turbulence, Yeager and Rutan found *Voyager*'s two-foot by seven-and-a-half-foot unpressurized cabin extremely confining. Yeager later admitted, "It was a lot more difficult than we ever imagined."

Yeager moved to California in 1977 and took up engineering design, acquiring skills and knowledge in the fields of aerospace design and commercial engineering draftsmanship. At the age of twenty-six, she learned to fly planes and became current in four categories of experimental canard composite aircraft. She set five world records for speed and distance, including one in which she surpassed *Voyager* partner Dick Rutan. In July 1986, six months before the world flight, she and Rutan flew *Voyager* on a 116-hour mission, setting a new closed-course Absolute World Distance Record. This achievement made her the first woman ever to be listed in the Absolute category.

Yeager has received honorary doctorate degrees, medals, awards, and honors for her courageous world flight, including the Presidential Citizen's Medal of Honor, presented only sixteen times in U.S. history, and the Collier Trophy, one of the most coveted aeronautical awards in America.

Yeager enjoys skydiving, wing walking, harness racing, and horseback riding. She heads Voyager Enterprises, Inc., a company devoted to the advancement of aerospace education.

What was it that attracted you to flying?

Initially, I wanted to fly helicopters. I had no particular background in flying, nor was I ever around anyone who flew aircraft. Helicopters were just something that fascinated me. I decided to find out what they were like to fly. I went to the local airport and enrolled in a flying school. It was recommended that I first take the fixed-wing portion of the course, which I did, and I received my license in 1978. When it came time to move on to helicopters, the company I was dealing with ran into financial difficulties, leaving my helicopter rating in limbo.

What aspect of your work on *Voyager* did you find most challenging?

It was so demanding; maybe that was the excitement of it. It's constantly discovering and exploring the unknown. There were no written rules or plans for *Voyager*. It was set a goal and find a way to make it work. The unknown, the theories, were only hearsay until we actually went out and tested the aircraft and collected data.

Voyager was much more than a record. *Voyager* was a milestone, a first in history. If you look at a pyramid, *Voyager* was the crowning point in aviation record setting. We had the chance to take that step. Each day offered something new. If you blinked, you missed out on something. It was self-motivating.

What do you enjoy most about your work?

I enjoy the people as well as the aircraft. I think what is most important is the educational values I've received and have been able to share. There's so much to learn. Even more exciting, there is so much developing in the aviation field.

What are important qualities for a test pilot?

I think dedication is important, and wanting to see technology improve is part of it. Also, a strong desire to participate in the future development of a field we all utilize daily and that is so important to everyone's needs. There is something about being on the leading edge of technology—there is no place better!

During the six years it took to prepare *Voyager* for the world flight, your team encountered technical difficulties, lack of funds, faulty equipment, and broken promises. According to what I've read, you kept the project going. What kept you going?

To me, a person can only be as good as his word. I made a promise. I said I was going to do this project, and I believed in it. Therefore, I was prepared to stay with the project until it was done.

When you were flying *Voyager*, you had quite a few harrowing experiences. How did you remain calm and collected when others in a similar situation would surely have panicked?

I don't know. I don't panic too easily. We flew *Voyager* sixty-seven test flights before the world flight. Each flight offered so many close situations, so we were well prepared for the unexpected. Difficulties became a normal state of affairs. When we experienced difficulties, it became automatic to pull out the checklist. With so much going on all at once, you have to remain calm so you can go through the procedures and make sure your partner is responding properly. The alternative is death.

I find it almost inconceivable that you and Dick Rutan survived in that tiny, unpressurized cabin for nine days. Do you marvel at that fact?

Yes! It was extremely small. You get your mind set to accomplish the task at hand, and with determination you can overcome a lot of things. You overlook the pain, the discomfort, and you learn to persevere without all the luxuries. The two of us worked well in the aircraft. *Voyager* was not a one-person airplane. It took both of us to complete the around-the-world mission. We were a team.

What do you think accounted for the success of *Voyager*?

A lot of years of planning and testing, a lot of luck, a lot of prayers from so many people, as well as a good working team. I think it is a combination of all those things. A number of instruments should not have functioned as they did, but the aircraft worked anyway.

Now that you've completed the *Voyager* project, what other project would you like to pursue?

I wish I had the answer to that, but I am still looking and evaluating. It would have to be something as hard, as challenging, and as involved as the *Voyager* project was. Now is a time of reflecting on what I've learned in the past and what I'm learning today. Then I will consider where I want to go from here. *Voyager* was very special. It was a very rare privilege to participate in something that is part of aviation history. A lot of pride comes with that accomplishment.

As a woman, have you ever experienced discrimination in your profession?

Not much. There are always a few people, but overall the people I work directly with accept me and help me tremendously. I know I don't know all the answers, and I know everyone is a source of knowledge. The best way to tap into their resources is to ask. And ask I do! I appreciate the information, the help, and the expertise that is offered me. I rely on the efforts and support of all the wonderful unsung heroes who are part of me.

Who were your role models?

I didn't really grow up with role models. Since I've become a pilot, I've learned of many aviation accomplishments, and I find I have a lot in common with those aviators' backgrounds concerning what they held in their hearts. But as far as someone whom I grew up forming my life after, I can't say that I've had a particular role model. I take bits and pieces from everyone I meet. I find good qualities in people, and I like to pull those qualities and hold on to them and try to make them part of me.

Anita M. Flynn

Profession: Research Scientist

Currently: Research Scientist, Artificial Intelligence Laboratory, Massachusetts Institute of Technology

Date of birth: June 10, 1960

Education: U.S. Naval Academy, 1978 - 1979
B.S., Massachusetts Institute of Technology, 1983 (Electrical
Engineering)
M.S., Massachusetts Institute of Technology, 1985 (Electrical
Engineering)

$\mathcal{A}$nita Flynn has contributed to numerous technological breakthroughs, such as developing vision algorithms for navigation, engineering novel people-finding pyroelectric sensors, and building one of the world's smallest [one cubic inch] robots.

At age thirty-one, she is one of the original members of the Mobile Robot Group of the Artificial Intelligence Laboratory at the Massachusetts Institute of Technology [MIT]. In developing autonomous mobile robots, Flynn and her colleagues have adopted a revolutionary approach to robotics. Instead of attempting to reproduce the full complexity of human thought in one large computer, they are creating an array of robots, each designed to perform a variety of complex tasks without having to think like people. Not surprisingly, the lab has been referred to "as one of the more intriguing places on the planet."

Flynn's creativity permeates her work. Her creative whimsy and team spirit were evident when in 1990, she organized an artificial intelligence fair. Exhibits ranged from robot boat races, face recognition contests, to demonstrations of current and ongoing research.

Flynn's research goals are to build gnat-size microrobots incorporating piezoelectric micromotors, three-dimensional gnat robot bodies, on-board intelligence, and integrated infrared/optical imaging sensors. Thus far, she and her group have four patents pending.

Flynn has published numerous papers on artificial intelligence and has been invited to talk about her research around the world. She is quoted as saying, "I'm what you would call a dreamer. But I also like to push on the small corners of those dreams to try to make bits and pieces of them happen." An ardent athlete, Flynn originally wanted to fly Navy fighter planes but transferred from the Naval Academy to MIT when she learned combat assignments were reserved only for men.

What drew you to a career as a research scientist?

It was never a major plan. Looking back, I suppose my naive algorithm for getting up and out was to choose the hardest path at every decision point. Not all decisions panned out. First, I went to the Naval Academy and spent a year as a plebe. It was the ultimate challenge, and it was great, but it was also the ultimate frustration. At that time [1978] many career paths, such as fighter pilot, were blocked to women. I quit after the first year, spent a year working odd jobs, and then went to MIT.

I always loved sports, and the Academy was heaven for the avid athlete, but MIT is the ultimate intellectual challenge. Engineering is creative, and the sole tradition at MIT is change. The challenge was to think of things nobody ever thought of before and change the world.

As an undergraduate, was your major artificial intelligence?

No, there isn't really a major in artificial intelligence. I studied electrical engineering. At MIT, departments teach and laboratories do research. Artificial intelligence is the name of a laboratory. It's the name of a field. People come to it from lots of traditional backgrounds.

What aspect of your work do you find most challenging?

The challenge is making things happen. It involves building an environment that nurtures creativity, setting up projects and a well-stocked lab so that tools and parts are right at hand and good people are drawn to it. It involves creating a group where ideas don't get squashed and avenues are always open for implementing your imagination.

Where do you get your research ideas?

Brainstorming, dreaming big, wanting to change the world, and having a certain drive. In our lab, it's sort of an underlying theme that we're going to build these robots, we're going to change the world, and, somehow, we're going to make it a better place. A lot of the specific ideas come out of mucking around in problems – thinking there must be a better way, then figuring it out. So the little ideas, which maybe later turn out to be important, come from just getting in, getting your hands dirty.

Ideas come from what we call hacking – working, programming, building things. You start out with a general idea. It's sort of a whole design process. You try something. If it doesn't work, you redesign it, then try it again. It still doesn't work, and you are totally frustrated, so you put it down and you go off and do something else. A week later, the answer hits you. It's sort of living the problem, being interested enough in it to be constantly thinking about it in the background.

What do you consider to be important qualities for a scientist?

A lot of drive, a lot of playfulness, and an attitude of "no squashing." You don't want to be surrounded by negative people. You should never think "that won't work" or "that's a dumb idea." It's so important to have an open mind and a creative attitude.

What do you think accounts for your success?

There's a lot of grunge work behind the flash. We always say that robotics is really just a deep theoretical study in connectors. It's not quite that bad, but working hard, saying yes to everything, and having a willingness to change direction mid-stride are a few of the ingredients.

What advice would you give someone interested in pursuing a career in science?

You have to enjoy the process, and you have to be at ease with delayed gratification. You have to be willing to take an idea that is very different and follow it, maybe realizing that today people aren't going to say, "Hey, it's a good idea." They might think it's totally off the wall. You have to accept that it might not work now, but later it's going to work; it is going to be the right thing.

If you unexpectedly had a month off, how would you spend it?

I would invent sleep capacitors and a suitcase that follows you.

As a woman, have you experienced discrimination in your profession?

No, but I think perception of discrimination is a matter of attitude. You can go through life with a chip on your shoulder, or you can go through life letting things slide off your back. If you ignore the little things, you can focus on making a positive contribution by, for instance, playing Tom Sawyer and painting the fence. If you are excited about what you are doing and having fun, others will want to join in.

I've known some women at MIT who were overly sensitive here; they had to fight all the battles. Anything that happened to them, they would get teed off and say, "That's discrimination!" The younger women had never been told they couldn't do anything, so they just assumed they could. It's a very different perspective to know that. I was in the middle, covering about an eight-year span. I could see both sides. For instance, I remember the dormitory I was in. All these freshmen women were going to row crew. It just never occurred to them that they couldn't row crew. But eight years earlier, there wasn't a women's crew team. Someone had to start it.

Government

Melissa Foelsch Wells

Profession: Foreign Service Officer

Currently: U.S. Ambassador to Zaire

Date of birth: November 18, 1932

Education: B.S., Georgetown University, 1956 (Foreign Service)

𝒟 escribed by Lawrence Eagleburger, Deputy Secretary of State, as "One of our most skillful ambassadors," Melissa Foelsch Wells is a career member of the U.S. Senior Foreign Service. She has served as ambassador to Guinea-Bissau, Cape Verde, and Mozambique and was appointed ambassador to Zaire in 1991. Wells is a charismatic diplomat and gifted linguist, who is fluent in German, Spanish, Italian, Portuguese, and French.

Wells joined the Foreign Service in 1958 after working as a secretary to the Bolivian ambassador in Washington, D.C. After many foreign and stateside appointments, Wells was appointed ambassador to Guinea-Bissau and Cape Verde in 1976. Her subsequent ambassadorial appointment was to the U.N. Economic and Social Council in New York. In 1979, Wells separated from the Foreign Service to become special representative to the U.N. secretary general for relief operations in Uganda. From 1982 to 1986, she was based in Geneva, where she was director of the Impact Program, sponsored by the U.N. Development Program, UNICEF, and the World Health Organization's Humanitarian Program. In 1987, she rejoined the Foreign Service and was named ambassador to Mozambique, where she served a three-year tour of duty.

Wells was born in Tallinn, Estonia, and immigrated to the United States with her parents at age four. She is married to Alfred Washburn Wells who, after retiring from the Foreign Service, became a town planner and an architect specializing in tropical architecture. They have two sons.

What drew you to a career in the diplomatic service?

I was a senior in high school, and we had Career Day. They trotted out the usual options for that time. This was a Catholic school, so first the convent was proposed as an option, then marriage, and then came the suggestions of being a teacher, a nurse, or an airline stewardess. I listened attentively to them all, and the only job that really appealed to me was that of the airline stewardess. I went to talk with her afterward, and she took one look at me and said, "Listen, dearie, you're much too tall!" Well, in my stocking feet, I'm nearly six feet tall, and in those days airlines had height regulations.

That event set me to thinking about what to do after I graduated. I had traveled a great deal as a child. I was not born in this country. I had lived over-seas with my parents, and I realized it meant a great deal for me to see the world. I sized myself up in terms of my academic qualifications at the high school level: I had a strong interest in social science, history, and civics. Putting all my interests together, I marched down to the public library and asked the librarian, "How do I learn about the diplomatic service?" She dug out a book that explained all about the U.S. Foreign Service, and I just took it from there.

I organized my courses at a local college in California so that I would be taking a program that was vaguely similar to the program at the Georgetown School of Foreign Service in Washington, D.C., which I wanted to get into. For financial reasons, I couldn't go there for the first couple of years, but then I did. After I finished the Georgetown School of Foreign Service, I joined the U.S. Foreign Service in 1958.

When you applied to join the Foreign Service, were you asked any "trick" questions during the oral exam?

There was a dreadful question about what are your marriage plans. They stopped asking that question years ago. But in my day, they had you over a barrel with that question. If you said, "I'd like to get married," they'd say, "Stop wasting our time, little girl." If you said, "I'll never get married," they'd say, "What's wrong with this lady?" (Laughter) Either way, they'd have you over a barrel. So I had thought this thing through as to how I was going to answer it. The first three or four minutes went by, and then the question came: "Miss Foelsch, what are your marriage plans?" I said, "Well, I don't have any at the present time. I am six feet tall and weigh two pounds more than Sugar Ray Robinson, and the right guy just isn't around." They laughed, which is exactly what I wanted them to do, and they got on with some other subject.

What is your primary function as ambassador?

My primary function is to represent the United States. It's only by being in the field and by being in the position of an ambassador of your country that you realize what a full array of means you have of representing the United States: by the way you act, interact, speak, and what you become interested in outside the straight and narrow path of communications with the foreign office or the chief of state. Through your personality, you can represent the United States – not necessarily U.S. policy, but, certainly what Americans are: how we feel, how we act, how we react. There's an openness, a sense of compassion, that we have. In many of the countries where I've served, I have gone out of my way to involve myself personally in the community. This, to me, is what the United States is about.

What aspect of your work do you find challenging?

I'd say it's two things really. One is leadership in the full sense of the word in terms of getting to know the people who work with you; getting them to understand the picture of where we are going, what we are trying to do at this post; and mobilizing their commitment to get it done. I've learned that people are the biggest asset you have once you get them to pull together. I think that's the most challenging aspect. The second is achieving specific targets, with a motivated staff, in terms of bringing about change that is of interest to U.S. policy.

What do you enjoy most about your work?

I think it is the idea of playing a part in U.S. policy and bringing about change. I'm obviously not writing policy on the seventh floor here at the State Department. But out in the field, being able to blend my perceptions of what I know, making recommendations as the ambassador and sometimes seeing them accepted and implemented, and helping the whole policy process along is very exciting.

What do you think accounts for your success?

You can't be honest and modest at the same time here! (Laughter) I'd say it is my leadership skill, my ability to mobilize people. If I may use a common expression, I can "turn people on" in terms of understanding a particular situation and what we are trying to achieve. I'm very good at that, and it doesn't mean just with my own team. I think I'm a good salesperson. When you have to do a job in terms of a *démarche*, you often leave behind what we call in diplomatic jargon a nonpaper. How you cover all the points and adjust them to the person you are selling to is important. If you've done your homework, you know exactly how he or she will react. I think I'm good at that.

Do you think current advancements in communications technology might one day obviate the need for exchanging envoys?

You can send a message by telex and hire the office boy to deliver it, but you need *me* to sell it. There is a lot to be said for human interaction, human dynamics, and so forth. You've got to know whom you are dealing with. You have to do much more than just follow the instructions in the cable.

With the prevalence of terrorism these days, what special precautions do you take as ambassador?

We have a whole panoply of physical security devices, but I think it's always wise to be aware of your surroundings. To give you an example, when I was in Uganda immediately after Idi Amin, I was held up at gunpoint. A car was passing, but it didn't continue to pass. It stayed alongside us. When I turned my head to look, I could see the passengers in the car looking out their windows, and they had guns pointed at us as we were driving along. They didn't shoot. I shouted to the driver to stop the car, and they pulled up in front of us. They pulled the driver out, and then I got out and they took the car. They left us standing there by the roadside, in the dark, in the boonies! To this day, I am terribly conscious of a car that is passing but doesn't keep on passing. This happened ten years ago, and still an alarm goes off in my head whenever that happens.

What are some of the perks that go along with being an ambassador?

Oh, usually you have a lovely house. I've had both ends of the spectrum. I've had lovely homes, and I've had pretty miserable digs. When I was appointed our first ambassador to Guinea-Bissau, it was an adventure. We were opening up the post. We had nothing. We had to find office space as well as living space. I lived in two rooms of the former officers' quarters of the Portuguese army. I had two refrigerators in my little sitting room, and I had filing cabinets in the bedroom. The lights would go out several times a day, and there would be no water. I remember sitting there one night in the dark, eating a can of California ripe olives for dinner, and thinking, "This is what it's like to be ambassador!" (Laughter) I am not knocking that. It was exciting. I always counsel younger people who have a chance to do unusual things to go for it. You must have a sense of adventure to be in the Foreign Service.

Is your current appointment to Zaire your ideal assignment?

When I came into the Foreign Service, we had this form that we called the "April Fool's Sheet" because it was due on the first of April and you were supposed to put down three countries where you would like to go. Today we bid on jobs, and it is very well organized. But back then, my first choice, both my first and second year in the Service, was Elisabethville (now called Lubumbashi) in Zaire.

You've been appointed ambassador to several developing countries where women are sometimes treated as second-class citizens. Have you ever felt that you were not accorded the respect due your rank because of your gender?

Never. I'm quite sure of that, and that applies even to before I was an ambassador. Maybe I have such tough skin that I just don't feel it! On the flip side, women who are very sure of themselves, which I am, irritate some men. You can sit there and not open your mouth, and a man will know that you are very sure of yourself. I can sometimes sense when a man feels uneasy working for me because I am a woman. I try to put him at ease, and if he realizes what's happening, it usually pays off very well.

What advice would you give someone interested in pursuing a career in the Foreign Service?

The Foreign Service is tricky in the sense that it is foreign. It's not a Pan Am ticket to romantic places for two weeks – you see the place, and then you come back. No! You get shipped out. You arrive with all your furniture smashed, and you are there. (Laughter) And two years will go by before you get reassigned. You may not like it, so you need a sense of adventure. I think that's the underlying quality that you have to have. Then the other aspect is that it is service. No matter what work you are doing, whether you are taking care of destitute Americans overseas through the consular section, writing reports, selling your government's policy on certain points, or whatever, it is service. And that to me means idealism and commitment. Put those together – adventure, idealism, and commitment – and what more could you want?

Has it been difficult juggling a career and a family?

It's been busy. I wouldn't say it's been difficult. I just assumed that was the way I would do it. If I were to do it again with the children, I certainly would want to spend more time with them when they were young. It was just impossible in those days. I took three weeks off to have my second child. I was at post in London, and that was all the time I could take. They've basically traveled with us to all my posts, with the exception of Uganda, because of the security situation there. When we left Brazil and went to Guinea-Bissau, we left the older boy in Brazil because he was close to applying to university. We just didn't want to fool around with correspondence courses, as good as they are. We kept the younger one on the Calvert System in Guinea-Bissau because there were just no adequate schools. We had the choice of the Soviet school, the East German school, the Cuban school, or the local school. We enrolled him in the local school in the afternoon so he could make friends and run around, and in the morning we would work on his Calvert. I use the royal "we," but my husband did all the work!

Who were your role models?

In terms of what I wanted to do, there just weren't any. Both of my parents had a tremendous influence on me. When I decided on the Foreign Service, they were behind me in spite of the fact that in those days, according to the newspapers, the State Department was full of "Commies." (Laughter) My father was a physicist, and he always wanted me to go into science. Lise Meitner, who was one of the first atomic physicists in Vienna, was always held up to me as an example by my father. He'd always mention proudly that I was going to be another Lise Meitner!

My mother had a career of her own. She was a singer, a soprano. She made a film in Hollywood, recorded, and gave concerts. She was glamorous. Somehow seeing my mother onstage, it never occurred to me that women couldn't do anything that they wanted to do. The world was my oyster! I think the attitude of your parents is very important.

What are you most proud of having achieved in your life?

The fact that my children have had a happy home. I had an unhappy childhood. My parents were divorced, and this loomed very large in my own mind. We have two boys, fully grown, fully launched at this point. But it gives me a great deal of satisfaction that they enjoyed a happy home. It's not easy. It takes two, with all due credit to my husband. It takes a commitment, especially with all the turmoil of traveling around the world, separations, and so forth. But, yes, that gives me the greatest satisfaction.

Gail Wilensky

Profession: Health Administrator

Currently: Administrator, Health Care Financing Administration, Department of Health and Human Services

Date of birth: June 14, 1943

Education: B.A., University of Michigan, 1964 (Psychology)
M.A., University of Michigan, 1965 (Economics)
Ph.D., University of Michigan, 1968 (Economics)

$\mathcal{D}$ escribed in the *Washington Post* as a "gritty marathoner" with the requisite "determination and willingness to face challenges," Gail Wilensky is a nationally recognized expert on a wide range of health policy issues. As head of the Health Care Financing Administration (HCFA), Wilensky directs the Medicare and Medicaid programs, that help pay medical bills for more than sixty million Americans. "In my job, there are two big areas to worry about," she says. "The first is to make sure the programs are running well. The second is the potential for impacting and setting precedents for other parts of the health system."

Wilensky came to HCFA from Project Hope, where she was vice president for health affairs. Prior to that, she was a senior research manager at the National Center for Health Services Research, where she designed and directed the analysis of the National Medical Care Expenditure Survey. She has published extensively on health policy and health economics.

Wilensky has served on the faculties of the University of Michigan and George Washington University and has held a senior research appointment at the Urban Institute. She is a member of the Institute of Medicine of the National Academy of Sciences and a former member of the Physician Payment Review Commission and the Health Advisory Committee of the General Accounting Office.

An avid jogger who runs six miles daily before work, Wilensky says, "It lets me cope with the stress I'm under far more effectively than anything else I can do." She resides in Washington, D.C., with her husband, Robert, a plastic surgeon. They have two children.

What drew you to the field of public health?

It was actually a two-stage process, because I deliberately avoided it for a while. I felt I was being encouraged to go into health because it was a woman's area. So my initial inclination, as an economist, was not to go into health. I changed my mind several years after I was out of graduate school because I am a public policy economist and health is an area of major government activity. Although I had some concerns about why I had been steered there, the notion that this was a major area for public policy is what changed my mind.

You said you were pushed into the public health field. How?

I had been encouraged by a male professor early on in my career to look at public health. My initial reaction as a twenty-four-year-old was, "This guy is trying to steer me into a woman's area, and I will have no part of it." It wasn't until several years later that an opportunity arose involving health economics,

changing my perception. Because the policy issues in health were so important, it really did seem like an interesting area to get into. That was a good
reason for me to enter it.

What advice would you give someone interested in pursuing a career in public health?

Follow it; there are more than enough opportunities. But get good technical
training. You will have much more impact with a rigorous quantitative
background, as well as knowledge about public health, than you will without
it.

What aspect of your work do you find most demanding?

There are two areas that I find most demanding in my current position as
HCFA administrator. First is the realization that I speak for the Department of
Health and Human Services and the Bush administration – not just for myself
or HCFA. The second aspect is the intensity of my days. I'm used to working
long hours six or seven days a week, but I have never been anywhere where
my days are as intense as they are now.

What do you find most rewarding about your work?

The number of areas and the important social policy decisions that come
under this agency, as well as the sense of being able to influence these
critical areas of health care in our country.

What do you think accounts for your success?

A willingness to work harder than most people and to do it with intensity and
concentration. I am well trained, and I have a good background in what I do.
Frankly, lots of people are well trained and intelligent, but I don't think there
are a lot of people who have the kind of background I have who are willing to
work any harder than I am.

Is there any other profession you would rather be pursuing?

No. If I had it to do again, I would have done a joint program in economics
and law. Unfortunately, they developed that program when I was about
halfway through graduate school, and it wasn't worth it for me to do it
sequentially. But I have always been interested in law, and I would have liked
to have done the joint program if it had existed when I went through. I think it
would have given me a somewhat different perspective, but I'm not sure I
would have wanted to do very much differently.

As a woman, have you experienced discrimination in your profession?

I have not personally experienced discrimination. There are a lot of reasons
for that, including good luck. When I was finishing graduate school and
starting to look in the job market, one of the older professors took me aside
and said, "You need to understand that if you ever are in direct, head-on

competition with a man and you are equally qualified, you are going to lose every time. But if you are noticeably better, you'll have a fighting chance." I was pretty angry; it never occurred to me, up until then, that might be an issue. But I decided I could live with those rules. My personal experiences have been that if you can demonstrate that you really are clearly better than other choices, you've got a fair shot. Those are pretty tough rules to live by, but it has been enough for me to feel that I have gotten opportunities that I wanted to have and that I don't personally feel that I have been discriminated against. That's not to say that I haven't come across some pretty sexist characters over the past twenty years. I've certainly seen that!

Has it been difficult juggling a career and a family?

Difficult, I suppose, but not by any stretch of the imagination impossible. I think there are two difficult aspects. The most difficult was that in the first few years, I didn't know any other women who worked full-time, were married, and had young children. I didn't have anyone to turn to who was in a similar circumstance. It wasn't until my oldest was about three and a half years old that I met someone more or less like myself.

I think probably the other difficult thing is when your children are at home – my youngest just went to college this year – you basically learn to do things very quickly. You don't have time to do anything in slow motion. You also give up the concept of having any time for yourself unless it is at very off-hours. One of the reasons I exercise at six o'clock in the morning during the week and eight o'clock on the weekends is I got in the habit long ago. If I wanted to steal a little time for myself, it had to be at a time that didn't come out of anybody else's time.

Who was your role model?

In a traditional sense, I don't know that I had a role model, but a lot of factors have made me what I am. My mother was a very influential force in my life because she imparted a sense of demands: the demands that I place on myself, the expectations that I have of myself, and the confidence to achieve what I want. She had a lot of impact on what I have been able to achieve. As a result I have tried very hard to serve, if not as a role model, at least as somebody whom younger women could come and talk to.

When I taught, which I did for five years, I let it be known that my door was open at all times to any of the women graduate students who wanted to come in and talk. It troubled me that there were very few women whom the graduate students could talk to who were more or less their contemporaries and who were married with young children. I thought it was important for them to understand that pursuing a career did not mean they could not choose other paths.

Sharon Pratt Kelly

Profession: Mayor/Politician

Currently: Mayor of the District of Columbia

Date of birth: January 30, 1944

Education: B.A., Howard University, 1965 (Political Science)
J.D., Howard University, 1968

"You are what you believe you are," says Mayor Sharon Pratt Kelly. "When I set out to become mayor, people thought it was amusing. People slammed the door in my face. I called them on the telephone, and they never returned my phone calls." Kelly surprised many political pundits by staging an upset victory on September 11, 1990, to become the Democratic party's nominee for mayor of the District of Columbia and went on to win the general election. Her campaign slogan was "Clean house," and her symbol was a shovel.

Described as a "fiery and charismatic public speaker," Kelly spent only a short time in private practice before joining the faculty at the Antioch School of Law. She soon gained a reputation as an advocate for the citizens of the District of Columbia, prompting former Speaker of the House Thomas "Tip" O'Neill to appoint her vice chairman of the D.C. Law Revision Commission.

Prior to running for mayor, Kelly was an attorney with the D.C. office of the Chicago law firm, Sidley & Austin. She is a member of the board of trustees of Howard University, her alma mater, and has been an active member of the Legal Aid Society. Nationally respected as a leader in the Democratic party, Kelly was the first woman to become treasurer of the Democratic National Committee, serving from 1985 to 1989.

Kelly is determined to make her mark on Washington, D.C., and has made it known that she is willing to be a one-term mayor if that is what it takes. "We are doing things differently from the way some of the power brokers are accustomed to things being done," Kelly said in the *Washington Post.* "If it means it doesn't translate in terms of their support at the end of four years, so be it. It will be clear at the end of the four years that we were here, we made a difference."

Kelly maintains that her best quality is her loyalty: "I'd go the last mile for a friend." A third-generation Washingtonian, her father is a retired D.C. superior court judge. Her mother died when she was young, and she was raised by her grandmother and aunts.

Kelly has two daughters, Aimee and Drew. She married banker-turned-entrepreneur James R. Kelly III on December 7, 1991.

What drew you into politics?

The need for change in D.C. The government had ceased to work for the people, and our youth were no longer being challenged to be prepared for the future. When I lost confidence in our city's former administration, I decided to heed the old saying that the best way to have a job done to your satisfaction is to do it yourself. So I left Potomac Electric Power Company to become mayor of the District of Columbia. I acted solely on my belief that I possess the talent, creativity, and tenacity to restore and enhance this city's greatness. District voters agreed.

What aspect of your work do you find most challenging?

Implementing the policies and procedures. Also, unlike any other city, the District has federal, local, and worldwide implications. I must address not only the needs and interests of a highly diverse city and business population, but also those of the House and Senate, plus hundreds of thousands of national and international visitors. Additionally, I must attempt to preserve the significance of this historic capital city, while enabling its growth and development as the icon of the future.

Are you eager to get up and go to work in the morning?

Every day presents a new challenge for me and for D.C., and because I have always eagerly accepted challenges, I enjoy coming to work. Each day is different, no day is easy, but every day is worth it.

How do you deal with pressure?

When the pressure is on, I try to take things one step at a time. When the day is over, I unwind by spending time with my family at home. A long time ago I learned that, just as precious diamonds are the toughest stones, life's best presents are the greatest challenges. Thus, I realize that when I am confronted with great challenges, I am in strong pursuit of goals worth reaching. So instead of directing my energy negatively to dwell on the strain, I keep it focused positively on the gain.

What do you think accounts for your success?

I believe that hard work and perseverance account for my achievements, but more importantly, the guidance and encouragement of my father, my aunts, and my grandmother have kept me motivated. In addition, having a program and an objective to which my mind was set helped me travel the path to success. When you have something to offer and you believe in yourself and your own abilities, there is nothing you cannot achieve.

Who were your role models?

My grandmother, Hazel Pratt; Patricia Roberts Harris; and Rosa Parks.

What advice would you give someone interested in pursuing a career in politics?

Make sure that you are involved with your community and know the problems and concerns. Be sure to reach out to every segment of the population — no exclusions, everyone counts. Pursue the office with honesty, integrity, and tenacity. Make sure that you have an agenda and stick to it, especially if everyone else thinks you're wrong! I've learned that when others think you're wrong, you're usually right on target.

Has it been difficult juggling a career and family?

In years past, yes. It is not easy to be a wife, mother, and career professional. But now that I am a single parent with two adult daughters, it is not difficult to juggle the two. Fortunately, I've always had strong family support, and when my daughters were young, if I had to be away, they were well cared for. My daughters have been very supportive of my career. In fact, while I was campaigning, they worked right alongside me. It was very much a family affair.

As a woman, have you experienced discrimination in your profession?

It's hard being a woman in any profession because often you have to work twice as hard to prove your worth. Women are often looked upon as fragile, sensitive, and weak. I've experienced many forms of discrimination, but I've never let it stop me. The key is to stay focused and put forth your best effort at all times. You can't be faulted for doing a good job, and hard work does pay off – I'm a witness!

Marcelite J. Harris

Profession: Military Officer

Currently: Vice Commander, Oklahoma Air Logistics Center, Tinker Air
Force Base, Oklahoma

Date of birth: January 16, 1943

Education: B.A., Spelman College, 1964 (Speech and Drama)
Squadron Officer School, 1975
Air War College, 1983
B.S., University of Maryland, 1986 (Business Management)
Harvard University's Senior Officers in National Security Course,
1989

$\mathcal{A}$t the Air Force's Office of Public Affairs, faces light up at the mention of her name. The promotion of Colonel Marcelite Harris to brigadier general on September 8, 1990, made her one of only fifteen women in the history of the Air Force to achieve the rank of general and the first black woman ever to do so. She has been described by her commanding officer as "fun to be with and also as tough as nails if she has to be." Harris attributes her rise through the ranks to being "just plain old me." To those who know her well, she has achieved her success by combining intuitive people skills with a firm grasp of military knowledge. In an interview published in the *Air Force Times,* Harris said she initially had a problem with self-confidence but overcame it by talking to herself, emphasizing optimism, and deciding that if she failed one day, she could succeed the next.

In her twenty-four year military career, Harris has compiled an impressive string of firsts. She became the Air Force's first woman aircraft maintenance officer and one of the first "air officers commanding" at the Air Force Academy in Colorado. In 1981, she was named the first woman maintenance squadron commander in Strategic Air Command. A little more than a year later, she became the Air Force's first woman director of maintenance and, eventually, the first woman deputy commander for maintenance. In 1988, she took over the helm of the 3300th Technical Training Wing, becoming the first woman technical training wing commander in Air Training Command. As the vice commander of the Oklahoma Air Logistics Center at Tinker Air Force Base, Harris is second in charge of a work force of more than twenty-six thousand men and women who repair parts, perform overhaul, and provide logistical support to some of the Air Force's key weapon systems.

Harris's decorations include the Bronze Star, Meritorious Service Medal, Air Force Commendation Medal, Presidential Unit Citation, Air Force Outstanding Unit Award, Air Force Organizational Excellence Award, National Defense Service Medal, and Vietnam Service Medal.

Harris is married to Lieutenant Colonel Maurice A. Harris, a B-52 pilot who is leaving the Air Force to study law. Maurice Harris has said that his wife has "an innate ability to make people want to do more, to light a fire if there isn't one, and diffuse it if there is one." The Harrises have two children – a son, Steve, and a daughter, Tenecia.

What made you want to join the military?

First, I needed a job. And second, I was exposed to the army while traveling overseas my senior year in college. I was with a speech and drama company doing USO tours in Germany and France. Just being in a foreign country and traveling excited me.

Did you have a hard time adjusting to military life?

No. I don't know what people are looking for, why they think military life is different. The service is similar to the way I grew up. There's discipline all through your life, and I think that's good and healthy. Society needs discipline; otherwise, we would run all over each other.

What aspect of your work do you find most demanding?

People problems are the most demanding – helping people work through their personal problems. Getting some of them solved tends to take a lot of energy.

What are you most proud of having accomplished in the military?

I guess the feedback I get from inspection reports. Enjoying the excellent feedback when higher headquarters comes and takes a look at me or tests me and the folks who work for me. That has always been a high for me. We do a fantastic job! That's when I really feel good.

Could you describe a typical workday?

Most of my days are filled with meetings. The meetings aren't just informational. They are planning meetings, they are strategy meetings, and they are info meetings. Then we leave the meetings, and we put a lot of what we discussed into action. I also handle an average of two people situations a day, where people want to talk to me about something happening in their life or I want to talk to somebody about something they've done. It's a very active kind of day. If I'm not behind my desk, I'm on the go! Sometimes I like to take a moment out to relax and talk with people: see how they're doing, let them know that I'm here, and find out if everything is okay. My day is also filled with my family. I have to get my daughter to the sitter, who gets her on a bus to school. Later in the day I pick my daughter up from the sitter, and I prepare dinner at night or I buy dinner to go. I make sure my daughter has her homework completed, and I check it. My husband and I spend some time together, maybe watching television or talking or playing games. Then it's to bed after the 10:30 news.

Do you ever get tired of wearing a uniform?

No. It makes it so easy to know what you're going to wear the next day.

How do you deal with pressure?

I like pressure; it keeps me on my toes. But there are times when I have to get away from it. I'll take a vacation, or I'll take a day of leave and simply do nothing. I like to read. I also like the theater. I like to get lost in fictional people's lives – that's the way I get away from pressure.

Is there any other profession you would rather be pursuing?

No, not at this time in my life. I wouldn't mind being a CEO of some major corporation someday, but that would come later, after the military has finished with me.

Has it been difficult juggling a military career and a family?

Sure, it's been a challenge. It hasn't been difficult, but it has been a challenge — once I got over the fact that I wasn't supermom! Before that, I was constantly disappointed in myself for not having things right. After the change in self-image, things seemed to fall into place a lot better. I also have a pretty cooperative family. That makes it easy handling some of these challenges. I'm on the road a lot, constantly on trips. When I am home, I try to make sure that I spend time with my family instead of with other people. We've got a lot of folks we know, but we enjoy being alone and doing things together as a family.

Is there friction because you outrank your husband?

None at all. I don't have any rank with my husband, and my husband doesn't have any rank with me.

Have you experienced problems with soldiers who are unwilling to take orders from you because you are a woman?

I have some problems with insubordination, but I don't think it's because I am a woman or because I am black. I think it's the individual. They might say, "Are you giving me an order?" And I'll say, "Yes, I'm giving you an order!" Several times when I was a lieutenant, a couple of guys didn't want to salute. One of them even told me he was a soldier and he didn't have to salute women. I haven't had any problems involving enlisted men in years because of the grade and the position I have. I just don't run into that.

You don't think there is much discrimination in the military?

No, I didn't say that. I'm talking about me. I wouldn't say there is much. I would say there is some. It may be subtle; some of it may even be covert. A lot of it is people just being unaware of their actions. They don't really mean to be discriminatory or prejudiced. They just are unaware that their actions send that kind of a signal. But some folks, they really want to hurt you because of what they perceive you to be. I don't think it's a widespread malignancy in the Air Force or any of the other services. I think the services have done a pretty good job of making people aware. Also, they have pretty strong guidelines and some rules on how the service doesn't abide and will not condone that kind of activity.

Who were your role models?

My mother; my father; Colonel Webb Thompson, who got me into aircraft maintenance; General Paul Harvey; General Ken Tallman; and my husband,

Maurice. I have not been exposed to too many women. Most of my role models have been men.

What advice would you give someone interested in pursuing a career in the military?

I'd probably give this advice for any job: above all, believe in yourself; believe in God. Take advantage of anything that comes along. Never close a door. There are going to be a lot of doors closed, and you should never close a door on yourself.

What do you think accounts for your success?

Not going around thinking I'm successful! I'm after completing the task at hand. If doing that makes you successful, who's going to complain?

Geraldine Ferraro

Profession: Politician

Currently: Campaigning for the 1992 U.S. Senate election (New York)

Date of birth: August 26, 1935

Education: B.A., Marymount College, 1956 (English)
J.D., Fordham University Law School, 1960

Since her historic campaign in 1984 as the first woman vice-presidential candidate on a national party ticket, Geraldine Ferraro has continued to be active in the United States and abroad as a lecturer, teacher, author, and policy expert. Her vice-presidential candidacy highlighted a lifetime of political achievement. Ferraro served as a Democratic congresswoman from New York's ninth congressional District for three terms from 1979 to 1985. While she was in Congress, even her detractors recognized her as one of the best instinctive politicians on Capitol Hill.

While putting herself through law school at night, Ferraro taught elementary school in the New York public school system for four years. One week after passing the New York bar exam in 1960, she married real estate developer John Zaccaro. She chose to retain her maiden name for professional purposes in recognition of her mother's support and devotion. Between 1961 and 1974, while raising three children, Ferraro maintained a private law practice. In 1974, she went back to work full-time as an assistant district attorney in Queens County. Four years later, she quit her job to run for Congress.

In 1983, House speaker "Tip" O'Neill passed over party members with more seniority to appoint her to the powerful Budget Committee. Her appointment as chairwoman of the 1984 Democratic Platform Committee won her almost instant party prominence. The combination of being the first woman to hold that post and her success in skillfully steering through a consensus platform document generated much media exposure, which encouraged Walter Mondale, the leading contender for the party's presidential nomination to select her as his running mate.

Ferraro remains active in the political arena through her political action committee, Americans Concerned for Tomorrow. She is an active participant in foreign policy debate as a board member of the National Democratic Institute of International Affairs and as a member of the Council on Foreign Relations. She served two years as the founding president of the International Institute for Women's Political Leadership.

In 1985, Ferraro published her first book, *Ferraro: My Story,* and is currently working on a book dealing with the tension between the rights of the media under the First Amendment versus the rights of an individual to privacy under the Sixth Amendment.

Ferraro and her husband reside in Forest Hills, New York. They divide their leisure time between a beach house on Fire Island and a winter home in St. Croix.

What drew you into politics?

The recognition that it was a way to get things done. I was involved in politics before I became a politician. I became involved in politics when I was in law school. I would come home at night and help work on state senate campaigns. I would work in the Democratic headquarters, stuff envelopes, that type of thing. I did this because I felt that as a citizen I had a responsibility to help elect people who I believed were right on the issues. That is how I got involved politically.

How I got into office myself was that I had been working as a prosecutor and found that I didn't like a lot of things that were going on. The laws were there, and I had to follow the laws, but I didn't think some of the laws covered the things I cared about. There were insufficient shelters for people, and no provisions were made for those shelters. The law was inadequate in how it dealt with women who had been abused. It gave them no protection to go home. So I thought that although I was doing my job, and doing it well, if I got into a legislature, I could do it better and I could make a difference in people's lives.

What aspect of campaigning did you find most demanding?

When I ran, I totally immersed myself in a campaign. When I ran for Congress the first time in 1978, I began work at 6:30 in the morning. I would be at subway stops at that hour giving out literature, and I would work until nine, ten, eleven o'clock at night to do candidate forums or whatever anybody wanted me to do. I'd do that seven days a week. I found it totally consuming. I think that is probably the hardest part – the total immersion.

When I was doing the national campaign, we hit five states in one day. I actually campaigned more than Ronald Reagan and George Bush put together as far as the number of trips and mileage are concerned! I also campaigned more than Fritz [Mondale]. I would not only have my speeches prepared; I would go over them. I would make sure that I was comfortable with them. I would focus on the local issues as I flew from one state to the other so I was fully prepared before I got there. The tension of having to be so immersed was the toughest part of the campaign.

What do you think accounts for your success?

I give my mother full credit for my success because she always said, "You can do whatever you want to do. Be whatever you want to be. Just work hard. You've *got* to do it! Between the two of us, we'll do it. Whatever you need, we'll do." She *never once* turned around and said to me, "You can't do it because you are a girl" or "You can't do it." My mother always said, "You can!" The fact that I really believed in myself, because my mother believed in me, is possibly the major contribution to any success I have had.

Has it been difficult juggling a career and family?

Yes, it is much more difficult for a woman than for a man because it's an obligation. We are the primary people responsible for family. A lot of working women have it a lot tougher than I do. I didn't go back to work full-time until my youngest was in school full-time. The kids would leave at 7:30 A.M. I would go to work five minutes away from where I live, and I would work from nine to five, unless we were on trial. I didn't have to worry that my kids would be home by themselves because I had a full-time housekeeper. The kids also had two grandmothers who were both literally within a five-minute drive from the house. And I had the most cooperative of husbands. It was hard to do, but not impossible.

Have you experienced discrimination because you are a woman?

Yes! I didn't within my family. My mother certainly afforded me the same educational opportunities as my brother. My mother did, though, allow my brother to go out a little bit more than me. She was much stricter with me socially, but that is the Italian culture.

From the outside, I do think women, especially of my generation, were discriminated against. When I was applying to law school, I was asked if I was serious because I was taking a man's place. I was one of two women in my class. We experienced not so much discrimination as sexism from some of the professors in the way they assigned cases. We were always given rape and sodomy cases – that type of thing. One professor always gave women bad marks. After my freshman year, they changed the identification on tests from names to numbers. We would be assigned numbers and the women did extremely well after that.

In work, I was in a woman's profession when I first started out – I was a teacher – and I wasn't discriminated against there. But when I went into the practice of criminal law, there was a certain amount of discrimination because there are certain cases that women generally don't handle. In addition, I didn't get an equivalent salary to a lot of the guys, but when I was appointed bureau chief, I took a look at the salary schedule and found that most of the bureau chiefs were making $30,000 – I'm going back to 1977 – and I was making $21,000. I went to the D.A. and asked him, "Could you tell me why there is such a difference?" He said, "Dear, you have a husband." I said, "Don't they have wives? I'm leaving!" He raised me a couple of thousand, but I told him, "It's good enough for now, but I'm looking around for a job."

There was discrimination even when I ran for national office. I mean, you tell me why people said genetically I wasn't able to understand throw weights. Evidently, they thought genetically I wouldn't be able to be the commander in chief if I were called upon to do so. I was constantly tested: I was tested on my knowledge, tested on my strength, tested on my toughness, tested on my emotional stability, tested on my psychology – that permeated the 1984 campaign. I hope that I did show people that women can grasp the issues that face this country.

Who were your role models?

I had two. The first was Eleanor Roosevelt. I met her in 1961. I was a new lawyer, new bride, and was so impressed by the woman. I had followed everything she had done. I grew up knowing my president was Franklin Delano Roosevelt. She could have sat down – because financially she was secure – and said to the rest of the world, "Let my husband do his thing, and let me relax and do nothing." She didn't do that. From the time she was very young, she really participated. She continued caring about important issues in the world long after her husband was dead. She was a public figure – a public leader – in her own right, and I admired her tremendously.

My mother, the second role model, worked for everything she ever had. She came from a family that was very poor. She was unable to get a formal education that would have made her life easier, but she took what life gave her, made the best of it, and made sure that her children had better. She gave us confidence and instilled in us the feeling that we could make a difference, not just for ourselves, but for others.

Elizabeth Hanford Dole

Profession: Public Service

Currently: President, American Red Cross

Date of birth: July 20, 1936

Education: B.A., Duke University, 1958 (Political Science)
Postgraduate work, Oxford University, Summer 1959
M.A., Harvard University, 1960 (Government and Education)
J.D., Harvard University, 1965

$\mathcal{E}$ lizabeth Dole's tremendous achievements in public service lend cre-
dence to Helen Keller's keen observation that "one can never consent to
creep, when one has the impulse to soar." Because of her commitment and
extraordinary dedication, Dole enjoyed a steady stream of influential government positions. She was appointed a federal trade commissioner by Richard
Nixon, was the nation's longest-serving secretary of transportation ever under
Ronald Reagan, and was the secretary of labor under George Bush. Currently,
Dole is the first woman to serve as president of the American Red Cross. She
declined her first year's salary of $200,000, saying that "the best way I can let
volunteers know of their importance is to be one of them."

Dole is known as a skilled conciliator, who, with a combination of charm,
diplomacy, and determination, is able to forge alliances between opposing
groups. One admirer has observed, "Men tend to become chivalrous – rather
than threatened – in her presence." Reputed to be one of the most capable
and politically astute women in Washington, Dole has served under every
president from Lyndon Johnson to George Bush. During the era of Johnson's
Great Society, Dole was a Democrat. She became an independent in the
early 1970s, and then became a registered Republican about the time of her
marriage to Republican Senator Robert Dole in 1975.

A 1988 Gallup poll named Dole one of the world's ten most admired
women. She has received numerous awards for her achievements in
government, including the Arthur S. Flemming Award for Outstanding Government Service.

Often described as the "second most powerful couple" in Washington, the
Doles reside in the same Washington apartment Robert Dole occupied
before their marriage. Both are early risers and regularly put in twelve- to
fourteen-hour workdays.

What drew you to a career in government service?

I've always been interested in making a difference, a positive difference, in the
lives of others. Government service offers tremendous opportunities to make
that difference. For me, the most rewarding times in my government service
career were not spent in smoke-filled rooms exchanging political gossip.
Rather, they were in classrooms, listening to at-risk youth and teen mothers
who were turning their lives around; in fields, meeting with migrant workers
who needed a voice; and in far-flung corners of the world where people
needed help. The opportunity to devote myself to these causes on a full-time
basis is what led me to the Red Cross.

Has it ever been a disadvantage being a woman in public life?

Frances Perkins, that amazing New Yorker, who, as Franklin Roosevelt's secretary of labor, was the first woman to serve in a president's cabinet, was once asked that same question, and she answered, "Only when I am climbing trees." For far too long, the progress of women in public life was a bit like climbing trees—with many of the branches placed just out of reach. But the last few years, I think, have been especially good ones for women in American government. More and more, we're gaining the confidence to reach out, grab the branches, and pull ourselves up.

What aspect of your work do you find most demanding?

I don't think I can pick out any one part of my job and say it has been harder than the others. Certainly one of the most challenging aspects of being secretary of labor was trying to reach a consensus between people in management and those in labor, who often hold opposing points of view.

My goals at the Labor Department were to make the workplace safer, to help those who are less fortunate receive the skills necessary to survive and succeed in today's workplace, and to be sure that when American workers retire, they receive the pensions and security they earned. These are goals worth achieving and worth the time and effort it takes to bring opposing views together.

What do you think accounts for your success?

Trying to do the very best I can in whatever I do. I think having a wonderful family has helped, too. In addition to being married to Bob, I have a mother who is my best friend and who has a great deal of wisdom and common sense, and I had a father and a grandmother who taught me many valuable lessons. I also grew up with a wonderful brother whom I greatly admire and from whom I learned much. I did have the advantage of a fine education at Duke and Harvard universities and was able to spend a summer at Oxford in England in 1959. But I think I learned more important things from my mother than anyone else.

As a woman, have you ever experienced discrimination?

I can't help but think back to my days as a student at Harvard Law School. There were 550 members of the class of 1965, and only 24 were women. On the first day of class, a male student came up to me and asked what I was doing there. In what can only be described as tones of moral outrage, he said, "Don't you realize that there are men who would give their right arm to be in this law school—men who would use their legal education?" That man is now a senior partner in a Washington law firm. Every so often, I share this little story around town. You'd be amazed at the number of my male classmates who've called me to say, "Please tell me I'm not the one! Tell me I didn't say that, Elizabeth!" And you know what? I just let them wonder!

Nancy Kassebaum

Profession: Senator/Politician

Currently: U.S. Senator from Kansas

Date of birth: July 29, 1932

Education: B.A., University of Kansas, 1954 (Political Science)
M.A., University of Michigan, 1956 (Diplomatic History)

"To be a good senator," Nancy Landon Kassebaum assured her audiences on the campaign trail, "you need to be willing to listen and able to work with people." Kassebaum is known in the Senate as a coalition builder and an independent legislator who places principles above politics. She has served as a U.S. Senator from Kansas since 1978. Her election marked the first time in the history of the United States that a woman was elected to the Senate without being preceded by her husband. "While women have always had important things to say, we never had sufficient access to a forum," she notes. "Fortunately, that is changing."

For Kassebaum, politics was a family tradition. She was four years old when her father, Alf Landon, then governor of Kansas, challenged Franklin D. Roosevelt's bid for a second term as president. After graduate school, she married Philip Kassebaum, an attorney, and returned to Wichita, Kansas, where for the next two decades her life revolved around her husband and raising their four children on a farm near the town of Maize. During that period, she was vice president of Kassebaum Communications, a family-owned concern that operated several radio stations; served on the Kansas Governmental Ethics Commission and the Kansas Committee on the Humanities; and was elected to the local school board.

The end of her marriage was the critical event that led to her decision to enter politics. After legal separation from her husband, she accepted a post in Washington as a caseworker for Senator James Pearson of Kansas. When Senator Pearson chose not to seek reelection in 1978, Kassebaum threw her hat into the ring. Upon learning that she was going to seek office, her ex-husband, to whom she remains close, advised her, "You have to want it enough to have a gnawing in the pit of your stomach that won't let you sleep. If you have that, then you can put up with the strenuous campaign."

Presenting herself as a homemaker, the mother of four children, and the daughter of Alf Landon, Kassebaum ran on the slogan "A Fresh Face, A Trusted Kansas Name" and won the election. To a critic who accused her of riding into office on her father's coattails, she responded, "I can't think of any better coattails to ride on!"

A popular senator, Kassebaum has been elected to three terms. She is a member of the Foreign Relations Committee; Labor and Human Resources Committee; Banking, Housing, and Urban Affairs Committee; and Special Committee on Aging. She also is credited with orchestrating passage of the bill imposing economic sanctions against South Africa.

When she has free time, Kassebaum enjoys cooking, hiking, reading, and spending a lot of time in Kansas. One friend who knows her well says, "If she had a chance to go to Rome, Paris, Bangkok, or Topeka, she would choose Topeka."

What drew you to a career in politics?

I grew up in a political family because of my father's active involvement as a candidate when he was the Republican nominee for president in 1936. I had always heard and enjoyed political discussions around the dinner table, and I enjoyed history and following the issues of the day. I think it came from always having an active interest as a young person campaigning in the days when you could tack up campaign posters on telephone poles. I just enjoyed it. I never ever thought that I would be actively involved as a candidate myself. When my own children were younger, I used to take them door to door campaigning for candidates I was supporting.

What aspect of your work as a senator do you find most demanding?

The demands are so constant. It's hard even when you are at home or in recess because you are always, to a certain extent, on call. It's always hard to get away from it. I think it is important to set time aside so you can read or go to a movie, or when I am at home in Kansas, to be able to get to the farm. Those kinds of things are important for one's perspective.

My job is difficult because it requires almost constant attention. It's also hard to take complex issues and try to involve the public in sorting through them. Usually people get their information from television, and frequently it's a cursory look. It's very easy to have special-interest groups target their own constituency and focus on one part of a problem. I feel that on the whole, communication is a difficult part of my responsibility.

What gives you the most satisfaction?

I love working with issues and with people. I do a lot of campaigning. It's the part that I enjoy the most. I don't enjoy fund-raising. I really like to work with the issues, whether the issue is health care, child care, education, etc.

Could you describe a typical day?

I get up about 6:30 and read the papers thoroughly before I come to the office, which is usually between 9:00 and 9:30. I'm here until seven or eight o'clock at night. Then I take work home with me. I don't do receptions, and I don't really do much in the evening unless it is a small gathering or Kansas-related. During the course of the day, I see a large number of constituents – it is surprising how many are in town for one reason or another!

Do you want to be president of the United States?

No.

Definitely not?

(Laughter) Definitely not!

What does power mean to you in your job?

I suppose it is being able to have influence – whether it's on legislation or the ability to get something for your state. By that I mean being able to talk to people – encourage businesses to come to your state – and being able to play a role in developing the well-being of your state and its people.

When you became a senator, were your expectations fulfilled upon assuming office?

Yes, because I didn't expect a lot. I worked here one year as a staff member, so I understood a bit about the day-to-day work of the Senate. Sometimes it can be very slow; sometimes it can be extremely nitty-gritty work. There is not a lot of what some would think is particularly glamorous work. It is a lot of hard work. Yet I would not be here if I did not enjoy it. It's not something you are forced to do! (Laughter) You do it because you look forward to being involved in the political arena. I don't think one should come expecting to change the world.

Are there days when you wish you were in another profession where you didn't have to deal with constituents and didn't have any social or political obligations?

Sure! I have a farm that I love. I love to read – that's the best way I deal with pressure. I can just curl up and read a book. It takes my mind off the day-to-day issues.

For women, I think, there are different pressures. I have an elderly mother who isn't well, and I spend all my free time back home with her because someone has to be with her all the time. When I am there, I can help. I think taking care of younger children or aging parents is probably more the responsibility of women, even when they are working, than it is of men. I know I would never have undertaken running for public office if I had small children. I feel I couldn't have balanced all those demands. On the other hand, some women do it very well.

I always thought Carla Hills [U.S. Special Trade Representative] was exceptional because of the skill with which she managed so many things. Carla raised four children through all her active involvement. I used to marvel to hear her tell how she would get up at five in the morning to take one of her children to a swimming lesson. She always was fully involved with her family and yet very capable in her outside work. I really respect women who have been able to balance family and active careers.

Initially, as the only woman in the Senate, did you experience discrimination or feel you were not being taken seriously?

Sure. There still are times! But I never felt that you should dwell on it because that takes up a lot of energy in a destructive sort of way. The important thing is to just go on and prove that you do understand [the issues].

Who were your role models when you first entered politics?

It is hard to say because you have different ones as you go along. My mother encouraged me to run for the Senate, even though she didn't particularly care for politics. Both she and my mother-in-law were very supportive of my running for office, far more so than my father. I don't know that I had anyone who was necessarily a mentor at that moment.

I've always enjoyed biographies and have been tremendously impressed with various people through history. Abigail Adams was one such person. Someone who I think has extraordinary intellect, ability, and conviction is Helen Suzman, who has been a member of Parliament and a leader of her party in South Africa for many years. She just retired in 1990 and was an early leader against apartheid. I always greatly admired General George C. Marshall. He was someone who I thought showed extraordinary devotion, dedication, and integrity in the service of his country.

What are your thoughts on the best way to prepare for a career in politics?

I came in a little differently, but I think it's terribly important to have roots in your community. It's important to be active in community projects so you know how to work with people who want to achieve something for their community and where to go to try to do that – whether it's through local, state, or federal government. I think it's very important to have a background in history and an enjoyment of politics. Some people are able to be extraordinarily skillful politicians without enjoying working with people, but I think it is best when you can combine both. People in politics have to enjoy it, or they just don't last very long.

What do you think accounts for your success?

Oh, I've never analyzed it. I suppose it's being well prepared and being viewed by your colleagues as effective. Also, being viewed as objective is important to being effective in politics, so that when you speak on a subject, people will pay some attention and you can garner support from a broad base.

Law

Alice Young

Profession: Corporate Attorney

Currently: Partner, Milbank, Tweed, Hadley & McCloy

Date of birth: April 7, 1950

Education: B.A., Yale University, 1971 (Asian Studies)
J.D., Harvard Law School, 1974

$\mathcal{A}$lice Young brings to the practice of law a unique cross-cultural perspective. "The Asian influence has made me much more sensitive to the possibility that things can be interpreted a different way," she says. As a partner with the New York-based international law firm of Milbank, Tweed, Hadley & McCloy, Young heads up the Japan Corporate Group, where she has negotiated contracts and financing for some of Asia's largest companies. Her practice includes clients not only from Asia but also from the United States, Europe, and South America.

Young exudes the relaxed confidence of a woman who dares to set her own style. She wears strikingly original clothes and freely admits, "I've never been comfortable in the corporate suit nor willing to conform to it." It is this élan, combined with her solid educational background, ease in dealing with people, expertise in corporate law and international business transactions, and facility with languages, that persuaded the partners of the San Francisco law firm of Graham & James to offer a thirty-one-year-old associate not only a partnership but also the responsibility of opening and heading up their branch office in New York City. The office flourished under Young's guidance, and she remained there until 1987, when she was lured away by her current employer.

In addition to a thriving law practice, Young pursues her interests in international affairs and the arts as an active member of the Council on Foreign Relations and the Business Committee of the Metropolitan Museum of Art. She is secretary of the Japan Society and trustee of the Aspen Institute and the Harvard Law School Association of New York City. She is also on the board of directors of Yasuda Bank and Trust Company, making her the only woman on the board of directors of a Japanese bank.

Born in Washington, D.C., Young is the eldest daughter of Chinese diplomat parents who were in the United States when the Communists took over China in 1949. Her father changed careers and became a professor of history and sociolinguistics. Young currently resides in Montclair, New Jersey, with her husband, Thomas Shortall, an investment banker, and their two children.

Did you always want to be an attorney?

Absolutely not. When I graduated from college, it was a different era and we had the luxury of thinking about what we wanted to do to change the world. I had been considering two possibilities. One was going to graduate school in Asian history, which was something that intrigued me a great deal. But having both parents in academia, I wasn't sure I felt enough of a personal commitment to spend four and possibly more years getting a Ph.D. and then teaching. The other possibility was law. In a sense, it was a way to get a professional degree yet have three more years to think about what I wanted to do when I grew up. So it was less a burning desire to become a legal practitioner and more a way of postponing growing up for a few more years but still having something to show for it.

Why did you decide to become a corporate attorney?

That was a more difficult decision. When I was in law school, I worked for the Office of Civil Rights and reviewed the affirmative action programs of Harvard, Yale, Connecticut College, and several hospitals and other institutions that received federal contracts. I was really appalled at the lack of inclusion of minorities and women. Initially, I had a strong desire to do something that involved government work to try to effect social change. My work was eye-opening in that I realized what a tremendous amount of bureaucracy there was. You could have the best intentions in the world, but it would take a very long time to effect change. One particular job, in one particular government office, wasn't going to do that. I got a strong dose of reality.

Corporate law intrigued me, particularly international law. Although most of the international work at the time was Europe-related rather than Asia-related, I liked the idea of being able to use my interest in other cultures and my legal skills. I had a certain fascination with the business world because it wasn't something I was particularly familiar with. Also, there might have been a slight rebelliousness because my parents are academicians and did not have a great deal of respect for the business world or for lawyers. In Asia, lawyers were not regarded as highly as scholars.

What do you find most exciting and challenging about your work?

I really enjoy almost every aspect of it. It's nice to have to think on your feet; you can never rest on your laurels. There isn't any one right solution to most of the issues I deal with. They're not cut-and-dry, black-and-white, cookie-cutter transactions. You wake up in the morning, and you wonder what new twists in the deal will develop that day.

I feel very much a part of a moving, breathing practice that doesn't stand still. There is a tremendous challenge in that. You have to keep learning, and ultimately that's what's exciting about any work.

Do you hesitate in crossing the line between business and legal advice?

The nature of my practice is such that I probably wouldn't be a very effective lawyer if I advised only in the narrowest legal sense. Many of my clients are foreign clients who may not necessarily be new to business in the United States but bring with them a very different perspective on business. They seek my business advice and would feel they were not getting the full value if I merely responded to the narrowest of legal inquiries and didn't ask the questions that would provide a broader legal context, as well as a business context. The same is true of my U.S. clients who are doing business in Asia or Europe. Often, they are seeking not just a specific answer to a legal question but some sense of judgment as to what would work from a business and cultural point of view. Some wonderful legal solutions can fall flat because of cultural differences or because business practices are different.

Do you think the deals you've worked on could have been done without your involvement or your cross-cultural perspective?

I was able to negotiate in a way someone without my background or experience could not have. Although I think I have a very American approach, which is part of my background and law training, my Asian cultural background gives me flexibility in changing my negotiating style from deal to deal. I think bringing that different perspective and flexibility resulted in deals that probably worked better for both parties. Even in purely American deals, which I do as well, having a different perspective gives me a little bit of an advantage either in being able to come at it from a different approach – catch people by surprise in a positive way – or come up with something a little more creative, which I think in complex deals is important.

What do you think accounts for your success?

A lot of hard work. An ability to discern opportunities, to see where something might be done differently or better. Also, law is a service – a people business – and that's an aspect I've always enjoyed. I genuinely like my clients, want them to succeed, and find their businesses interesting. I think that shows.

What advice would you give someone interested in pursuing a career in the law?

I would say find a niche in an area you really enjoy, because I've seen too many lawyers who are very unhappy with the practice they're in. Law is an umbrella for a lot of different types of practices. I think it's very important to figure out what areas of interest you have outside the law and find a practice that combines them. Then I think you'll be happy with what you do. If you try to segregate what you do day in and day out in a law practice from what you are most interested in, then I think there's always going to be a tension.

Who were your role models?

There have been a lot of people whom I have looked up to, but not specifically in my profession. The support I've gotten has really been from women friends, both those who work outside the home and those who work full-time at home. I never had a mentor; but there have been a lot of people along the way who've been very helpful.

As a woman, have you experienced discrimination in your profession?

I would say yes. It was partly due to my age. When I was starting out in practice, I looked fairly young and there still weren't a whole lot of women in law. Therefore, I think I was taken less seriously than I would have been had I been a man. But, as time went by, it was harder to detect whether it was discrimination. Now, because of the area of practice I'm in and because I have some unique skills, it hasn't been an issue.

For years, I never had women clients, particularly when dealing with Asia. The only women who came to meetings were bringing in the tea or coffee. There were no women in senior management positions in Asia, unless they happened to be the daughter of the owner or had inherited ownership of a company. Now, however, certainly in the United States, a lot of investment bankers, CFOs, and senior executives are women. I think there's a tremendous camaraderie among us.

I still think there is a tremendous amount of discrimination. I don't think I have suffered from it as much because of my unique skills. In fact, it was an advantage being a woman at times. It's less and less true now, but there were times in my practice when I'd go to a cocktail reception and there would be maybe eight hundred men and two or three women. If you made a good impression as a lawyer, it was easier for people to remember you because you were a woman. That was an advantage for me in many instances.

How do you contend with the pulls of a demanding career and a growing family?

I don't really view them as in opposition but in terms of making choices and deciding priorities. It clearly forces you to decide what's important and what isn't. I've gotten rid of a lot of things that aren't as important as I thought they were at one point in my career. I probably attend fewer cocktail functions. I don't go for that one last client development project. I often remind myself of the adage, "No one on their deathbed has ever said I wish I had spent more time at the office." I honestly believe that part of my being a really good lawyer has been that I have had interests outside the law.

Coping with my children, I think, has forced me to be more mature than I otherwise would have been and has been invaluable in my learning to cope with my practice. So I don't view any of it as having to choose one or the other. It's always been trying to put everything in balance. My day-to-day law practice is very important to me. Of course, the care for one's family is a deeper emotional one. There is such an extraordinary joy in having my son say to me, "Mommy, please give me another hug." I don't know that I could ever duplicate the joy of giving birth to my children and then watching them grow as human beings.

I don't know whether you can have it all, but I'm trying very hard. (Laughter) It just becomes a matter of priorities: when you have a sick child and a meeting to attend, you go to the sick child. It's not so difficult to figure out what makes sense.

I also have other interests. I'm very involved in the Aspen Institute, a corporate think tank that tries to teach values to leaders in corporate America and globally, leaders who can tackle world issues, family issues, and environmental issues as well as company issues. I think that's very important. I have some involvement with the Metropolitan Museum. I'm very interested in foreign policy, so I've tried to be active in the Council on Foreign Relations. I really want to have a full and balanced life. I have a lot of friends, whom I'd like to keep forever. You can't keep friends if you never see them, so I try to keep in touch.

These are what's important to me. It's a difficult juggle. I don't want to diminish it as far as saying it's a snap or there's no problem to it. I deal with guilt and on occasion feel that I'm not doing anything right. I have those anxieties, but I think I've been able to keep in perspective what's important and what is less important.

Sandra Day O'Connor

Profession: Jurist

Currently: Associate Justice, U.S. Supreme Court

Date of birth: March 26, 1930

Education: B.A., Stanford University, 1950 (Economics)
L.L.B., Stanford University, 1952

$\mathcal{R}$onald Reagan described Sandra Day O'Connor as "a person of all seasons, possessing those unique qualities of temperament, fairness, intellectual capacity, and devotion to the public good which have characterized the 101 brethren who have preceded her." President Reagan named Sandra Day O'Connor to the Supreme Court on July 7, 1981, and the Senate unanimously confirmed her on September 22, 1981, making her the first woman ever to serve on the highest court of the land. O'Connor is described by friends and colleagues as both "warm and down-to-earth" and "reserved and self-contained." Her sister, Ann Femandez, says, "I've never seen her lose control, and I doubt anybody else has."

At Stanford Law School, O'Connor graduated third in a class that included William Rehnquist, the current chief justice of the Supreme Court, who ranked first. While an editor of the *Stanford Law Review,* she met her husband, John Jay O'Connor III, who was a year behind her at Stanford Law School. They were married soon after her graduation in 1952.

Seeking employment after law school, O'Connor interviewed with several law firms in San Francisco and Los Angeles, but none of them were ready to hire a female lawyer. One firm offered her a position as a legal secretary, but she opted instead for public service and worked as a county deputy attorney in San Mateo, California.

After her husband's graduation from law school, she accompanied him on a three-year tour of duty with the U.S. Army in Frankfurt, West Germany, where she worked as a civilian lawyer for the Quartermaster Corps. By 1957, the O'Connors were back in Phoenix, where the first of their three sons was born. O'Connor subsequently opened her own law firm and served as a member of many civic and local boards. She also worked on behalf of the Republican party.

When a seat in the Arizona Senate became available in 1969, Governor Jack Williams chose O'Connor to fill it. The following year, she campaigned for the same senate seat and won handily over her Democratic opponent. In 1972, she was elected majority leader, becoming the first woman to hold that office in any state senate in the country.

Toward the end of her second full term in the senate, O'Connor opted to move from the legislature to the judiciary. After a hardfought election, she won the position of Maricopa County Superior Court judge. Preferring law to politics, she resisted the urgings of Republican leaders to run against Democrat Bruce Babbitt in the 1978 gubernatorial election. The following year, Governor Babbitt selected O'Connor as his first appointee to the Arizona Court of Appeals.

An ardent exercise enthusiast, O'Connor organized a half-hour morning exercise class for women employees at the Supreme Court. Her son, Scott, relates that one of her favorite Christmas gifts is a set of golfing rain gear. "Her free time is so precious," Scott says, "that she's not going to let a little thing like rain get in the way." O'Connor also enjoys swimming, skiing, and tennis, as well as cooking gourmet meals. She relaxes with her husband and three sons at her parents' 155,000-acre Lazy B Ranch in southeastern Arizona.

What drew you to a career in law?

I took a class as an undergraduate at Stanford from an inspiring professor. He was a lawyer, and he showed how the law could serve society in beneficial ways.

What is most demanding about your work?

As a member of the nation's highest court, I am called upon to resolve some exceedingly difficult legal issues. There is never as much time as I would like to have to work on each case that we consider.

What do you think are important qualities for a judge?

Humanity, common sense, and integrity, among others.

What do you find most challenging about your work?

Trying to resolve some of the most difficult legal issues in our nation.

Could you describe a typical workday?

Workdays are very long and are spent mostly reading and writing. It is rather like an academic life.

What do you think accounts for your success?

I have been fortunate to be at the right place at the right time. I also have tried to do the best I could with each job, without regard for monetary reward.

How do you deal with pressure?

I try to analyze each case and problem as it comes and to make decisions based on careful study and preparation. Then I do not look back and second-guess that decision. Instead, I go on to the next problem.

When you were raising a family, how did you manage to pursue a career?

It was never easy. We tried to keep our children active and busy after school and on holidays. There wasn't any "Miller time!"

If you unexpectedly had the day off from a busy work schedule, how would you spend it?

In an active outdoor sport such as tennis, golf or skiing.

What do you think accounts for the greater acceptance of women professionals compared to when you graduated from Stanford Law School?

Gradually, public perceptions concerning the role of women began to change. It was the result of strong advocacy and government and private action to raise the public consciousness.

Is there any other profession you would rather be pursuing?

Absolutely not.

Elizabeth Watson

Profession: Police Officer

Currently: Chief of Police, Houston

Date of birth: August 25, 1950

Education: B.S., Texas Tech University, 1971 (Psychology)

E lizabeth Watson, a seventeen-year Houston Police Department veteran, is the first woman to head a police department of one of America's ten largest cities. As Houston's chief of police, Watson commands a force of four thousand police officers, 10 percent of whom are women. When she joined the force in the early seventies as a rookie, Watson was told to sew her own uniform because uniforms were only issued to men. Today she is so widely praised that she has joked, "Nobody could be as good as I sound." During her career, Watson has been involved in virtually every aspect of law enforcement.

Watson's father, a NASA aerospace physicist, encouraged his daughter, who was shy as a child, to speak up in class. He would tell her, "You are as smart and talented as anyone you will ever meet." Her younger sister, also in police work, was the first woman captain of the Harris County (Texas) Sheriff's Department. Watson's husband, Robert, is a sergeant in the Houston Police Department. They have three young children. On more than one occasion, her ten-year-old daughter has urged, "Now, Momma, tell the Mayor you have to get home tonight because we need to talk."

What drew you to a career in police work?

Actually, it was a recommendation from my mother, whose father and brothers were police officers in Philadelphia. She suggested that I might find police work interesting. Quite frankly, I disagreed with her that it was any kind of job for me to get into. Nevertheless, I was in the job market, so I thought I'd try it for a little while until I could find something more suitable. But once I got into it, I liked it.

What was your family's reaction when you were appointed chief of police?

My mother and one of my sisters were very concerned about my taking a job that was so high profile, so difficult; where there would be so much criticism, not of me personally, but just because of the position itself. They wanted me to do it, but they were reluctant to be adamantly supportive. Everyone else – my husband and my other brothers and sisters – said, "Go for it."

What do you find most challenging about your work?

The most challenging aspect is trying to reach so many audiences, trying to be everything to everybody. I think balancing the profession – the career aspect – with the home life is a full-time job. Trying to meet all the various demands is very difficult. The public, the city council, the community, and the people in the department all need a piece of me, and, of course, I travel.

How do you deal with job stress?

I have a newborn, and I find that going home at the end of the day and rocking him is a great way to put things in perspective.

Are you able to leave work behind when you go home?

Definitely! I don't have a choice. When I go home, I have a baby, a five-year-old, a ten-year-old, and, of course, my husband. It's not a matter of consciously doing it; I just don't have another choice.

Has there been a rise in police brutality in the United States?

I think all police departments at this particular point in time are reverberating from the Los Angeles incident where a motorist was beaten by police officers. There is a negative perception of police, and sometimes perception becomes reality. I am not aware of statistics that would suggest that there is an increase in police brutality. Our own number of complaints against officers is down. For the last year, we had only four instances of excessive force that would meet federal guidelines in terms of what the attorney general would be looking at, and those were not committed by police officers. They were committed by nonclassified personnel, such as we have working in the jails.

One of the things that is important to understand is that every department has a different definition of brutality, which in police terminology is called excessive force. In Houston, excessive force is any act that causes discomfort, whether or not there is apparent physical injury. If a person complains that he was mistreated, we call it excessive force. Our own definition is very broad because we take it very seriously. When we find an instance of excessive force, we terminate employment. We do not think there are degrees of excessive force. If a person abuses, we don't need him or her. That's the position management takes. I think it's not quite accurate to say that there is an increase in excessive force. I can remember the riots of the sixties, and then there was a period in the seventies when there were rampant claims of brutality. I don't think we're seeing that now.

Do you think the danger of police work combined with a relatively modest salary has deterred qualified candidates from joining the force?

Yes, I do. I think that the policing profession is not viewed by many as a profession but rather as a job. Indeed, I had a conversation with one leader in the Hispanic community who was talking to me about the issue of education. He said, "You really need to drop your educational requirements because if there is a Hispanic who has some college education, he's going to want to be something more than a cop." As soon as he said it, of course, he knew it wasn't exactly the right thing to tell me! But nevertheless, I think that's the sentiment. I think he blurted that out because that is what people feel: if you really have talent, education, and intelligence, there ought to be something else to do. Why risk so much for so little?

In recruiting for the force, what do you look for in a candidate?

We have a rather extensive screening capacity. We look for a minimum of two years of college education. We look for people who have an interest in community service. We put candidates through a psychological screening, both before they enter the academy and before they are able to graduate, so we can be sure that we have a person who is psychologically suited to dealing with people in a compassionate way. It's a difficult thing to determine, but we do the best that we can. We're looking for people who are bright, who are service-oriented, and who are creative.

What advice would you give someone interested in pursuing a career in the police force?

Go for it! I think it is one of the rare occupations that provides an almost endless array of opportunities for personal growth. There are so many different aspects. When you think about policing, you probably think about the uniformed officer in the patrol car, but we have helicopters, mounted patrol, canine officers, investigators, and officers who are involved in planning, computer programming, and teaching. Not too many occupations have so many different facets.

As a woman, have you ever experienced discrimination in your profession?

I would say there have certainly been instances where I received treatment that was as a result of my gender. Discrimination has a negative connotation, but it is not always negative. When a person is singled out because of gender, it may be positive or negative. I've had both. I have had opportunities to work in some places that were very coveted because I was a female. They were looking for a female, and there were relatively few of us. On the other hand, I've had to work on assignments that I didn't want because I was a woman. So I would say, on balance, it works both ways.

Have you encountered much insubordination from male officers?

No, not at all. They are very respectful.

Has it been difficult juggling a career and a family?

Difficult, yes. I would say less difficult than it might have been if I didn't have a very supportive family. My husband is very supportive. I also have brothers and sisters who live very close to me geographically and are able to help out when my schedule gets too demanding.

What person or persons have made a difference in your life?

When I am confronted with situations that are difficult, I would say that my father and mother are probably paramount. I try to reflect on what my father might have told me either unconsciously, subconsciously, or consciously. I find that helps me a lot. From a professional standpoint, I rely very heavily on people in the profession who really made a contribution. Lee Brown, my predecessor as chief, who is now commissioner of New York City, was really a mentor for me. I learned a lot from him, and I still call to consult with him.

What do you think accounts for your success?

I think that I have certainly been very fortunate and have had a lot of good luck. I never expected to achieve the position I now hold. I viewed each position as though it were going to be where I would be spending the rest of my career. So I worked very hard to be the best that I could be in each position. One of the unexpected benefits was that others noticed my efforts.

Science
and
Medicine

Jacqueline K. Barton

Profession: Chemist

Currently: Professor of chemistry, California Institute of Technology

Date of birth: May 7, 1952

Education: B.A., Barnard College, 1974 (Chemistry)
Ph.D., Columbia University, 1979 (Inorganic Chemistry)

$\mathcal{I}$n 1988, Jacqueline Barton became the only woman ever to receive the prestigious American Chemical Society Prize in pure chemistry. It has been said that "the results of her work are so tiny they can't even be seen under a microscope. But in the world of chemistry, Barton's achievements are far from small." By designing molecules that communicate with DNA, Barton has opened new vistas in science that may one day lead to more effective disease treatment.

Barton is an inspiring teacher who is able to communicate her passion for science to her students. While at Columbia University, Barton was a National Science Foundation (NSF) predoctoral fellow and studied platinum chemistry. Thereafter, as a National Institute of Health postdoctoral fellow, she studied biophysics at Bell Laboratories and Yale University. Barton then became an assistant professor of chemistry and biochemistry at Hunter College, City University of New York. In 1983, she returned to Columbia and three years later became a professor of chemistry and biological sciences. In the fall of 1989, she assumed her current position at the California Institute of Technology (Caltech).

Barton has been the recipient of some of the most coveted awards in her field, including the Harold Lamport Award in Biophysics from the New York Academy of Sciences; the Alan T. Waterman Award from the NSF, awarded to the outstanding young scientist in the United States; the National Fresenius Award; and the American Chemical Society's Eli Lilly Award in Biological Chemistry. In 1991, she was awarded a MacArthur Foundation fellowship.

Jacqueline Barton is married to Peter Dervan, a professor of chemistry at Caltech. They have one daughter.

What drew you to a career in chemistry?

As a young girl, I wasn't exposed much to science, but mathematics always fascinated me. I thought it was fun. When I continued into college mathematics, it had a certain abstract quality. But when I started studying chemistry, I discovered that this was one way of combining the abstract and the real. What really made a difference for me was getting into a laboratory, seeing the reaction happen, seeing things change colors, and trying to understand what was happening on a molecular level.

What do you think is the most common misconception about chemistry?

That it is difficult. It is not. I think part of the problem and part of the challenge is to get past the boring stuff and give students, at a much earlier age, a feel for what we do as chemists. You can go through training in chemistry as an undergraduate at the best colleges in the country and not know what chemists actually work on, what passions drive us, what we study. I think we have been remiss in not getting that excitement across to people.

What do you find most challenging about your work?

It's challenging on all levels. It's challenging to try to help young scientists develop and to achieve specific ends in research. It's incredibly challenging to work as a team and to try to design a molecule to do something, then see whether or not it does it. The work I'm involved in – designing molecules that look at DNA structures – is very exciting.

When you go to the lab to do research, is there a sense of excitement that "today I might make an important discovery"? Or is lab work not that spontaneous?

The next new result is always exciting, but when you get the next result, you don't have a sense that it's over, you have done it. The wonderful and addictive and fascinating thing about this process is that when you get to a result, it comes with another question, and it makes you want to probe further and ask the next question, do the next experiment. It's incremental information. We're always learning something, and we try to design a framework that will teach us something no matter what the result. Sometimes you go in with one point of view, and you're totally surprised with what you find. Then you really learn something!

What is it like to learn something totally new?

There isn't another high like it! That's what makes you want to do the next experiment. That's what makes you want to learn more and discover more.

Is chemistry more of a collaborative effort or more of an individual pursuit?

I have a research group of about twenty men and women. Some are graduate students working toward their Ph.D.'s; others already have their Ph.D.'s and want to learn more. In some respects, we all function together. Our overall goals are the same. The questions we are addressing are the same. But everyone has his or her own individual project. So we're all solving different aspects of the same puzzle.

In my lab, we do a mix of different kinds of chemistries: inorganic chemistry, synthetic chemistry, and a little bit of physical chemistry and biochemistry. We also interact with biologists and physical chemists. In that respect, it's collaborative in that we take advantage of all the information that's available to us and interface with different disciplines.

Has it been difficult juggling a career and family?

It is difficult. My life has changed a lot recently. A couple of years ago, I remarried. My husband is a chemistry professor at Caltech, and we just had a child. I can't imagine having a child at a younger age when you are coming up in the ranks. It's a constant juggle.

Have you ever considered leaving the academic world to become a scientist/ entrepreneur?

Never. Teaching is very much a part of what I do and who I am.

What do you think accounts for your success?

Perseverance, creativity, curiosity, and luck. I also work very hard. The pursuit of excellence and doing it right are important to me.

As a woman, have you ever been discriminated against in your profession?

No. When I look at my role models – women chemists of an older generation – they all have stories to tell about how they were discriminated against. The good news is that I don't have a story to tell.

Who were your role models?

Bernice Segal was my teacher of chemistry in undergraduate school at Barnard College. She was an absolutely fantastic teacher. Now, being a teacher myself, I appreciate her all the more. She was a tough lady, wouldn't take no for an answer, and expected nothing less than your total commitment. She scared the hell out of you if you didn't do it right. I have tremendous respect and admiration for her. She was one of my first role models.

What advice would you give someone interested in pursuing a career in chemistry?

Go for it, and enjoy it. Chemistry is fun, and whatever you are going to do, you have to have fun. If it's fun, you will become involved in it, immersed in it, and dwell on it. To have a career in chemistry, you have to be committed. Chemistry also requires a concern for excellence.

What are you most proud of having achieved?

I feel very good about the recognition I've received from the chemistry community. Based partly on the work in my lab, we're reaching the point where a woman can be considered a good chemist, not just a good woman chemist. In terms of the work we're doing, I feel very proud of having brought the tools and techniques of inorganic chemistry to bear on the study of DNA and RNA structures. I feel good about melding the techniques of one discipline together and trying to understand, probe, and in some respects, broaden inorganic chemistry.

Marianne Ruth Neifert

Profession: Pediatrician

Currently: Medical Director, Lactation Program at Women's and Children's
   Hospital, Presbyterian/St. Luke's Medical Center (Denver)

Date of birth: January 10, 1948

Education: B.A., University of Hawaii, 1968 (Chemistry)
   M.D., University of Colorado School of Medicine, 1972

$\mathcal{M}$ arianne Neifert is pediatrician at Presbyterian/St. Luke's Medical Center in Denver, mother of five children, and author of a monthly medical column for *McCall's* magazine titled "Ask Dr. Mom." Her field of professional interest is the physiology and clinical management of lactation. As the medical director of the Lactation Program at Women's and Children's Hospital, she has received numerous grants to conduct research, published extensively, and received wide recognition as one of the foremost experts in her field. She is also an associate clinical professor of pediatrics at the University of Colorado School of Medicine.

Neifert's other activities include working as medical director of the Mothers' Milk Bank of Denver, and serving as a member of the Professional Advisory Board of La Leche League International, an ad hoc reviewer for the *American Journal of Diseases of Children* and *Pediatrics,* and an executive board member of A Chronicle on Drug Abuse.

In 1984, Neifert was named one of the Outstanding Young Working Women of America by *Glamour* magazine. She coauthored the child care book *Dr. Mom: A Guide to Baby and Child Care* and coedited the medical textbook *Lactation: Physiology, Nutrition, and Breast-Feeding.* Her most recent book is *Dr. Mom's Parenting Guide,* published in 1991. Neifert's husband, Larry, is a management consultant and conducts management seminars for businesses.

What drew you to a career in medicine?

There is no doubt that part of the attraction was the academic challenge. I was always a good student and medicine was an area that was a definite academic challenge. And it was nontraditional for women. From the time I was a little girl, I just knew that I wanted to break some of those barriers. I didn't want anything to be denied me because I was a girl. I was from that generation where if you were interested in medicine and you were a girl, you became a nurse. A part of me wanted to do the nontraditional thing. I also was very interested in people's welfare. I was one of five siblings – the middle child – and I was always the one who took care of family members when they were sick.

Why did you decide to become a pediatrician?

I became a parent at a young age. I married at eighteen and had my first baby at twenty. My son was six months old when I started medical school. From the moment I became a parent, I was a changed person, particularly beginning my second year of medical school. We started doing some clinical rotations, and I remember being at the hospital and rotating through pediatrics.

Immediately it was clear that, because I was a parent, I had extra insights and was drawn to the topic. I think from that time on, I knew pediatrics was the area where I could make the biggest contribution, and it certainly held a tremendous interest for me.

What aspect of your work do you find most challenging?

There are so many challenges. It's somewhere between being exciting and being overwhelming! I'm involved in various aspects of medicine. I find unique challenges in all of them. I first think in terms of interpersonal relationships, which is a big part of clinical medicine. I consider it always to be a challenge to be nonjudgmental. In medicine, you meet all kinds of people with personal needs and hurts. One of the hardest parts is seeing them and their problems without bringing your own background of biases and judgments to bear, helping them without clouding the picture by judging how you would react in a certain situation.

I also participate in research. I think clinical research, for me, has been the most humbling aspect of medicine. I definitely find research to be challenging. You have to keep an open mind and see the data in an objective manner. You have to accept how difficult research can be when you design a study and imagine how it's going to go, then every possible thing that can go wrong does.

When I went into medicine, I had this fantasy that you could study hard enough and learn everything. I was used to getting a perfect score on an exam and knowing all the answers. It was such a shock to get into medicine and realize you can't know all the answers; you may not be able to make a diagnosis; you may feel impotent and not sure how to help somebody. I was unprepared for the reality of knowing you can't always cure and you have to do the best you can and just provide comfort sometimes.

Obviously, in pediatrics, one of the most heart-wrenching things is to have to work with families that have life-threatening problems with a child, a baby who dies, or a baby who's handicapped. We always think of medicine as making people well and sending them out with a smile on their face. But a big part of medicine is helping people adjust to situations that can't be changed: their baby might be mentally retarded; their child might be dying of cancer. I think many people in medicine withdraw their emotions because it is so painful. Yet it is at these times that people need to know you care. Even if you can't physically change the reality of their particular crisis, you have to hang in there with them.

How do you deal with pressure?

One of the things I tend to do with pressure is to focus on the thing that I perceive to be the biggest crisis at the moment. I'm not saying that is the best way to deal with pressure, but it's a way that has worked for me. Essentially, I deal with the thing that is due first. That works well, except for long-term projects like writing a book. Pacing myself for long-term projects has been an issue that I've had to struggle with. It also helps to put things in perspective, to periodically ask myself, "Will this thing that is creating so much pressure matter a year from now?" Trying to distinguish the urgent from the important is a constant issue for me.

How do you relax?

I don't relax very well! (Laughter) I have some outlets that mean a lot to me. I'm very involved in my church. I teach a Sunday school class, and I'm involved in Bible study. Once a year, our family takes a family vacation, which is a wonderful time to refuel and reenergize. We go on a camping trip. There are no phones and no beepers. Nobody can reach me. All the children come, and they bring their friends. It's quite a tradition. I find that very relaxing. Also, I like to read and talk with my family and extended family on the telephone. I have a corporate-level phone bill! Three of my kids are long distance now, but I just love to talk with them, and that's relaxing for me.

Could you describe a typical workday?

A typical workday for me is very atypical. There really is no routine. I think that is partly a reflection of the fact that I like to shift gears from time to time. I am not in a traditional pediatric practice. I don't arrive in the morning and have patients scheduled every fifteen minutes throughout the day. I am in a unique program.

As a pediatrician, I became quite interested in breast-feeding, and during my training in the early seventies, breast-feeding began to increase in popularity. It had been at an all-time low for some decades. Now it is again, you might say, a community norm. But there remains a huge gap in the knowledge of health professionals. The clinic that I'm in sees women and babies who are referred to us for problems with breast-feeding. Our clinic also conducts several breast-feeding research projects. In the course of a day, we might look at data, work with subjects, or work on the design of a new research project. A typical day would also involve writing and submitting grants or planning ahead to find another funding source to apply to. We also train health professionals, so we may have a nurse or a physician from another state rotating through our clinic to gain firsthand experience in solving breast-feeding problems.

I also do a lot of writing and speaking. During the day, I might be putting a slide show together, going down to Children's Hospital to talk with the residents about breast-feeding, speaking to nurses, or giving a parent talk at a community function. To be honest, a typical day also would involve at least three phone calls from my kids. They tend to perceive me as always available to them, which is something I've tried to cultivate, since I've been gone from them so much.

What personal qualities are most valuable to you in your profession?

I think I have good people skills. I have been blessed with a lot of empathy for people. I'm a good listener. Parents, particularly women, perceive me as someone who understands their parenting struggle. I think where I've made my mark in pediatrics is by supporting parents, which enables them to give their very best to their child. I help children indirectly by helping their parents.

I am lucky to have a high energy level. I can get by on little sleep for long periods of time, and I'm pretty enthusiastic. Another important quality is the willingness to take risks, which is something I've had to work on all my life: the willingness to get outside my comfort zone, to stretch, to fail, to pull myself up and try again. There is a saying: "Successful people are willing to do that which unsuccessful people are not willing to do." I think that applies to me.

What advice would you give someone interested in pursuing a career in the medical profession?

Well, I would give several pieces of advice. The first comes from Winston Churchill. During the war, he gave a graduation speech at the boys' school he had attended years earlier, and he simply said, "Never give up. Never give up. Never give up. Never, never give up." I say that to any woman who wants to go into the field of medicine. There are so many qualified women who could make such wonderful contributions, but because of one little setback, they abandon their medical careers. I see this all the time. Women take the medical college admissions test during the last year of college, and if they get low scores, they just walk away from medicine. My advice is don't walk away. Take the study courses. Do whatever it takes to raise your score. Don't let one setback discourage you. Persevere and have willpower. Get the support and help you need to reach your goal. Never give up.

Also, we need to get rid of all our stereotypes about medicine. You don't have to be Marcus Welby or Ben Casey. There are so many ways to make a contribution in medicine. Don't get locked into a stereotype. Don't say, "I can't be in medicine and have a family or be a well-rounded person." Emphasize your personal attributes; you will be amazed at the unique way you can make a contribution.

Has it been difficult juggling a career and a family?

I would be dishonest if I said it wasn't difficult, but the rewards outweigh the difficulties. I would not have been willing to forgo having a family. My family means a great deal to me. Difficult is not the right word. When I think about the word juggling, it has such important imagery when you visualize what you have to do. There is always some aspect of your life that's up in the air — very vulnerable, very precarious — and could come crashing down at any moment. You have to focus from time to time on a child's needs, a marriage's needs, a career's needs. I think it's largely a triage system. Luckily, needs come in and out of focus. One moment a family issue is most pressing; another moment your career is at a dangerous turn or you have a crisis at hand. The challenge is not to be lulled into believing that everything at work is always a crisis, your family will always be there for you, or you'll have time for your children another day.

My message to young women coming up in the ranks is this: "If you don't put your family first, nobody else in your profession is going to put your family first for you. There will always be pressures to drop your family to take care of a work-related crisis. But if you're not careful, that can string out into a lifelong pattern of putting your career ahead of your family. Don't take your family for granted." I am so fortunate. I've been married twenty-five years, and I had five children in a span of seven years. I don't for a minute take my family for granted. A lot of it has involved shifting gears and turning to whoever seemed to be the neediest at the moment. Juggle is a very good word.

Also, I have a husband who let me do nontraditional things before that was fashionable. My husband deserves a lot of credit for being tolerant and supportive. Even in terms of my children's support, there were many times when they could have said, "Why aren't you there for us?" Instead, they always focused on how proud they were to have a mother who was a doctor and who was making a contribution. In fact, they tended to overglamorize the things I did.

As a woman, have you experienced discrimination in your profession?

I experienced discrimination at two points in my career. First, when I was applying to medical school. I got in, but, looking back, no medical school admissions committee today would be allowed to make decisions based on the information they used in 1968. I graduated from college in three years. I practically had a four-point grade average. It never occurred to me that I wouldn't get accepted to medical school. When I applied, I was married and pregnant, and my husband was serving in the Vietnam War. The committee wanted me to wait until my husband came back from the war to see how we did with the baby. They encouraged me to postpone going to medical school another year. Everything worked out in the end, but I do feel that was clearly discrimination, because their advice was based on the fact that I was a woman, I was pregnant, and they doubted I could juggle a family and medical school.

The second time I was discriminated against was more painful. I was in academic medicine for ten years – 1975 to 1985 – and I absolutely loved my job as a faculty member in the Department of Pediatrics. But in retrospect, there were clear differences in my mind between what happened to junior female faculty and what happened to junior male faculty. I had a definite lack of mentorship. I feel I was pigeonholed in low-level positions. I was viewed more as a drone. That was a sad thing for me. I had the privilege of being a role model for others and being a medical student adviser. I think I made an important contribution, but there were disappointments, and I think that was largely due to the lack of mentorship.

Today almost all women medical faculty are in junior-level positions. Very few get tenure or full professorships. I think we have a few more years to go before we achieve equality in academic medicine. Little by little, I think we can make these changes in academic settings, but I think that's one of the final places for parity in medicine that needs to be tackled.

Who were your role models?

I had a lot of role models. The difference between a role model and a mentor is you choose a role model and a mentor chooses you. I had lots of role models, but I lacked mentors who invested in me.

My parents were role models and mentors. They had five children. My mother was a schoolteacher. My father was a tremendous Mr. Mom way back when nobody was doing that. I wouldn't ever have dared to try to juggle a large family and a career without having seen them do it successfully.

There were two male physicians who I think were exemplary role models. They modeled professionally and personally what I wanted to be as a doctor. One was the late C. Henry Kempe, who was a pediatrician and chairman of the Department of Pediatrics at the University of Colorado School of Medicine when I was a medical student there. The other, Watson A. Bowes, Jr., was a faculty member in the Department of Obstetrics and Gynecology, and he is now at Chapel Hill, North Carolina. He represented what I wanted to be as a clinician and as a person. He has such integrity and such generous personal qualities.

As a woman, I think of people such as Eleanor Roosevelt. She meant a lot to me. She was a strong woman who was able to make an impact, be heard, and say what was on her mind.

Antonia C. Novello

Profession: Physician

Currently: Surgeon General of the United States

Date of birth: August 23, 1944

Education: B.S., University of Puerto Rico, 1965 (premed)
M.D., University of Puerto Rico, 1970
M.P.H., Johns Hopkins University, 1982

$\mathcal{A}$dministrator, researcher, lecturer, and author, Antonia Novello is first and foremost a physician. Her motto – "Good science and good sense" – sums up what she brings to her position as the nation's surgeon general.

Novello was sworn in as the fourteenth surgeon general of the U.S. Public Health Service by Supreme Court justice Sandra Day O'Connor on March 9, 1990. The historic White House event, attended by President George Bush, marked two firsts: Novello became the first woman and the first Hispanic to hold the position. As surgeon general, Novello advises the public on health matters such as smoking, AIDS, diet and nutrition, environmental health hazards, and the importance of immunization and disease prevention. She also oversees the more than five thousand members of the Public Health Service Commissioned Corps.

Novello entered the U.S. Public Health Service in 1978 after working in the private practice of pediatrics and nephrology (a branch of medicine concerned with the kidneys). She worked at the National Institute of Health, where she served in various capacities. She is also a clinical professor of pediatrics at Georgetown University School of Medicine and the Uniformed Services University of the Health Sciences. She is the author of numerous scientific articles pertaining to pediatrics, nephrology, and public health policy. Novello was the first woman president of the Pan American Medical Society.

As a child growing up in Puerto Rico, she was afflicted with a congenital malformation of the large intestine that left her weak and needing frequent surgery. The condition was not corrected until she was eighteen. Her father died when she was eight, and her mother supported the family as a school principal.

Novello's husband, Joseph, is a psychiatrist and medical journalist.

How do you handle the stress that comes with being surgeon general of the United States?

If I hadn't been married for twenty-one years to a wonderful man, it could be a lot more stressful than it is. Also, my husband is a psychiatrist. (Laughter) One thing is certain: a supportive family is very important in handling the stress of the office, because you can never leave the office behind. What is also helpful for me is that in addition to being a psychiatrist, my husband is a media doctor and journalist. I never had to deal with the media before, so it's wonderful having a husband who knows how to handle it.

I must also say that a lot of the pressure comes from the demands I put on myself. I believe it is important that I see and touch as many people as I can. Maybe, because I am a woman and a minority, many problems are attached to my office that other surgeon generals would consider incidental rather than of deep concern.

What issues in particular are you alluding to?

The issue of minorities and the issue of women. I take them very seriously. Whether it is a reality or not, I believe that how I handle this job will determine whether I open or close doors for many other people who will follow me. Whatever I say or do will be judged not only for what Antonia Novello said or did but also for what the woman surgeon general who is also Hispanic said or did.

There is a lot of work to be done. Many people in America don't know that the surgeon general is female and Hispanic. But through the work of this Hispanic surgeon general and the fact that I represent all Americans, they will realize that it is not unreasonable to give jobs of this visibility to someone who in another time would never have had this opportunity. So I really do put a lot of effort into making sure that my speech is good, that I deliver it the best way I can, and that when I mix with people, I have one-on-one contact with as many of them as possible so they realize that behind this job is a woman who listens to their concerns and feels with them. Every time I take even one little step in that direction, I feel rewarded.

What is your mandate as surgeon general?

The role of the surgeon general is to be the voice of the people on health issues. I see my role as that of an ombudsman, the person who brings what people need and want to the attention of policymakers. The surgeon general walks a very fine line between the needs of the people and the needs of the government. As the speaker for both sides, you have to make sure you understand the issues on both sides and try to make each side understand the other. My role is that of an independent broker and an ombudsman of care. Being the voice of the people can be quite daunting.

What aspect of your work do you find most challenging?

The greatest challenge is the knowledge that I represent the people, most of whom I may never see face-to-face. I have to learn to see through their eyes and truly understand their health needs. Most importantly, I must speak to them in a way that helps them understand that even though the things they might want are not likely to be obtainable, I tried to accomplish these things for them.

Having lived with a chronic illness until adulthood, has that affected your outlook?

First of all, it made me want to become a doctor. Secondly, it really brought home the fact that despite the best medicine and the best doctors, some patients fall through the cracks. I truly believe I was one of them. It convinced me that one has to take charge of one's own life and health without expecting somebody else to be wholly responsible.

Is that your main message as surgeon general?

My message is that nothing is impossible. Someday, when I am able to talk in depth about all the things that happened during the first eighteen years of my life, people will realize that if I made it, anybody can. That is why sometimes I feel a little impatient with people who use illness as an excuse for failure. I am not criticizing others for not accomplishing what I did. I am only saying that I know what it is like to go through a lot of pain and still reach one's goals.

Why did you decide to become a pediatrician?

It was because I was such a sick child and my pediatrician was a very nice human being. I bet you would find that a lot of doctors end up practicing in areas of medicine in which they or a family member had experience as a patient – either positive or negative, but especially if they were treated well. Pediatrics represented such an area for me.

Why did you give up your pediatric practice to go into public health?

After being on call every other night every other week, and after paying all my bills, I made about $7,000 after a full year in practice. I was very uncomfortable charging patients, and that discomfort was quite obvious in the total billings at the end of the year. But that was not the big issue. The issue was that I felt the practice of pediatrics, confined as it is to one patient at a time, was not the best way to help many. That was why public health became such a challenge. Also, because I am a nephrologist, I realized that in the practice of medicine, the government has a lot to say and do. I felt the time had come for me to find out how the government had an influence on my life and in turn how I could make a difference in a lot of other people's lives. That's when I decided to go beyond pediatrics and become a public health officer and specialist.

As surgeon general, you wear a vice admiral's uniform. Does that mean you are a member of the armed forces?

As surgeon general, I am a member of the uniformed services, and I meet on a regular basis with the other three surgeon generals of the armed forces. The seven uniformed services, four of which are armed services, include the Army, Navy, Air Force, Marines, Coast Guard, Public Health Service, and National Oceanic and Atmospheric Administration. As surgeon general, I have a very good relationship with the Department of Defense. In Operation Desert Storm, our duty was not to carry arms, but to make sure that we would be able to take care of the needs of the American people who stayed behind in communities where their doctors had been incorporated into the Reserves. Some others in public health – very few – were able to help in taking care of those injured or sick as a consequence of the war. That is part of our public health mandate. But to bear arms and go to the Persian Gulf, I would have needed an executive order from the president. The last time that happened was in the Korean War.

What is your greatest concern regarding the health of the nation?

My biggest concern is providing adequate health care for all. Everyone has to play a part, from the one who delivers medical care to the one who pays for it to the one who makes sure the system is not extended beyond its capacity. Unless we get together and make sure the employer, the employee, the payer, and the deliverer of the care share the responsibility, the government alone cannot address this issue in a workable way. Among those who need care, I worry foremost about the children who come from poor families and have no one to speak for them. My biggest concern today is that the children of the United States of America, whom no one really pays any attention to, are going to be the generation in charge of this country by the year 2013. They have to be cared for and treated as seriously as if they could vote and were participating in the labor force. I have to speak on their behalf because they have no vote and no power. When we open our eyes in the year 2013, when most of us baby boomers would like to retire, there will be no labor force if we do not make sure that today's children have an opportunity to grow up healthy and educated.

What statistics do you find particularly alarming?

There are so many distressing numbers for children's issues, but one statistic that I find particularly worrisome is that only one out of every six children is immunized in this country. I believe immunization should be a right, not something that is available depending on resources. I strongly believe that when children are born, they have the right to be vaccinated.

What do you see ahead for women who are working, have children, and are taking care of aging parents?

I am acutely aware of the many problems women in general face. Many women are caretakers of children and of aging parents. They suffer from stress because they don't know whose needs to take care of first and their own needs are neglected. Any agenda for addressing the problems of women must consider the entire life cycle of women, not just the reproductive years. I am following very closely the agenda of the Department of Health and Human Services as we look ahead to the next two years to implement the women's agenda, which will examine the women's life cycle, from their reproductive life to their psychological life to their empowering life.

When I look at the epidemics of today, I see them as they affect women and children. The AIDS epidemic alone takes close to 50 percent of my time. It affects minorities disproportionately, and it has women in despair. Women and children with AIDS need a lot of help and support. They get insufficient attention because it is still looked upon as an epidemic of IV [intravenous] drug users and their partners. I believe that by the year 2000, it will have become evident that the epidemic is heterosexual. It is urgent to get information out to all women to protect and educate them so there will be no unnecessary fear or stigma attached to AIDS.

As a woman, have you experienced discrimination in your profession?

I have not experienced that much discrimination as a woman, but I have experienced discrimination as a Hispanic. I believe that is why I work so hard to prove to those who discriminate that I am not in any way less qualified because I come from a Hispanic background. For example, I just came through U.S. customs, and I was asked, "Are you a U.S. citizen?" I didn't know at that point whether to laugh or throw a punch at the questioner! In every situation where I sense prejudice, I try to be so good in my actions and my work that I make the person feel like a worm. (Laughter)

Taking into consideration the fact that Dr. Everett Koop had seven years to grow into his uniform, so to speak, are you comfortable with the job yet?

People forget that the first four years Dr. Koop was the surgeon general, not many people knew who he was. I am the beneficiary of Dr. Koop's success in the creation of the position as one deserving of respect and high expectations.

I have a feeling people realize the agenda is different, the way I handle the agenda is different, and the person behind the agenda is different. I am being watched, but I'm also being given time to grow. I have said growing into a job can be likened to the development of a child: first we crawl, then we walk, then we run, and sometimes when we run, we leap. In time, I hope to leap like Dr. Koop. Meanwhile, I would say that in the course of fifteen months, I have already stopped crawling and am walking. I can look back and say I have come out very strongly against underage drinking and for the need for accurate product labeling. I have also produced a comprehensive guide for the care of patients with AIDS and have taken a very strong stand for vaccinations for all children as their right. I feel confident that people appreciate my efforts and realize that I am following my agenda, by which I will be judged.

What do you think accounts for your success?

I think my success comes from having come through the ranks and showing people that if you work hard, you can be successful. Maybe it is the pediatrician part of me always trying to speak for those who cannot speak for themselves. Maybe it is the Latino part of me, where a hug and a pat on the back are natural. I think people realize I am not a fake. I think I come across as a normal person addressing issues from an office that is not ordinary.

What important lessons have you learned in your life?

Well, I've learned people listen to the surgeon general, they trust the surgeon general, and they want to like the surgeon general. Whenever I have a message, I really weigh it before I deliver it to the people because I want to make sure that I say it in a positive way. I don't want to close any doors, and if I have to, I try to leave a window of hope open. I truly believe people are tired of negative messages. I want to let them know that despite the fact that they might have done something unhealthy for years, there is still hope that if they change their habits, they can affect their life in a positive way.

Who was your role model?

My mother. She's a very strong woman. She studied all her life to achieve despite poverty. She still believes education is the key to success. When things were very tough, she never made me feel my illness was a burden. Yet she never tolerated my being weak, and because of that, I never felt I was different from the rest of the children. Now when my mother and I reminisce, she always tells me, "I just don't know how we did it!" (Laughter) She never made me feel I was ill or defective or that there was anything I couldn't do. She would listen if I complained, but she would always say, "Okay, where are we going next?"

How would you like to be remembered as surgeon general?

It's a little too early to ask me that. I would hope to be remembered in the same way Dr. Koop is. He got the message of AIDS out to the people, and he continued what Luther Terry did with respect to the danger of cigarettes. I would like to be remembered as the pediatrician who brought the kids' issues to the forefront and made sure the children's agenda became as important as any other agenda. Also, being a woman, I hope to be remembered for bringing women's issues to the forefront, for alerting people that despite some of the ethical, legal, and moral issues that affect women, we should be united rather than divided by any one issue.

Judianne Densen-Gerber

Profession: Psychiatrist/Attorney

Currently: President, Odyssey Institute International, Inc.

Date of birth: November 13, 1934

Education: B.A., Bryn Mawr College, 1956
LL.B., Columbia University Law School, 1959
M.D., New York University Medical School, 1963
J.D., Columbia University Law School, 1969

J udianne Densen-Gerber has interwoven careers as a psychiatrist, attorney, pioneer in drug rehabilitation, and author of legislation against child pornography. She is president of Odyssey Institute International, Inc., and the founder of New York City's Odyssey House, one of the first drug treatment centers to treat addicts without relying on heroin-substitute drugs. "If you ask what is the thread running through my career," she has said, "I would say I help people in tremendous pain."

After obtaining a law degree in 1959 to satisfy her parents who were both lawyers, she proceeded to medical school, where she gained the distinction of becoming the second woman in the United States to earn dual degrees in law and medicine. The drug treatment program that she developed at Odyssey House was such a success that it has expanded to several states, as well as to Australia and New Zealand. Densen-Gerber helps addicts by emphasizing what she believes to be the root cause of drug addiction, "the individual's sense of hopelessness and lack of self-confidence." Among the first psychiatrists to believe that a drug addict, given the proper treatment through group therapy and individual development within a structured setting, could be cured, she initiated a pioneering treatment program for addicted mothers and their babies and established a separate residence for adolescents. Odyssey House was built on the premise that no one would be turned away and everyone would be given an equal chance.

In her work with drug addicts, Densen-Gerber discovered that a large percentage of them had been sexually abused as children. Based on her observations, she wrote the federal legislation that created the National Center on Child Abuse and Neglect within the Department of Health, Education and Welfare (HEW). She launched the Child Advocacy Program to help sexually abused children. She also worked with legislators to write a federal statute prohibiting child pornography and collaborated on the writing of similar statutes in thirty-seven states and in the United Kingdom.

Densen-Gerber is the author of several books, including *Drugs, Sex, Parents, and You,* (which she coauthored in 1972 with her thirteen-year-old daughter, Trissa Austin Baden), *We Mainline Dreams: The Odyssey House Story,* and *Walk in My Shoes.*

Densen-Gerber is married to Michael M. Baden, M.D., a forensic pathologist. They have four children, all of whom are pursuing careers in medicine. She has been described by an acquaintance as "one of those people who, when you're with them, it's like being at a party."

You have combined so many disciplines with psychiatry. What motivates you?

(Laughter) I call myself a reluctant dragon. I am very existential. What motivates me is whatever clinical problem presents itself in my office. I like to respond to new and exciting ideas and to think through solutions.

What do you think is the most common misconception about psychiatry and psychiatrists?

My husband once said, "Psychiatry is gossip." It's not. It's a combination of the art of timing, the ability to communicate and listen, and science. The most common misconception about psychiatry is that anyone can do it, that psychiatry is not much more than self-help, which is not true. There is much value in self-help groups, and they are good adjuncts to good psychiatry, but there is so much more that you have to know about how the mind works. The mind is very complicated, and it is an endlessly exciting trip to see how it sees things and reacts.

What aspect of your work do you find to be most demanding?

Addressing social ills and bringing legislation such as the reporting laws in child abuse and child pornography to bear on situations that cause psychiatric damage.

What qualities do you think are important for a psychiatrist to have?

The ability to listen — that is the most important quality — and the ability to communicate so that the patient can hear.

What do you think accounts for your success?

Three generations of excellent female role models. One of my grandmothers was a real estate agent, and another of my grandmothers chained herself to the White House (in the crusade for women's suffrage rights). My mother is well into her eighties and was a very successful lawyer specializing in FCC work. During my childhood, neither my mother nor my father nor my grandparents showed any sexist attitudes. I did not learn until I entered professional school that there was any bias against women.

Did you have any other role models?

At the time I became dually certified in both professions, I was the second woman in the nation to do so. Certainly, I had role models as I mentioned, in my female antecedents. I am also extremely fond of Abigail Adams. I have had the privilege of knowing Margaret Thatcher, Congresswoman Lindy Boggs, Queen Elizabeth, and Indira Ghandi. They are women to inspire us all. All of them have combined careers with motherhood and marriage.

As an attorney and a psychiatrist, how do you combine the two professions?

Mostly by seeing patients and abstracting from those patients' social problems, then working on legislation to alleviate the problems or working in the courtroom on significant cases.

What do you find most challenging about your work?

The fact that one sees a clinical picture such as child abuse, drug abuse, or satanism, and the stages of denial that society goes through. The fact that people accept so many wrongs as a given. The difficulty in obtaining remediation on a social issue – this is really one of the most difficult things. I also have a very strong feeling that we have to reevaluate our Constitution and our Bill of Rights because they do not provide the protection for children that is necessary. The First Amendment should not be interpreted to protect child pornography. The establishment clause should not protect satanism, which at this time is considered a religion – a 5013 charity. I find it difficult to believe that you can get a tax deduction for giving money to promote Satan.

How do you deal with patients' problems? Do they linger in your mind?

The majority of the patients I treat present social issues such as satanism, drug abuse, and child abuse. Therefore, my legal background permits me to take the tremendously difficult problems and translate them into social action and legislation such as the child pornography laws. So I get release by doing something. When I finish a patient hour, I have to turn that hour off. I cannot linger thinking it through, or I would be overwhelmed, particularly since I am now involved in a lot of satanic cult deprogramming. I often consult with friends and colleagues regarding problems that I need to think through or when I need other insights. I also play very hard and read a great deal. I just turn myself off. I schedule leisure time to think, read, or do things unrelated to the type of material I am professionally presented.

What do you find most satisfying about your work?

Watching a patient get better, get married, get a job or a promotion, or being invited to attend a christening. In fact, I will soon be going to a christening. A patient, who was an incest victim and unable to marry until age forty, is going to have twins. That is very satisfying.

Has it been difficult juggling a career and family?

Of course it has been difficult. I wrote a book on that subject called *Walk in My Shoes.* I believe that it can be done, and I am very opposed to the concept of the mommy track. I have never, because of family obligations (including nine pregnancies), missed more than three days of work.

What is the driving force in your life today?

Getting older, I suppose (laughter), and coping with that. The things that concern me most are the plague of AIDS and the high rate of divorce (66 percent) in marriages of thirty years and over. I am very concerned about the quality of life in this great country. In my own life, what concerns me most is keeping stimulated and being able to confront new problems and new ideas.

As a woman, have you experienced discrimination in your profession?

There is no way of overestimating the amount of discrimination that one experiences professionally because one is a woman. It ranges from receiving funding letters from Columbia Law School addressed "Dear Brothers in Law" to not being allowed to use the elevator in said law school when I was in the eighth month of pregnancy and wished to go both to class and the ladies' room.

There is definitely a glass ceiling. I hit the glass ceiling very early in life. I didn't know I was hitting it. People objected to my earning capacity as a CEO of fifty-one hospitals worldwide. It is very difficult to appear before local, state, and federal legislative committees in which the men are called "doctor" and I am called by my first name. It goes from minutiae of discrimination to discrimination on a larger scale.

I tend to be the kind of person who gets to the heart of the matter right away. I have very little patience because I have so much to do, so I am not exactly the world's best diplomat. I remember at one point being told by a very distinguished gentleman, "If you don't want to be treated like a woman, don't act like one." I told him, "I don't know how to act like anything else. I am one."

Is there any lesson that you've learned that might have made your life easier?

I know that I was too much of a workaholic in the beginning, and I should have learned a certain mellowness in the setting of priorities before I turned fifty. It would have been nice if I had been able to do that in my thirties. I would have enjoyed life more. Until 1984, I was the CEO of fifty-one treatment centers worldwide, and I traveled around the world three times a year. I underestimated the terrible personal and physical toll that so much traveling could take.

What are you most proud of having achieved?

I am most proud that in spite of all the difficulties that a career woman has in mothering, my children have all elected to study medicine without any pressure from us. The eldest is an obstetrician, the second is a medical anthropologist, the third is studying infectious diseases, and the fourth is entering Brown University as a premed student, tending toward psychiatry.

Jon Randolph

Peregrine Wolff

Profession: Veterinarian

Currently: Director of Animal Health, Minnesota Zoological Garden

Date of birth: November 16, 1959

Education: Middlebury College, 1976- 1977 (Biology)
University of Vermont, 1977- 1979 (Animal Science)
D.V.M., New York State College of Veterinary Medicine at
Cornell, 1984

$\mathcal{A}$s director of animal health at the Minnesota Zoological Garden, Peregrine Wolff is responsible for the care of fourteen hundred animals. One of the disadvantages of caring for zoo animals, observes Wolff, is that 70 percent have to be sedated before they can be treated. Another obstacle is that animals instinctively hide their illnesses because, in the wild, signs of weakness mark them as easy prey. Thus, they tend to be very sick by the time they show symptoms of their condition.

In late 1989, Wolff assumed her current position at the Minnesota Zoological Garden where, in addition to being responsible for the clinical care of the animals, she also conducts and assists in research and conservation projects. She has been named an assistant clinical professor at the University of Minnesota's Veterinary College and has conducted zoo medicine workshops for Latin American veterinarians.

Wolff has done extensive research in the field of veterinary medicine and has written numerous articles on the subject. She chairs the Infectious Disease Committee of the American Association of Zoo Veterinarians. Her husband, Mark Spreyer, is an ornithologist and writer. During her free time, she enjoys gardening, bird-watching, and her many pets.

What made you want to become a veterinarian?

I was always interested in working with animals, and I actually wanted to be a zoo veterinarian when I was young. My father was a professor, and we spent a lot of time on sabbatical in Europe. We visited many zoos over there. I really enjoyed zoos at an early age and I think my parents, particularly my father, were very interested in animals. My mother was interested in medicine. So the two interests just naturally went together.

What aspect of your work do you find most challenging?

Without a doubt, dealing with some of the political problems. Most zoos have government funding of some sort, which always brings along a bureaucratic machine. Taking care of the animals is the easy part; it's dealing with the people and the politics that's hardest and most challenging. Also, medicine is changing very rapidly. A lot of new drugs come out every year. Since we work with so many species, just keeping up on the literature is a challenge.

What do you enjoy most about your profession?

I really enjoy working on the animals and helping sick animals recover. I like to see the progress we make in solving problems – not necessarily medical problems, but working out new management problems that may make the species do better in captivity. Contributing to that animal's or that species's survival is what makes me feel good in my job.

Do you get a chance to practice much preventive medicine?

We try. I would like it if all we had to do was preventive medicine. That's what a lot of zoo veterinarians are trying to strive for. We try to give annual exams to most of the animals. Every year they get vaccinations. They are on a routine worming program. We have a neonatal protocol for baby animals. Also, to protect our collection, we quarantine any animal that comes into the zoo. Before they are released into the collection, they must have a physical exam and three negative fecal exams to make sure they have no parasites. We are also working on a nutrition program, and we have nutrition consultants to help us with the diets of all the zoo animals.

Is there much of a difference between your work and that of a veterinarian who is in private practice?

When I was a student, I worked with veterinarians in private practice. I think private practitioners have a much more scheduled day. They see patients in fifteen- to twenty-minute exams, and if something more needs to be done, they'll set aside time to do surgery or further workups. Most of the animals they work with don't have to be immobilized before they can touch them. That makes everything go a lot more quickly.

I don't think most private practitioners have as many meetings as we do. We work with a lot of management issues, and I think we have more extensive paperwork. I feel we write up more extensive records mainly because we immobilize the animals and much of what we see is not routine. The majority of our collection in the zoo is composed of threatened species. Also, treating a wider range of species, we are responsible for a greater volume of literature. I think they have a more predictable day, but when we are working on a rare animal, I don't think that we are under any more pressure than private practitioners because they are usually working on an animal somebody dearly loves.

As a woman, have you experienced discrimination in your work?

I wouldn't say that it has been blatant discrimination. I don't think anyone has come out and said, "You can't do that because you are a woman." I attended veterinary school at Cornell, and my class was the first that was over 50 percent women. That was in 1980. Now even more women are in veterinary school. But there are still certain attitudes in school. For instance, it is assumed that the people who work with the large animals are men. Also, you would hear things like "Well, you'll get out and practice for a few years and then have a child, and that will be the end of the work," or "We're investing in someone who is not going to be as productive in her career as a man."

I don't think that I've been passed over for a job because I was a woman. But you still get the little things, like some men refer to you when you are with other women as "girls" and that sort of thing. I haven't experienced anything that has been blatant; it's just been subtle manners of speech, the way people are treated, that type of thing.

Who were your role models?

Three veterinarians I worked with where I grew up: two large animal veterinarians and a small animal veterinarian. All three of them were men. The person who was responsible for my zoo career, in a sense, was Gerald Durrell. I read a lot of his books as a child. He was an animal collector back in the fifties, and he started a zoo in the Channel Islands in Jersey. I ended up spending six months working there. There were no women role models in my life, other than my mother, who encouraged my medical leaning. At the time, there were no women veterinarians or even women working in zoos whom I knew about.

What advice would you give someone interested in pursuing a career as a veterinarian?

It is a lot of hard work. When I went to school, it was much harder to get into veterinary college than it was to get into medical school. People really have to look at the financial commitment involved, because I don't think for the amount of money you spend on your education, as compared to a physician or maybe even an attorney, that you necessarily get the respect or the financial return they do. I think it is a rewarding career and allows you a lot of diversity. If you want to become a veterinarian, you really must enjoy the work. You should want to achieve personally as well as see advancement in the field of veterinary medicine. There is a tremendous amount of opportunity, but you have to be aware of the realities as well.

What do you think accounts for your success?

I am dedicated, I work pretty hard, and I am generally very easy to get along with. I respect other people, and I don't treat people on a hierarchy. I think people appreciate that, especially support staff. I respect what is important to people. When you are dealing with zookeepers, their animals are very important to them. If you work hard, care for their animals, and try to do your best, they really appreciate it.

Is there any other profession you would rather be pursuing?

I'd like to do more frontline conservation work. I'd like to save species in their natural habitat. That would be my goal. I'd like to make zoos obsolete by keeping animals where they are supposed to be, and that's in the wild.

Index by Name

Index by Profession

More good books from
WILLIAMSON PUBLISHING

To order additional copies of *Working Women for the 21st Century,* please enclose price per copy ($13.95, paper; 19.95 hardbound) plus $2.50 shipping and handling. Follow "To Order" instructions on the last page. Thank you.

THE WOMEN'S JOB SEARCH HANDBOOK
Issues and Insights into the Workplace
by Gerri Bloomberg and Margaret Holden

Delves into the issues that keep women of all ages out of the jobs they want and deserve ... and often out of the workplace entirely. They tell it like it is — not like we may wish it were. Covers your initial mindset, turning volunteer work into bonifide work experience, reentering the job market after many years at home, where to start. With this book, if you want to work at a job you love, you can do it!

252 pages, 6 × 9,
Quality paperback, $12.95

INTERNATIONAL CAREERS
An Insider's Guide
by David Win

If you long for a career that combines the excitement of foreign lifestyles and markets, the opportunity to explore your potential, the promise of monetary and personal reward, then learn from David Win how to get off the stateside corporate ladder and into the newly emerging areas of international careers. Now's the time!

224 pages, 6 × 9, charts and sources
Quality paperback, $10.95

AFTER COLLEGE
The Business of Getting Jobs
by Jack Falvey

Wise and wonderful ... don't leave college without it. Filled with unorthodox suggestions (avoid campus recruiters at all costs!), hands-on tools (put your money in stationery, not resumes), wise observations (grad school! — why pay to learn what others are paid to learn better). This is a job-search book with a real difference that will make a real difference in your life no matter what your age!

192 pages, 6 × 9
Quality paperback, $9.95

STUDY ABROAD: The Astute Student's Guide
by David Judkins

Learn here about the various kinds of study abroad opportunities – who the "major players" are, what the lesser-known, unusual programs offer, how to pick the right program for your budget, your personal needs, your academic goals. All programs and all students are not equal; creating the right match is essential.

304 pages, 6 × 9, charts
Quality paperback, $12.95

WHAT'S NEXT?
Career Strategies After 35
by Jack Falvey

Falvey explodes myths right and left and sets you on a straight course to a satisfying and successful mid-life career. Bring an open mind to his book and you'll be on your way. A liberating book to help us all get happily back into work.

192 pages, 6 × 9
Quality paperback, $9.95

BIKING THROUGH EUROPE
A Roadside Travel Guide with 17 Planned Cycle Tours
by Dennis & Tina Jaffe

The Jaffe's experience and knowledge of cycling through Europe makes for a one-of-a-kind book with 17 fabulous routes for you to choose from plus wonderful field-tested recommendations for accommodations, side routes, restaurants, and shops. These cycle vacations are dreams come true!

304 pages, 6 × 9, detailed maps & routes
Quality paperback, $13.95

To Order:

At your bookstore or order directly from Williamson Publishing. We accept Visa and MasterCard (please include number and expiration date), or send check to:

Williamson Publishing Company
Church Hill Road, P.O. Box 185
Charlotte, Vermont 05445
Toll-free phone orders with credit cards:
1-800-234-8791

Please add $2.50 for postage and handling. Satisfaction is guaranteed or full refund without questions or quibbles.